Early praise for *Beyond Legacy Code*

Beyond Legacy Code presents a fresh perspective on the modern software development process. Engineers will find solutions to their day-to-day challenges. Non-engineers will gain an appreciation for the challenges and difficulties of making software.

➤ **Stas Zvinyatskovsky**
Senior Principal Software Architect, Yahoo

David helps us see how we got where we are. He gives us things to do that will help us. He gives us deep matters to think about. This book is a gift to people who care about software. Take advantage of it.

➤ **Ron Jeffries**
RonJeffries.com

If you feel stuck and powerless to improve your software delivery process, this book will offer years of experience distilled in just a few core ideas. This is a great book for anyone starting on a journey toward frequent iterative delivery, and for those people who tried adopting an agile process and failed to get the big benefits.

➤ **Gojko Adzic**
Partner, Neuri Consulting LLP

This book provides great discussion on what things I can do to make customers happy and also to keep them happy as their needs change.

➤ **David Weiser**
Software Engineer, Moz

It's a good read for any developer or manager, working on any type of code in any company.

➤ **Troy Magennis**
   Author of *Forecasting and Simulating Software Development Projects*, CEO Focused Objective

David's explanations are so clear I am hopeful even managers of development teams and leaders running companies who build custom software will pick up this book and understand these practices that allow us to build software that is economical to own, maintain, and enhance.

➤ **Jim Fiolek**
   Software Architect, Black Knight Financial Services

Throughout the book there were points that gave me a sense of relief—where I would think if only we could get people to follow these few principles our life, and software, would be so much easier and less stressful.

➤ **Nick Capito**
   Director of Software Engineering, Unboxed Technology

We fight to make every line of code we write part of a real live product. Find out how that fight sometimes leads us astray. Find out how to make you and your team much more productive in building real live products that customers want now AND tomorrow.

➤ **Michael Hunter**
   Geek, Hacker, Principal Engineer, Architect

Beyond Legacy Code

Nine Practices to Extend the Life (and Value) of Your Software

David Scott Bernstein

The Pragmatic Bookshelf

Dallas, Texas • Raleigh, North Carolina

Many of the designations used by manufacturers and sellers to distinguish their products are claimed as trademarks. Where those designations appear in this book, and The Pragmatic Programmers, LLC was aware of a trademark claim, the designations have been printed in initial capital letters or in all capitals. The Pragmatic Starter Kit, The Pragmatic Programmer, Pragmatic Programming, Pragmatic Bookshelf, PragProg and the linking *g* device are trademarks of The Pragmatic Programmers, LLC.

Every precaution was taken in the preparation of this book. However, the publisher assumes no responsibility for errors or omissions, or for damages that may result from the use of information (including program listings) contained herein.

Our Pragmatic courses, workshops, and other products can help you and your team create better software and have more fun. For more information, as well as the latest Pragmatic titles, please visit us at *https://pragprog.com*.

The team that produced this book includes:

Jacquelyn Carter (editor)
Potomac Indexing, LLC (index)
Liz Welch (copyedit)
Dave Thomas (layout)
Janet Furlow (producer)
Ellie Callahan (support)

For international rights, please contact *rights@pragprog.com*.

Printed in the United States of America.
ISBN-13: 978-1-68050-079-0
Printed on acid-free paper.
Book version: P1.0—August 2015

Contents

Foreword

Legacy

A legacy is the part of the dead that remains influential.

A life that leaves a legacy has been a good one. Not so for software. We use the polite term "legacy" for code that has lost all sense of vitality even though it might run every day and exert the unchanging influence of past decisions on all who for whatever reason are unable to walk away.

We distinguish software from hardware. We call hardware hard because we think of it as fixed, unlikely to change without screwdriver in hand. We call software soft because it is made up of ideas, expressed as code, loaded into hardware to make something useful.

The irony of our industry is that code turns out to be "harder" than hardware when it is thought to be finished and the developers dismissed.

Software comes to life when developers express wants and needs as decisions in the logic of programming. It's like making something out of nothing until we recognize all of the careful reasoning that goes into making the new life the one we want.

Agility

We say an organization is "agile" when it responds to threat and opportunity in ways uniquely of the moment. An agile organization is informed by history but not shackled to practice encoded in software not likely to be revised soon.

A double handful of thinkers, myself included, chose the term "agile" to describe the fresh emphasis we had all observed given to software that remained immediately adaptable to changing needs. Such forces are felt most strongly in new software development but do not disappear in any way for software so important that it should be kept alive and healthy for a lifetime.

The thinkers took issue with management practices such as "fortune telling," wherein software developers were asked to make predictions about the future of a cooperative process and were then judged competent or incompetent by how many predictions came true.

The thinkers took issue with development practices such as "big design up front," where anticipation of every possible alternative was judged the most likely way to avoid "bit rot" in downstream maintenance.

The thinkers then cast their advice for both developers and managers as the "manifesto for software development," which attracts more attention today than it did at its founding over a decade ago.

The manifesto is not without weaknesses. It has fallen short in two ways. It fell short when its brevity led readers to think of it as general wisdom rather than specific advice on how to write software.

The manifesto also fell short when "development" mentioned in the title led readers to apply the advice only on new projects and then only until they first go "live."

Work

Paid developers must recognize their obligation to deliver lasting value to others and that simply doing as they're told is insufficient to the task.

The intricacies of programming can compound when applied carelessly, creating a burden for programmers that's nearly impossible to shed. Agile methods in general, and this book in particular, describe a way to work within an organization respecting this reality.

This book revisits practices that have been proven over and over for two decades to be both effective and still surprisingly difficult to adopt.

The phrase "Agile in name only" describes organizations that go through the motions prescribed in countless books and then reap little benefit. This book dissects the motions and the reasons behind them. It is only with the logic of Agile firmly in hand that one can diagnose "in name only" disappointments.

The relentless fall in the cost of computing in turn raises the real value of well-made software. Where businesses respond, fortunes are made. As barriers to entry evaporate, every business must make software well to survive.

Strangely, the proliferation of cheap computers has made programming more difficult. The most Agile developers, the so-called "polyglot programmers," know that their skills are rarely appreciated outside Agile organizations.

David Bernstein explains how and why Agile methods work. He digs deep into his own experience of this revolution to tell stories from his own experience that illustrates the value of these practices.

Beyond Legacy Code makes clear what has to happen in order to successfully adopt these practices and get the most out of them.

Ward Cunningham
Portland, Oregon

Acknowledgments

First and foremost I'd like to thank my wife Staci Bernstein, for giving me the space and support to work on this book and to follow my dreams, and our miniature poodle Nicki, who kept me company the whole time I was writing, editing, and rewriting.

I'd also like to give special thanks to Ward Cunningham for writing the foreword to this book and for all the encouragement he's given me.

Writing a book is a major undertaking and this book involved the support of many people, for whom I am deeply grateful. Thanks to my associates, colleagues, and clients for conversations and support throughout the process.

I'm deeply grateful to those reviewers whose dedication to make this book better gave selflessly of their time and expertise to provide feedback, especially Scott Bain, Heidi Helfand, Ron Jeffries, Jim Fiolek, Stas Svinyatskovsky, Ed Kraay, James Couball, Pat Reed, Stephen Vance, Rebecca Wirfs-Brock, Jeff Brice, Jerry Everand, Greg Smith, Ian Gilman, Llewellyn Falco, Fred Daoud, Michael Hunter, Woody Zuill, Gojko Adzic, Troy Magennis, Kevin Gisi, David Weiser, Nick Capito, Sam Who, Michael Hunger, Ken Pugh, Max Guernsey, and Chris Sterling.

Finally, I'd like to thank the many thousands of software developers who have attended my classes over the last three decades. I'm grateful to have learned so much from you all!

Introduction

This book will help you drop the cost of building and maintaining software.

If you're a software developer, you'll learn a set of practices to help you build changeable code, because when code is used it often needs to be changed. For managers working with software developers, this book will show you how investing in nine essential practices will help your team work more efficiently to deliver software that doesn't devolve into legacy code. And to do that, you need more than just a technical to-do list—you need a firm understanding of the principles that add the *why* to the *how*.

Every day, we lose time, money, and opportunities because of legacy code.

Different people have different definitions for "legacy code," but put most simply, legacy code is code that, for a few different reasons, is particularly difficult to fix, enhance, and work with.

And there's a lot of it out there. Virtually all software that I've seen in production is legacy code.

The software industry as a whole hasn't put enough value on maintainability, so businesses wind up spending a great deal more to maintain code than they initially spent to write it. As we'll see in Chapter 2, *Out of CHAOS*, on page 19, inefficiencies in how software is built costs businesses at least tens of billions of dollars every year in the United States alone—and this is hardly just some abstract figure on a ledger sheet somewhere. We feel the effects of legacy code every day. Software is expensive, buggy, and hard to enhance.

People from inside and outside the industry have taken sides and argued for or against certain project management methodologies—a lot of which contain some truly brilliant ideas—but in order to effect lasting change for the better, we first have to come to a mutual understanding of the fundamental goals of software development.

This book isn't just about creating better software; it's about creating a better software industry. It includes the best of what I've learned in the last thirty years as a professional developer. The first two decades of my career were spent doing traditional Waterfall software development where systems were planned, built, and tested in distinct phases. The problem was, the way we planned to build software turned out to be fraught with many unforeseen issues that forced us to make serious compromises in both quality and budget.

But over the last decade things have been changing for me, and for other software developers I know, who have been practicing an Agile software development methodology called Extreme Programming (XP). Instead of trying to figure everything out up front, we figure things out as we go, designing, building, and testing little bits of software at a time.

XP practices such as test-driven development and refactoring have taught me valuable lessons for decreasing both the risks and the costs of building and extending software. Using these practices has shown me a range of different approaches for solving software problems. Can applying these practices reveal ways of building higher-quality, more maintainable software?

I say the answer is a resounding *Yes!*

Early in my career as a programmer, I was assigned to reconcile stock data from the Standard and Poor's feed into my client's proprietary database. Until then the process was done manually, which was error-prone and took, on average, fourteen hours each day to complete. I had to automate this process, but the best approach to accomplish this was not clear to me at first.

After a few weeks, and after writing over forty pages of code, I had a flash of insight that involved reorganizing how I processed the data. Within a few hours I had finished the project and slashed out all but five pages of code. What I thought would take me several more months when I came into work that morning turned out to be finished before I left that evening. Since then I have had many flashes of insight that have revealed underlying patterns in problems that, once recognized, showed me how to rapidly build highly maintainable solutions.

This is but one example of dramatic differences in productivity between alternate ways of approaching the same problem. I've heard many similar stories from other developers. Perhaps you have your own stories of when you had a flash of insight and suddenly a difficult problem became simple.

In my professional experience, the difference between highly productive developers and average developers can be profound. I've spent most of my career studying those rare individuals who are many times more productive than average software developers. What I've learned is that these people weren't born that way. They've simply formed some different distinctions than the rest of us and perhaps follow some unusual practices. All of these things are learnable skills.

As a young industry we're still figuring things out and learning to distinguish what's important from what's unimportant. Building software is very different from building physical things. Perhaps some of the challenges facing the software industry are rooted in a misconception of what software development actually is. In an effort to understand software development, to make it predictable, it has been compared to manufacturing and civil engineering. While there are similarities between software engineering and other fields of engineering, there are some fundamental differences that may not be obvious to someone who isn't actually writing software on a daily basis.

The fact that software engineering is not like other forms of engineering should really come as no surprise. Medicine is not like the law. Carpentry is not like baking. Software development is like one thing, and one thing only: software development. We need practices that make what we do more efficient, more verifiable, and easier to change. If we can do this, we can slash the short-term cost of building software, and all but eliminate the crippling long-term cost of maintaining it.

To that end, I offer nine practices that come from the Agile methodologies of Extreme Programming, Scrum, and Lean. When not just adopted but fully understood, these nine practices can help prevent the code we write in the future from becoming legacy code.

And though there is a lot of code out there that's either impossible to fix or already slipping into obsolescence, we can use these same practices to slowly dig our way out of the mountain of legacy code we've already accumulated.

These nine practices will help development teams build better software, and help the industry as a whole stop leaking money, time, and resources.

I've seen these nine practices work for my clients, who build some of the biggest and most complex software ever created. I know it's possible to achieve extraordinary results using these practices, but just "using" them by no means guarantees success. We must understand the principles behind the practices in order to use them correctly.

These are interesting times, and we get to be part of them. And while we are pioneers venturing into uncharted territory, there are guiding lights. The nine practices in this book have been guiding lights for me in my career as a software developer and beyond. I hope they become guiding lights for you as well.

How to Use This Book

Beyond Legacy Code: Nine Practices to Extend the Life (and Value) of Your Software is about developing software, but you don't have to be a software developer to understand it.

How software is written may be an alien concept to most people, yet it affects us all. Because it has become such a complex activity, developers often find themselves trying to explain concepts for which their customers, and even their managers, may have no point of reference. This book helps bridge that communications gap and explains technical concepts in common sense language to help us forge a common understanding about what good software development actually is.

Getting different kinds of readers on the same page with technical practices is no easy task, but to that end this book is designed to help five different groups of people share a common understanding of software development:

- software developers
- software development and IT managers
- software customers
- product and project managers from any industry
- and literally anyone interested in this vital technology

I've tried to make software development accessible to everyone by borrowing elements of personal story telling and drawing on a wide range of anecdotes, analogies, and metaphors to illuminate technical concepts. It's hard to generalize about software development and so it's easy to find exceptions to a lot of what I say, but there's usually a deeper insight to be found.

To make this book accessible to nondevelopers and focus on the importance of these practices, it's not written as a *how-to* book. There are already several good books on everything from story writing to refactoring (see the bibliography). While this book does offer lots of practical advice, what makes it different and most valuable are the discussions of *why* the technical practices are useful. This approach helps nondevelopers, like our managers and stakeholders, understand some of the issues and challenges developers face when building software.

Part I: The Legacy Code Crisis

In Part I, *The Legacy Code Crisis*, on page 1, I confront the significant issues facing the software industry head on and find that billions of dollars are lost every year due to poor software development processes.

Much of the software that runs our lives is buggy, brittle, and nearly impossible to extend, which is what we mean when we say "legacy code." How did we get here and what does that mean, not just in terms of the software industry but also in terms of all the other people and industries it touches?

If you're already familiar or perhaps even frustrated with the software industry you'll find more than just "preaching to the choir" in these pages. You'll also find a deeper insight into why things often don't work out as planned when building software, and lots of good reasons why better approaches are needed.

Even for software industry insiders, Part 1 can put these significant challenges in their proper context. Managers and developers alike may discover a fresh perspective on the problems we, as an industry, are facing every day. As one manager said to me, "It added arguments to my arsenal." It may help you spread the message that at least we have to recognize that there is a problem before we can solve it.

If you come from outside the software industry in particular, I all but guarantee that Part 1 may surprise, even shock you.

Part II: Nine Practices to Extend the Life (and Value) of Your Software

In Part II, *Nine Practices to Extend the Life (and Value) of Your Software*, on page 43, with the problem clearly stated, the remaining three quarters of the book moves past the doom and gloom and into a set of practices that provides a real, workable solution, beginning with practices that are most useful for managers.

In Chapter 5, *Practice 1: Say What, Why, and for Whom Before How*, on page 59 and Chapter 6, *Practice 2: Build in Small Batches*, on page 73, I offer some hands-on recommendations for not just how better to begin implementing a complex software development process but to manage that process all the way through to completion. These two practices will be of particular interest to those of you coming from outside the software industry, with advice that can easily translate to any project management environment. By adopting these practices you can...

- operate more efficiently
- save money in both the short and long term
- create higher quality software
- increase customer satisfaction and repeat business

The next seven practices are much more software developer specific and present technical practices I found most helpful in my career.

I've seen these practices both succeed and fail. Software development teams have applied best practices but with poor technique so they didn't get the value they were hoping for. The difference between teams that are successful with these practices and teams that aren't comes down to understanding why these practices are important in the first place. That's what this book stresses.

And though these are ultimately technical practices, I urge managers—in any industry—to open your minds to the basic concepts. Know the challenges your developers face, and share with them the fact that there are practical, start-right-now practices that can move that team from floundering through broken processes to a new level of efficiency and effectiveness.

As you read through the descriptions of these practices, I urge you to think about why these practices are valuable before studying how to implement them on your project. This will help you learn how to use the practices more effectively.

Though I do recommend reading—and adopting—all nine practices, feel free to adopt the practices in any order you like. I certainly recognize that everyone coming to this book will have specific issues and specific needs, which is why I organized Part II as nine individual practices. Concentrate on what will help you most and help you fastest, but please don't stop there.

I'm Not Planting a Flag, I'm Opening a Door

How you read this book, and what you take from it, is up to you. I've tried to avoid circling the wagons around terms like Agile, Scrum, or XP. I want *Beyond Legacy Code: Nine Practices to Extend the Life (and Value) of Your Software* to change the way people think about the still-new profession of software development and help bring it into the mainstream. I want to open up discussion throughout the software community, where we too often take sides, argue details while missing the bigger picture, and otherwise dig ourselves into trenches when we should be sharing ideas based on a single common goal: to build the best possible software.

Online Resources

The code examples in this book can be found online at the Pragmatic Programmers web page for this book.[1] You'll also find a discussion forum where you can ask questions and receive feedback, as well as an errata submission form where issues with the text can be reported, plus a lot more.

---

1.   http://pragprog.com/book/dblegacy

Part I

The Legacy Code Crisis

Am I the only one? Does anybody else notice—or care—that so much software doesn't work as promised, or doesn't work for long, and is often nearly impossible to fix?

Software is far from 100% successful. But how is the software development industry really doing? What percentage of software projects are successful? And what do we even mean by "successful" or "failed"? How do we measure those things?

I've asked a lot of people these questions, both inside and outside the software industry. Most people outside the industry find these strange questions to ask—"You mean some projects are unsuccessful?"—while the people inside the software industry might be tempted to ask, "You mean some projects are successful?"

CHAPTER 1

Something's Wrong

Something was wrong.

There was no trust within the organization. Their heavyweight software development processes got so much in the way they couldn't really produce code anymore. The whole company was in a death spiral—their entire $750 million business was at stake.

You might have been one of the core developers on this team. Their core developers were brilliant, but they also had a second level of junior developers and offsite or second-site teams that were allowed to slip into an attitude of "code monkey-ness"—micro-focused on building "just this feature," not thinking about how that single feature would integrate into the whole and unaware that some of the things they were doing were going to cause big problems in the short term and even bigger problems later on.

Even though the development effort was being led by very smart, experienced professional developers, the software that was being created didn't follow good standards and wasn't easy to work with. The whole development team didn't understand the reasons behind the technical practices. They ended up cutting corners here or gaming the system there, creating little sub-teams—or even "teams of one"—operating with a different set of standards and an incomplete view of the whole system. This made integrating code a nightmare-like experience that no one looked forward to.

Or you might have been one of the managers responsible for getting this software done, shipped, and earning rather than costing money. Their managers were smart and experienced, too, and in the end just as frustrated, even demoralized, as the developers. This company's managers saw deadlines slip, watched as unstable release candidates were passed into production, and try as they might they just didn't know what to tell the developers to help them do things right. So management's response was to add more process, which eroded even more trust, and deadlines slipped even more.

Too often, organizations can let the relationship between development, QA, and operations devolve into antagonism, which is what happened to this struggling company. Neither developers nor management understood exactly why they needed to step back and look at how they approached their work, but the reality of their burn-down rate made it clear that they had to.

I was the third consultant they hired, and the first not to address it as a "people issue." What I saw was a *legacy code* issue. Their software was brittle and hard to work with. The company had grown by leaps and bounds over the past ten years and their code had suffered as a result.

The company had been trying to "go Agile" for years, but while many of their teams did institute some of the Agile practices, their existing code was constantly getting in the way, throwing off estimates and slowing them down. They knew they had to address both their existing legacy code as well as all those bad habits they'd accumulated along the way that got them into this situation.

We focused on the solid engineering practices we'll cover in this book and *why they work*. And I wasn't kidding when I said that the developers and managers alike were smart, experienced professionals. They listened, opening themselves to a collaborative process in which they were amenable to change. They put the necessary effort into fixing what was wrong with both their software and their processes.

If you were a software developer there, you would have noticed you were no longer getting calls at 3 a.m. because servers were down. You would have started getting fast, positive feedback from the tests you were adding that let you know your code was still working as you intended. With the rest of the team, you would have devoted 20% of your effort to cleaning up existing code and you would have seen that effort start to pay back in a big way—within just a year.

If you were part of the management team there you would have seen team members collaborate more effectively. You would have stopped being terrified of losing "critical resources" (individual developers) that could tank the company by deciding to get a job somewhere else, leaving no one else able to unravel that single developer's code. You'd also see a shift in the team's attitude as developers began to deal with the legacy code issue rather than pretending it didn't exist.

It took several months, but as the quality of their code started to improve, so did the team's velocity. The team's estimates became more reliable and they began to consistently meet deadlines again without having to cut corners.

They started to break down walls, both literally and figuratively. Departments began to talk to each other. Working together, they restructured the way they did QA and the way they handled requirements. Testers sat with developers to figure out how to validate release candidates automatically. In time, they went from a largely manual two-week testing process to validate release candidates to a fully automated testing process that happened, in most cases, in less than two minutes. This saved them huge sums of money each year and gave them the foundation to transform their organization.

And the bottom line was: People began to care again.

This is a true story. I've seen it play out time and time again. And if you're a software developer, or if you manage software developers, and fear you're even now heading down this death spiral, this book will show you how to do what this company did to turn things around. If you're struggling, you're not alone.

Something's wrong with the way most software is built and maintained. But it doesn't have to be that way.

What Is Legacy Code?

Software is different from everything else in our world. When we understand its nature and how it needs to change over time, we can find ways to increase the fitness of the code we build so it's less costly to maintain and extend.

In his book, *Working Effectively with Legacy Code, page xvi [Fea04]*, Michael Feathers asks what we think about when we hear the term "legacy code":

> If you are at all like me, you think of tangled, unintelligible structure, code that you have to change but don't really understand. You think of sleepless nights trying to add in features that should be easy to add, and you think of demoralization, the sense that everyone on the team is so sick of a codebase that it seems beyond care, the sort of code that you wish would die. Part of you feels bad for even thinking about making it better. It seems unworthy of your efforts.

We know how software becomes legacy code. Like everything else, software tends to go through a life cycle. Programs are created, used, patched, and eventually retired. Software, like a living thing, also dies, if only because the operating system it runs on becomes obsolete. And like doctors, software developers can at best only postpone the inevitable. If a patient gets more quality time to live than she would have otherwise, the treatment is considered a success. But we all know that someday, the inevitable will happen for all of us, and the same thing is true with software.

Over the course of a program's lifetime code gets hacked and modified, which often weakens the design so the software gets harder and harder to work with. And since most software written today is effectively unchangeable, we end up having to replace more than we fix.

This has even given rise to a newly emerging field called "software archaeology," a term coined in 2002 by the Pragmatic Programmers, Dave Thomas and Andy Hunt.[1] When I'm looking at a system that was built years ago with no documentation and poorly named variables, I sometimes feel how an archaeologist must feel pondering the mysteries of a lost and ancient civilization from a shard of pottery. It's just so little to go on.

When we look deeper into the shortcomings of how we build software, we can see how this leads to the creation and propagation of legacy code. If we can appreciate how challenging it is to try to estimate the time, cost, and processes of achieving something we've never done before, and how different software engineering is from other forms of engineering, then we can begin to understand where legacy code comes from and what we can do about it.

Michael Feathers further defines legacy code as any code without tests. This is because, like me, he places a high value on good automated unit tests that exercise code and validate it's being used as intended.

But having good unit tests presupposes that you have good, testable code, which is often not the case with legacy code, so you'll have to clean up the code and put it into a better state. That's often easier said than done. Making untestable code testable can involve re-architecting an entire system, and although there are techniques that can help, it can end up being a lot of work.

There are no easy answers, no quick fixes for legacy code. In Chapter 2, *Out of CHAOS*, on page 19, we'll see exactly how all pervasive this problem is and how much it's costing industry. A problem of this magnitude calls us to step back and look at it from different angles. If the solutions we've applied in the past haven't been working, then maybe we should look for different solutions.

---

1. Hunt, Andy, and Thomas, Dave. "Software Archaeology." *Software Construction/IEEE Software* March/April 2002. http://media.pragprog.com/articles/mar_02_archeology.pdf

Down the Waterfall

Borrowed from the manufacturing and construction industry, the Waterfall Model of software development was described in 1970 by Winston Royce[2] as a series of stages for building software—but on the next page he said it wouldn't work. Apparently, no one ever read that far.

Once the dominant methodology for building software, the Waterfall Model is simple in concept, providing these seven distinct steps to be followed in this order:

Stages of Waterfall Development

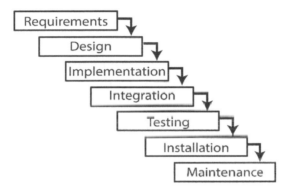

Requirements

Information is gathered from subject matter experts and prospective users to create a requirements document. This is a written set of instructions that tells us what features we're supposed to be building in the current release. Features are things that the software *does*.

Design

Software is then designed to fulfill the written requirements. The design is usually in the form of design diagrams and other artifacts that *describe* the design. This is not the code itself, but rather another document: diagrams and descriptions of how the software will be built. Unlike a blueprint, which specifies everything needed to build a building, software architecture isn't nearly as precise or complete.

---

2.   http://agileconsortium.pbworks.com/w/page/52184647/Royce%20Defining%20Waterfall

Implementation

Following design is the implementation phase, where code is written to conform to the design. Coding is simply a matter of fulfilling the design as detailed in the design artifacts.

Integration

After all the code is written the integration phase begins. During integration, all the code each team member wrote is put together. This is typically the first time all the code is assembled into a single computer program.

Testing

Once the software is integrated the testing phase begins, verifying that the software behaves as intended. This involves running a series of tests that exercise the software to prove it works.

Installation

In the installation phase the software is released to the user. This may involve distributing the program on CD and mailing it to the customer or making the software available online for download.

Maintenance

Finally, we have the ongoing maintenance of the software, in which problems are fixed, new features are added, and updates are made.

The Waterfall Model makes complete sense for building bridges or manufacturing widgets because it's more efficient to group feature requests into releases. But software development is not a manufacturing process. Software developers don't assemble programs from prebuilt parts. Sure, some parts can be prebuilt, but most of the parts we need we have to build or modify—even invent—ourselves. And we rarely know for sure what we'll have to build, modify, or invent until we get there, however robust our architecture.

Playing All or Nothing

The way we accumulate risk in a Waterfall software development project has some striking similarities to playing the odds in Las Vegas.

In traditional Waterfall development, in order for *anything* to work, *everything* has to work. Programmers don't see their code run with the rest of the system until integration—one of the last stages before release—when all the separate pieces of code are brought together to make a whole.

When we put off integration until the very end, we're basically playing roulette where we have to win ten times in a row in order to succeed.

One mistake in the way even a single line of code was written, and a program won't compile into executable code, or if it does compile it crashes when you run it. This is what we lovingly refer to as a "bug."

Many bugs *only* show up during the integration phase and not before. When we integrate at the end of the project, it creates a huge unknown all through the development process. And since integration has been put off, any necessary fixes and mysterious bugs become big and expensive problems that require a tremendous amount of effort (and associated cost) to fix. I couldn't imagine a riskier and more error-prone way of writing software.

And this is why it's so expensive to make last-minute changes in software. It requires a great deal of manual effort to retest and re-integrate the code. It's possible that making a small change in one area can affect many other areas of a program, so it's often prudent to retest the whole system whenever any changes are made to any part of the system. If this is left as a manual process, it can get exorbitantly expensive and very much discourages any last-minute changes that may come from important new information and better ideas gained later in the development cycle.

Why Waterfall Doesn't Work

When building software over long release cycles, developers may not see code run until months after it's written. They might build a "testing harness" so their code can be reached in a debugger (software that lets you detect bugs in other software) and stepped through one statement at a time, but this is not the same as running the code in the way it's meant to be run in the context of the whole system.

This is one of the main problems with batching features up into releases. It may make a lot of intuitive sense to batch things up. This is how we construct things. If you're building a house you want to get everything you need to build the foundation over to the job site so you won't have to stop that step waiting for more concrete, or whatever. Then you want to drop all the lumber so you aren't paying for carpenters to sit around waiting for a few more ceiling beams, and so on.

This is one of the main differences between virtual things and physical things. As it turns out, batching things up *doesn't work well in the virtual space.*

And it's not just that batching is inefficient—and we're going to talk about the inefficiencies as we start to look at the cadence of different release cycles—it forces us to build things that are *unchangeable.* This is far more subtle, but vitally important.

Only when you build things incrementally can you put the joints in to allow you to expand it later. You don't even think about it when you optimize for building software in releases. In the Waterfall world it's just never a priority and never an issue. No one builds a house with later room additions in mind. You build the house the blueprints call for. And how often does someone add a room addition to a house? Compare that to how often a new feature is added to software.

Recipes vs. Formulas

There's a difference between a recipe and a formula. You can make, say, marinara sauce from a *recipe* and it will taste the same as the marinara sauce made by someone else from the same recipe, but only if both cooks follow that recipe in exacting detail. But if one cook adds a little more pepper, and someone else uses more basil and less oregano, it's still marinara sauce. On the other hand, if two bakers are making bread and one alters the balance of water, flour, and yeast, that bread will fail to rise—it'll be ruined. Baking bread requires a *formula*.

We have to start seeing software development not as formulas to be followed in exact detail, but as recipes open to the creative interpretation of individual chefs to be adjusted according to the specific situation.

Programming is not a "paint by the numbers" kind of activity except in the most mundane types of tasks. Many tasks require breaking new ground and moving into uncharted territories. Software development has many *contraindications* where the "right" approach in one situation is the wrong approach in another situation.

This sense of stepping into the unknown tends to force traditional Waterfall processes to get increasingly more complex in an effort to predict and moderate the parade of unknowns. But making something more complex doesn't automatically make it better, and this can quickly get out of hand.

Separation of Development and Test

"It's my job to get through this as quickly as I can and do my best to hit all the features I've been asked for, but the QA team is the angel on my shoulder so I can afford to be sloppy, to just take a wild stab at it because my job is to create the rough draft and then I have this 'coauthor' who's going to be there to perfect it."

How many times have you, as a software developer, thought or said that—or as a manager, heard it said? But the QA team really isn't a software developer's "coauthor." All QA can say is, "Go back and try it again. Oh, and by the way, your time has run out."

How could we possibly win when we set ourselves up like this? And yet this is business as usual, and is a big problem because it encourages developers to not pay attention to what they're doing in the moment.

This problem isn't limited to just Waterfall development. The majority of software development projects still have a separate QA effort with manual parts that take days or even weeks to validate release candidates.

Stimulus and response have to be as close together as possible in order for us to change our habits. When developers don't see the consequences of our actions until months later, it doesn't properly register. It's as if we're living by the motto:

> It's not my job to find the errors; it's my job to create them.

Like Waterfall, other popular project management methodologies like Six Sigma and Total Quality Management, which were highly successful in providing consistency and quality of manufactured goods, have significant problems when applied to software. Ironically, we spend so much time focusing on the checks and balances of the methodology that we don't have any time to focus on putting quality into the product.

Traditional software development practices, with a focus on predicting the future and pre-measuring workflow, end up forcing developers and managers alike to find ways around the intrusive nature of the process in an effort to simply get their work done.

When "Process" Becomes "Busy Work"

When I was a programmer at IBM we had a rule that every line of code had to include a comment from the developer. This had the unintended effect of driving developers to use bad naming conventions for data and functions because the code would be "explained" in the comments. People started reading the comments instead of the code. But at crunch time developers would often update the code but not the comments, putting comments and code out of sync with each other. And an outdated comment is worse than no comment at all. This turns the comment into a lie, and we don't want lies in our code.

Suppose I have a line of code that reads

```
x++; /* I am incrementing x here */
```

I don't need a comment like that one (/* I am incrementing x here */). I can assume the reader understands the basics of the language. Excessive comments are noise at best and at worst they're lies, however unintentional.

When I see a large number of what I call "what comments"—comments that describe *what* the code is doing as opposed to *why* it's doing it—I get the sense that the developer who wrote it was nervous, concerned as to whether or not the reader would understand what the developer was doing in his code. Code should be self-expressive, and this is best accomplished by naming things well and using consistent metaphors to make software easy to follow and clear.

Excessive comments can become an excuse for not writing good-quality code. The practice of using block comments to provide a multiline description for a section of code—instead of putting that behavior into its own private method that can be called with an intention-revealing name describing what the method does—makes code harder to read and leads to methods that do too much.

There's no reason to believe that IBM had anything but the best intentions behind this commenting policy. In fact, I think the whole software development Road to Hell is paved with good intentions, but until we begin to understand the true nature of software development we may be doomed to apply management "solutions" that do more harm than good.

For example, I knew a company that required twelve major documents to be written and signed off on by all department heads before a line of code could be written. Because things went wrong in the past there was a distinct lack of trust between management and the developers. Ironically, most of their problems were actually caused by their complex process and not a lack of caring on the part of the developers. Management's response was to add more processes, which made things go even further awry.

It's fair to assume from the beginning of any project that the people involved want to do their best and deliver a quality end result. But somehow we can go from being ready and excited to contribute to disengaged and ambivalent—ready to game the system.

People feel disengaged when they're either powerless to influence an outcome or simply *feel* powerless to influence an outcome. This can happen in small ways to all of us every day. Conversely, the most powerful way to get people engaged in something can be summed up in a single word: respect.

Concrete Management

Modern management techniques developed as a result of the Industrial Revolution. Those early managers walked along the factory floor with stopwatches, timing workers in their various tasks and giving them a simple command: *faster!*

But in software development there's no repetitive task with one simple set of criteria to determine if it's done correctly and that we can "do faster." Sure, we wiggle our fingers at the keyboard but what we are really doing is thinking, visualizing, modeling, and embodying those models into code. Every task is different and finding solutions involves constantly learning new things.

Managers want to assure themselves that developers are doing the right things, but the deeper question is:

What are "the right things"?

What are our goals when building software? What principles do we follow? Most professionals in other occupations can easily answer this question, but I've met few software developers who can.

Managers attempt to answer the question "What are 'the right things'?" by trying to measure productivity—that old production line manager's stopwatch—or by imposing more complex schedules, even though this often has the opposite effect and ends up *de*motivating people. The more processes we add, the worse it gets because *process cannot dictate creativity*. We have to recognize that software development is fundamentally a creative process.

Here Be Dragons

We use maps to get around, to plan our trips, to clearly define a Point A, a Point B, and the shortest route between the two. Though the Latin phrase *Hic sunt draconnes*, or "here be dragons," didn't appear on ancient maps the way most people think it did, it's become synonymous with a place we don't know yet, somewhere that has yet to be explored. Those places at the far edges of the map are scary, full of monsters...and most of what a software developer does lies somewhere in that territory.

Everyone knows it makes management—almost anyone in fact—feel comfortable if we rely on numbers, charts, and deadlines. But to do great things in any profession means to venture into the unknown, and the unknown can't be easily quantified.

So if software development takes place mostly in the territory of the "dragons," why, how, and what do we measure in software development?

We measure to identify areas of improvement, add predictability, reduce risk, and so on. But beyond all that, we measure so we can feel more comfortable moving into the unknown. We measure so we can take educated guesses as to how long a project will take, how much it will cost...

But however educated, they're still just guesses.

Ultimately, we measure because it gives us the feeling that we understand and are in control.

But these are just illusions.

Guesses and illusions can give us the confidence we need to move forward, but they can also give us bad information that leads us in the wrong direction, and we end up paying for that later.

It should be no surprise that the more challenging the project we have to manage, the less accurately we can quantify our progress, at least at times. When we build virtual products, we must be comfortable thinking more abstractly about our process. And measuring progress when developing a virtual product isn't obvious to most people.

Traditionally, software development managers have created schedules allowing for time to design, code, and test a system. This phased approach helped everyone get a sense of a project's progress. Unfortunately, it often turned out to be a lie. Eight months into a nine-month project, we'd find we were six months behind schedule. How did this happen?

Well, we were always six months behind; we just didn't find out until the eighth month, when it was too late to do anything about it.

Managers always ask developers when they think they'll be done with a given task, and very often developers say they don't know. Developers aren't trying to be evasive, and they aren't making some kind of power play. They simply do not know. There's a joke in the software development industry that goes something like this:

Developers have three states:

> *finished,*
>
> *not yet started,*
>
> *and almost done.*

Estimating Unknowns

The reason we rarely know how long a particular task will take is that we've never done it before.

It's possible, and in fact probable, that we'll miss a step. We might assume there's already some code written and available to do a particular subtask of what needs to be done and find out that there isn't any, or we'll discover that this unique task we need to do isn't so unique after all and there's a library that has exactly the functionality we need. More than anything we need to think things through, and we can never do that as effectively as when we're actually performing the task.

The tasks we perform when writing software are vastly different moment to moment, day to day, month to month, and project to project. Of course, there are similar things that we do all the time—designing, testing, coding, and so forth—and there are similar techniques we use and similar ways of approaching problems. But the problems themselves, and their solutions, are often markedly dissimilar to ones we've encountered before.

I know companies, particularly larger companies, that devote a very small percentage of a team's time to writing code. A lot of times this shows up in the guise of trying to improve quality.

For example, a great deal of effort is placed on writing internal design documents and keeping them up to date throughout the development process. In a process like this, all design documents are valued equally, but many, though once useful, end up being abandoned and are clearly not as valuable.

If the customer isn't paying us to write these extensive analysis and design documents, then why are we doing it? The answer is that we believe it helps us understand and express the problem so that we can better approach a good solution. But we often wind up wasting most of our time on issues that don't ultimately provide value to our customers. When we are focused on measuring meaningless things, like actual time vs. planned time using estimates that were based on false assumptions, then we are starting out on the wrong foot.

Developing software is risky. It's rarely done well and the software is practically obsolete moments after it's written. Faced with this increased complexity, the traditional approach to fixing problems in software development is to create a better process. We rely on process to tell us what to do, to keep us on track, keep us honest, keep us on schedule, and so on.

This is the basic philosophy behind Waterfall development. Because changing code after the initial design phase is difficult to accomplish, we'll prevent changes after the design is done. Since testing is time consuming and expensive, we'll wait till the end of the project so we have to test only once. This approach makes sense in theory but is clearly inefficient in practice. In many ways what we're doing is purposely avoiding what is painful or difficult, not because it helps us build better software, but because it's hard, takes more time (at least, more time than we initially estimated), and costs more money.

An Industry of Amateurs

The software industry has been called an industry of amateurs, and sadly, in many ways this has been true.

There's no generally accepted body of knowledge software developers are expected to have, and there's a huge diversity in the way developers approach problems. Knowing a programming language doesn't make you a software developer, just like knowing a written language doesn't make you a writer.

Many computer science curriculums don't prepare students for careers as software developers. They do teach discipline and rigor but focus on the mathematical side of programming, which isn't what most software developers do. It's like insisting that before you can become a painter you must first demonstrate you can solve complex differential equations. But software developers themselves come from diverse backgrounds and often approach problems in different ways. As a result, communicating design ideas and reaching consensus can be difficult.

Science and engineering disciplines rely on generally accepted standards and practices, but there are very few agreed-upon standards and practices in the software industry. This is partly because the problems we solve are so diverse from each other and partly because we are such a young industry.

The best developers I know have managed to figure things out for themselves. There's a lot of reinventing the wheel in software development.

In civil engineering, there may be disputes on the aesthetics of a building but not on its construction. Given the size of the structure and the materials being used, there's a prescribed amount of reinforcement needed and a well-defined process for construction. Building construction codes have been adopted based on these principles. This is not the case with software.

I don't think we'll ever end up with *The Software Engineering Handbook* like we have *The Civil Engineering Handbook*. Civil engineering is—no pun intended—concrete, whereas software engineering is abstract. It happens in a virtual domain that we cannot see, hear, smell, or touch.

That makes it difficult for most of us to comprehend. We're not used to thinking that abstractly, and we don't yet understand the context for software development. We cannot yet describe the laws that affect the virtual domain the way forces like gravity affect the physical domain.

In contemporary medicine, the overarching context was summarized by Hippocrates when he said, "First, do no harm." The goal of the doctor is to heal her patient, and while a doctor may have to harm her patient in order to save him, like amputating an infected leg, the purpose of her intervention is ultimately to save her patient's life.

But there is no equivalent of the Hippocratic Oath for developing software—no statements to guide us to make the best choices.

There are a seemingly infinite number of choices we can make at any step of the software development process. Understanding the best trade-offs for a given situation involves understanding what we gain and what we lose with each option.

In order to solve problems like the one described at the beginning of this chapter, both software developers and managers need to start with a shared understanding of the nature of software and how software needs to change over time so they can build code that's more resilient to change. We have to fill in that giant gaping black hole where our fundamental knowledge is supposed to be.

The challenges that the software industry faces are also opportunities for those who are willing to see them and gain the huge benefits they offer. Our failures in this young industry are pointing us to better approaches that challenge our fundamental assumptions and show us better, more effective ways of working.

And we have to have the courage, not just to ask some difficult questions but to move past our entrenched opinions, our closely held beliefs, and our exclusive communities. We have to work together to answer those questions and work toward a better, more efficient, more reliable, and more quality-oriented profession.

Retrospective

Something's Wrong with the way most software is built and maintained. In a typical Waterfall environment we wait until the very end to see if the thing is going to work, and when bugs present themselves, they're difficult, time-consuming, and therefore expensive to track down and fix.

In this chapter, we discovered...

- Most people have little knowledge of how software is constructed and how software becomes legacy code—software that's difficult and expensive to work with—and how to prevent it from happening.

- Batching features into releases is inefficient.

- Traditional Waterfall processes lead to the creation and propagation of legacy code.

- Software engineering hasn't yet established its core principles or a common body of knowledge every software developer must know.

The Waterfall Model of software development promotes the creation of hard-to-maintain software. The Waterfall methodology works well for constructing buildings, but it doesn't work well for constructing software where batching up features into releases is risky and expensive. Traditional management techniques often don't apply to software either and developers don't yet have a common body of knowledge they can share.

I saw the negative impact these ideas had on the projects I worked on but had no idea how profoundly they affected other projects. Next, we'll look at the software industry as a whole and how it's doing.

CHAPTER 2

Out of CHAOS

If you're like me, you know that something's wrong with the way most software is built and maintained but you're having trouble finding the hard facts that might lead to that conclusion. Without this data it may be hard to convince your team members or managers that legacy code is not just a cost of doing business but a true crisis in progress. And we all need to be aware of the key issues that cause software projects to fail if we want to avoid them.

We are, by and large, a fairly unstudied industry, especially considering how much is at stake in terms of how software affects all other industries worldwide. The Standish Group has at least tried to get to the bottom of the young, complex, and chaotic software industry. While they agree their data might not tell the whole story, it's clear to anyone who has been a software developer for a while that the success rate in our industry isn't very high.

I've seen projects I've worked on struggle and even fail, but I never thought for one minute that the entire industry might be in crisis, losing tens of billions of dollars a year to broken software development processes. But as someone who advises some of the biggest software companies in the world, I wanted to find out how typical my experiences were. So I turned to the largest, most highly anticipated, and now most-often quoted study in our industry, the Standish Group's CHAOS Report.

The CHAOS Report

The Standish Group[1] is a research organization that studies the software industry. Their flagship study, appropriately named the CHAOS Study, looks at a broad cross section of software development projects and evaluates their success based on various criteria. The study includes 34,000 software projects

---

1.   http://www.standishgroup.com

in a range from shrink-wrap software and operating systems to custom applications and embedded systems. The ten-year rolling study includes a wide range of different software projects and different sponsors. Every year they drop 3,400 projects that they were looking at from ten years ago and pick up 3,400 new projects.

The Standish Group sent questionnaires to 365 respondents, covering 8,380 applications in an effort to sort projects into one of three categories:

Successful

The definition the Standish Group uses for success of a software project is that it was "completed on time, on budget, and with all the features and functions as originally specified."

Challenged

Challenged projects are a bit more difficult to classify. These are projects that were completed, but with some compromises either to budget—they went over cost—or to time—they shipped late—or they shipped with fewer features or less functionality than planned.

Failed (Impaired)

A failed project is any project that was canceled—it never saw the light of day. Typically, projects are canceled and fail for reasons outside the developers' control. A project can fail for any number of reasons: insufficient funding, a shift in the market, a shift in company priorities...

In 1994, the CHAOS Study[2] reported that 16% of the 34,000 projects they tracked were successful, 53% were challenged, and 31% failed. Ten years later, in 2004[3] 29% were successful and only 18% failed.

CHAOS Report

2.   http://www.projectsmart.co.uk/docs/chaos-report.pdf
3.   http://www.infoq.com/articles/Interview-Johnson-Standish-CHAOS

In 2010, the CHAOS Study[4] reported that 37% of projects were successful, 42% were challenged, and 21% failed. Just two years later, in 2012[5] 39% were successful and only 18% failed.

While this is a vast improvement over the years, it still means the odds are against us making a software project "successful," and the odds are worse than one in three that any one project will be successful, at least as defined by the Standish Group.

I believe that the increase in success in the 2004 study may be largely due to more maturity in the industry and greater adoption of Agile methodologies throughout the industry. But even with new ideas like Agile, the chances are only one in three that we'll be successful.

I've worked with some very large organizations and for most, but not all of them, the success rate is much worse. Those that are not exclusively software development companies sometimes have success rates in the 5% range.

The software industry wanted this study so badly there was quite a bit of excitement leading up to it. But it wasn't too long after its release that excitement turned into some significant questions, and not about the study's findings, but about the study itself.

Refuting Standish

There is a need to provide some objective criteria for any study, but in particular the Standish Group uses a highly inaccurate definition of success: "completed on time, on budget, and with all the features and functions as originally specified."

But "originally specified" in terms of budget, time, and features is never going to be anything but a best guess. And there is no data on the fitness of those software projects once they're in the marketplace.

---

4. http://www.versionone.com/assets/img/files/ChaosManifest_2011.pdf

5. http://www.versionone.com/assets/img/files/CHAOSManifesto2013.pdf

Initial specifications depend on our knowing *precisely* what we want this software to do, *precisely* how we will go about making it work, *precisely* how long that will take, *precisely* what challenges may crop up along the way...and leaves *precisely* no room for better ideas.

The Standish Group's definition of success is nothing more or less than a recipe for failure. It depends on the entirely fallacious concept that we can precisely predict any of this stuff, let alone all of it. But what may be even worse, it assumes that we begin every project knowing exactly the best way to do everything and so leaves us no room to experiment, discuss, revise, rethink...get a better idea.

In their paper "The Rise and Fall of the Chaos Report Figures,"[6] IT industry researchers J. Laurenz Eveleens and Chris Verhoef showed that the Standish definitions of *successful* and *challenged* projects were misleading and one-sided and that they ended up perverting the estimation practice, which resulted in meaningless figures.

All the CHAOS Study really measures is the ability of project management teams to estimate time and cost, and the effort put into building requirements. But as Eveleens and Verhoef point out, the Standish definitions don't consider a software development project's context, such as usefulness, profits, and user satisfaction.

Meeting the initial targets is more a definition of *failure* since it assumes we didn't learn what the customer really wants and how to build a better program than initially specified. All we have to do is go for done: Ship the thing on time, on budget, and with only the basic functionality first outlined in the initial requirements.

By the Standish Group's definition, a project is "successful" even if:

- The program crashes a month later.

- The user comes back and wants to add a simple feature that can't be done, requires a huge investment in additional time and money, or introduces a range of new bugs.

- Bad code in that system propagates for years to come, creating a massive technical debt in legacy code.

- It's the last piece of software that customer will ever buy from us.

---

6. Eveleens, J. Laurenz, and Verhoef, Chris. "The Rise and Fall of the Chaos Report Figures," *IEEE Software*, 2010, 27(1) http://www.computer.org/csdl/mags/so/2010/01/mso2010010030-abs.html

This tends to indicate that most of the projects the CHAOS Report identifies as "successful" may not actually be successful at all.

By the same token, projects classified as "challenged" by Standish may not have met their originally estimated functionality, schedule, or budget but may have become successful in the marketplace.

The only thing we really know from the CHAOS Report is that "failed" projects were canceled during development and were never released to the user.

These simple criteria never get deeper into the question of *why* projects fail, or why projects become "challenged" in the first place. So it ends up just saying: "We screw up a lot, for some reason."

I'm not willing to leave it at that.

Why Projects Fail

We don't like to talk about failure. Failure tells us there's something we don't understand. But failure does happen, and it's perhaps more prevalent in software than most other industries. While the methods of the CHAOS study may be in question, the fact that the software development industry has considerable room for improvement cannot be refuted. Regardless of how the data are collected, no one works in our industry very long before realizing that it's more likely a new software project will fail than succeed. This has made software development an "iffy" proposition at many companies, and failures often attract national attention.

This isn't just happening to startup companies on shoestring budgets. We're also talking about some of the largest and most well-funded organizations in the world.

In 1994 the Federal Aviation Administration canceled a major project to upgrade its air traffic control system after spending 2.6 billion taxpayer dollars. The Ford Motor Company simply walked away from a new purchasing system in 2004 after spending as much as $400 million. According to an April 2014 article in *The Washington Times*,[7] the cost to repair the glitchy Obamacare website will reach $121 million, which is $27.3 million more than the site cost to build in the first place.

And this sort of thing happens *lots* more often than every ten years.

---

7. Howell Jr., Tom, and Dinan, Stephen. "Price of fixing, upgrading Obamacare website rises to $121 million," *The Washington Times*, April 29, 2014. http://www.washingtontimes.com/news/2014/apr/29/obamacare-website-fix-will-cost-feds-121-million/?page=all

According to Standish, a failed (impaired) project is "cancelled at some point during the development cycle." This definition avoids the ambiguities inherent in their definition of challenged and successful projects. It's clear when a project is canceled.

But most projects aren't canceled because the software development effort has failed, but for other reasons that have more to do with changing business priorities and evolving market needs. Whatever the reason for a project being canceled, it usually happens for reasons outside development's control, whereas it's more common for projects to become "challenged" due to poor programming practices or other technical reasons.

For our purposes, let's break this complex problem into three key factors that drive this low success rate:

1. Changing code
2. Fixing bugs
3. Managing complexity

Something's Changed

Software doesn't change by itself; it stays exactly as it was written. Windows 7 didn't evolve into Windows 8 by process of natural selection. But if software is being used it will need to *be changed*, and someone will have to take active steps to change it—and this is a good thing. It means people are discovering new ways to get value from that software. The only time software doesn't need to change is if it's never used.

Adding features to software is a common request, but until recently we didn't have a disciplined way of doing it. Often the teams that maintain code are not the teams that originally wrote it, and even when the developers who wrote the code are asked to extend it, they often have a hard time remembering why they designed a program the way they did.

In many cases, developers actually require more time to read code than it took to write it, so if changes will be extensive they often opt for rewriting pieces of code rather than bothering to try to figure it out. Instead of taking the time to understand the existing design, many teams faced with adding new features to existing code will hack it in any way they can, which can degrade the overall quality of the system, making it more difficult to extend the code later.

The cost of adding new features to existing software can be astronomically high. This is because most software was not designed to handle new features and will have to be redesigned before the feature can be added. This can be risky and expensive, so instead developers end up adding code on top of code. The intertwined nature of software makes it difficult to add features without suffering a domino effect. A new feature introduces a new bug that leads to another bug, then another and another, and so on. Extending software that wasn't designed to be extendable is like trying to add a new knot to an already knotted piece of rope.

Changes to code, even minor ones, often require the entire system to be retested. For most programs, this means a huge manual effort to rerun all the tests for a system in order to verify nothing was broken in the process of adding the new feature.

If all this sounds a little like a house of cards, you're mostly right. Developers too often write code that is *unchangeable*.

Infestation

Software often fails because of bugs and bugs are expensive to fix. They can amplify the cost of development by an order of magnitude, halt projects, and cripple systems.

Software developers don't usually spend a lot of time fixing bugs. Some bugs are pernicious and take time to fix, but most are trivial. What isn't trivial is *finding* the bugs in the first place.

A recent version of Mac OS X, for instance, has somewhere in the neighborhood of 85 million lines of code,[8] or the equivalent of nearly 1,200 copies of *War and Peace*. Think about what it means having to read through a single manuscript that's 1,200 times longer than one of the world's longest novels to find one typo.

But one typo can crash an 85 million–line program.

So the real question is how do we make bugs more *findable?* Or even better, how do we *prevent bugs from being written in the first place?*

I was a bit surprised and somewhat embarrassed when I finally recognized that the bugs in my programs were written by me. Developers write bugs just like they write code. The only difference is they aren't paid to write bugs.

There are different kinds of bugs: typos that get past the compiler, design flaws that are more of a systemic problem, and everything else in between.

---

8. Information Is Beautiful. "Codebases: Millions of lines of code," v 0.71, October 30, 2013. http://www.informationisbeautiful.net/visualizations/million-lines-of-code/

Bugs are often the tip of the iceberg, and fixing one can cause several more to manifest. Software is often written in a way that intertwines it with itself, and bug-fixing can quickly degenerate into a Whac-A-Mole kind of experience where a simple fix you thought would take a few minutes turns into a seemingly endless ripple of changes through a system.

I've been dealing with bugs for many years as a developer, but I've only recently started to see them for what they really are: flaws in my software development process.

And like insects, software bugs need the right conditions to breed.

Crisis of Complexity

In 2002, the National Institute of Standards and Technology (NIST) said:[9]

> Software is error-ridden in part because of its growing complexity. The size of software products is no longer measured in thousands of lines of code, but in millions. Software developers already spend approximately 80% of development costs on identifying and correcting defects, and yet few products of any type other than software are shipped with such high levels of errors.

Eighty percent of development costs are spent on "identifying and correcting defects"! That leaves only 20% of our budget to create value. Apparently we are so rushed and make so many mistakes that it requires 80% of our costs to go back and fix. No wonder developers have so little time! But the solution to this dilemma can't be found in platitudes like, "Do it right the first time." As we will see, the real problem and solution are far more complex than that.

Most software is written in a way that often makes it harder to read than it was to write. It's full of dependencies—one piece of code depends on another, which depends on another, until the entire system is one big knotted mess—with every developer at least partially "reinventing the wheel" as they write code, so there's little or no predictability in how a particular feature might be modeled.

Add this to another interesting fact brought to light by the CHAOS Report...the percentage of features that end users actually use. Out of over 34,000 software projects the Standish Group found that only 20% of features were often or always used and a whopping 45% of features were *never* used.[10]

---

9. National Institute of Standards and Technology. "Software Errors Cost U.S. Economy $59.5 Billion Annually: NIST Assesses Technical Needs of Industry to Improve Software-Testing," June 28, 2002. http://www.abeacha.com/NIST_press_release_bugs_cost.htm
10. Fowler, Martin. "Build Only the Features You Need," July 2, 2002. http://martinfowler.com/articles/xp2002.html

And by never used I don't mean features like restoring a backup. We don't restore backups every day. Though rarely used it's still very important. By never used I mean never, ever, *ever* used!

The developer who wrote it may have run through it in the debugger, but aside from that no customer has ever seen it.

How did these features get built in the first place if nobody wants them? Part of the answer is marketing. It might have looked good on a bullet list of features, or the customer thought they might have wanted it so they included it in their laundry list of features, knowing, on a Waterfall project, that they'd get only one chance to list everything they needed.

But developers are also guilty of overbuilding. We think, *I'm right there in the code and I can add this feature in just a few minutes—it'll cost nothing.* But what we don't realize is that while it may have cost nothing to add the feature, it could cost a small fortune to maintain it in the future.

And when we string together one "small fortune" after another, after another, after another, across the entire software development industry, the cost of developing, maintaining, and extending software becomes a rather large fortune. But we don't stop there—we add those large fortunes together, too, until, as the late Senator Everett Dirksen once said, "A billion here, a billion there, and pretty soon you're talking about real money."

The Cost of Failure

Many of the published studies on the software industry are ten or more years old and have not yet been superseded by newer studies. However, many of the findings in these studies are still relevant as of this writing.

I've asked thousands of professional software developers who've attended my classes over the years what percentage of software projects they feel are successful. I get answers ranging from 5% to 30%.

Even though we hadn't yet discussed the report, this anecdotal data isn't far off the CHAOS Study's findings. The developers' answers reflect something we all know, regardless of having hard statistics to back us up or not:

Our industry has a long way to go before it's as effective and efficient as it should be.

If software development projects fail more than they succeed, what does this mean for the industry, for customers, and for developers? We can add up the money we lost in development time and resources for a failed project, but we can't put a price on lost opportunities.

We hear about failures like the baggage handling software delaying the opening of the Denver Airport for more than a year and costing $560 million.[11] We don't tend to hear about the smaller failures that happen all the time, and add up quickly.

Today software is at the heart of virtually every business, embodying policies and procedures for nearly everything we do. More and more companies are finding themselves in the software business as well as whatever other business they were in.

A Billion Here, A Billion There

A 2002 NIST report titled "The Economic Impacts of Inadequate Infrastructure for Software Testing"[12] found that software defects cost the U.S. economy nearly $60 billion annually.

Let's put that into perspective:

- $60 billion is bigger than 70% of the world's 180 economies by gross domestic product.[13]

- If you combined the entire estimated net worth of Facebook founder Mark Zuckerberg with the entire estimated net worth of Amazon founder Jeff Bezos, it would be about $60 billion.[14]

And that's $60 billion lost *every year*.

In the United States alone.

Granted, these figures are difficult to pin down with total accuracy, but because this issue is so vital to all the rest of what we're talking about here, let's look at other attempts to quantify the cost of software failures.

11. Calleam Consulting "Case Study – Denver International Airport Baggage Handling System – An illustration of ineffectual decision making." (2008) http://calleam.com/WTPF/wp-content/uploads/articles/DIABaggage.pdf

12. National Institute of Standards and Technology. "The Economic Impacts of Inadequate Infrastructure for Software Testing," May 2002. http://www.nist.gov/director/planning/upload/report02-3.pdf

13. Serafin, Tatiana. "Just How Much Is $60 Billion?" Forbes (blog), June 2006. http://www.forbes.com/2006/06/27/billion-donation-gates-cz_ts_0627buffett.html

14. Forbes 400. http://www.forbes.com/forbes-400/list/#tab:overall

New Studies, Same Crisis

In "Software Project Failure Costs Billions: Better Estimation & Planning Can Help,"[15] author Dan Galorath found studies that "generally agree" the cost of software project failures are in the "50 to 80 billion dollar range annually." If that's true, we lose either the entire capitalization of the Ford Motor Company on the low side or China's Sinopec Group (the world's fifth largest corporation) on the high end.

In his influential whitepaper "The IT Complexity Crisis: Danger and Opportunity,"[16] Roger Sessions sounded the warning:

> The coming meltdown of IT; the out of control proliferation of IT failure is a future reality from which no country—or enterprise—is immune. The same IT failures that are eroding profitability in the United States are impacting the economy in Australia. IT failures are rampant in the private sector, the public sector, and the not-for-profit sector. No place is safe. No industry is protected. No sector is immune. This is the danger, and it is real.

That's a whole lot of bad news. We screw up more than half the time and it's costing us a fortune.

Even if the NIST's $60 billion annual loss estimate is off by as much as 50%, is a low eleven-figure annual loss any more acceptable than a mid-eleven figure annual loss? And every manager has to stop and ask: "How much is my organization contributing to that eleven-figure loss?"

These massive costs to develop software are only dwarfed by the even greater costs to maintain software. With up to 80% of the cost of software happening after the initial release,[17] companies can spend five times more to maintain software than they initially spent to build it. Roughly 60% of these costs go to enhancements while 17% go to error correction, as shown in the graph on page 30.

Why is the cost of maintenance so high? Simply put, it's because we don't value maintainability enough to make it a priority so we build software that's risky and expensive to change and no one knows the economic impact of that.

---

15. Galorath, Dan. "Software Project Failure Costs Billions: Better Estimation & Planning Can Help." *(blog)* June 7, 2012. http://www.galorath.com/wp/software-project-failure-costs-billions-better-estimation-planning-can-help.php

16. http://simplearchitectures.blogspot.com/2009/11/it-complexity-crisis-danger-and.html

17. Glass, Robert L. "Frequently Forgotten Fundamental Facts about Software Engineering," *IEEE Software* archive, 18(3), May 2001, pp. 111–112 http://dl.acm.org/citation.cfm?id=626281

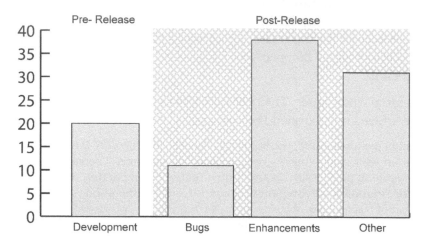

Pre-Release vs. Post-Release Costs
Percentage Cost of Ownership for Software

But even if we're not sure how to measure success and failure and how to track all the money lost in every corner of a massive industry, we're pretty smart people, and when we're willing to say, "We could do better," we start to at least try to do just that.

Retrospective

Out of CHAOS comes a sobering view of the massive cost of maintaining legacy software. With suspect research methodologies and numbers in the ten of billions of dollars, clearly this is an industry that's wasting a tremendous amount of money, effort, and customer goodwill.

In this chapter, we discovered...

- Inefficiencies in the ways we build software cost businesses a fortune every year, and we can and must address that crisis.

- The most widely quoted study of the software industry, the CHAOS Report, is fundamentally flawed yet its final conclusion—that our industry has a long way to go—is right.

- The major studies on the software industry agree that we are losing at least tens of billions of dollars a year in the United States alone to broken software development processes.

- Legacy code is a global problem, and one we all have a share in creating, so we must all take responsibility for solving it.

The Standish Group's CHAOS Report looks at the success rate of software projects across our industry. It says most projects aren't successful but defines "success" so poorly that the study isn't useful. Regardless, other studies confirm that poor software development practices are costing industry at least tens of billions of dollars a year.

Even though it appears that most software projects are doomed to be unsuccessful, some projects are successful and many of them take a different approach to development. I began to look for alternative approaches for building software. Let's take a look at some new ideas from smart people who are positively affecting software development.

CHAPTER 3

Smart People, New Ideas

By the turn of the millennium a group of highly successful software developers realized that in terms of software development process, less is more. Taking a different approach, they strove to find a lightweight process for developing software. Initially, they called it the "lightweight software development process," but fearing it might not be taken seriously enough, they renamed it the "Agile software development process."

It may be fair to say that the "grandfather" of Agile was W. Edwards Deming and his concept of Lean, but it wasn't until after the introduction of Agile that Mary Poppendieck brought Lean principles to software development. And building on the Extreme Programming philosophy behind Agile, Ken Schwaber and Mike Beedle wrote *Agile Software Development with Scrum* [SB01] to help teams implement Extreme Programming in their shops more quickly.

All of these were steps in the right direction, and as we saw in some of the CHAOS statistics and from other sources, they have begun to combat the rampant inefficiency in the software industry. However, we'll need to look deeper into these "new" ideas to see how and why some very smart people have only managed to make incremental changes for the better as much as a decade and a half later.

Enter Agile

When the eminent statistician W. Edwards Deming went to Japan in 1950, as you can imagine, he found a nation in tatters. Barely five years past the end of World War II, Japan's infrastructure was still largely in ruins. The rebuilding of Japan was an uphill struggle at best, an impossible dream at worst. But Deming, originally part of a team sent to help plan the 1951 Japanese Census, began to work with top engineers and managers not to simply rebuild the nation's economy and industry to pre-war levels but to jumpstart it in ways that no one had yet imagined. As much as any single individual, W. Edwards Deming was responsible for Japan's post-war "Economic Miracle."

But it wasn't a miracle.

The ideas that Deming brought with him focused Japanese business on the concept of continuous quality improvement. That required the establishment of quality-first standards and a commitment from all levels of an organization to focus on quality of workmanship and maximum value to the customer. Deming's ideas were incorporated into the culture of Toyota Corporation, which adapted it into a notion they called Lean, and of course this worked quite well for Toyota.

Lean is a process that has been proven over the last two decades and brought back here when Toyota opened plants in the United States. There are now several Toyota plants in the United States, and they're still able to operate with phenomenal efficiency, even with a very different American work ethic. As it turns out, it's the processes, not the people. Toyota has an excellent set of processes, and their success has brought about significant transformation in the rest of the automotive industry, and in many other industries.

What Deming looked for was *waste*, and how that could be eliminated. In manufacturing, inventory is considered a waste because it's taking up space, which means it's not just freezing your capital but costing you money, every day, to warehouse it. Until you release it to the customer you're realizing negative revenue from it. This is easy to understand and goes all the way back to the 1920s when Henry Ford wrote about just-in-time supply chains.

But what is the waste in software, which unlike cars, doesn't require a delivery of steel, another delivery of tires, and so on?

Lean says waste in software development is any task that's started but not yet complete; it's work-in-progress. I would even go so far as to say that anything that isn't software, or anything that doesn't provide direct value to the customer, can be seen as waste.

This philosophy is shared by Agile software development, which encompasses project management methodologies including Extreme Programming, Scrum, and Lean. Although this isn't a book about any single-source methodology, a lot of the practices we'll discuss as we move through the book were outlined back in 2001 in the now-famous Agile Manifesto, which stated, "We are uncovering better ways of developing software by doing it and helping others do it."[1]

At the core of this process is the promise to "satisfy the customer through early and continuous delivery of valuable software." In other words, rather than create more process to assure quality, they suggested less process so developers have more time to focus on applying solid engineering practices. They introduced technical practices, such as test-driven development and pair programming, that supported creating changeable software that was easy to deploy, maintain, and extend.

Smaller Is Better

Long-distance runners often talk about setting shorter mental goals for themselves as they run. "I'm going to make it to that lamppost" feels possible—easy even—especially compared to a twenty-six-mile marathon. Then once you get to that lamppost you set a new goal: the big tree. Then the red car. And so on.

Software developers aren't always sure—in fact we're almost never sure—how long a project is going to take. And there are a lot of reasons for that, none of which is laziness. The profession of software design is, in many ways, barely past the starting line, and we're not exactly sure we can finish a marathon. We can't see the finish line from the starting line—we're not even sure in some sense how long the race actually is. The finish line might be twenty-six miles away, or it might be thirteen miles away or fifty-two. Or we know where the finish line is, but have no map, no prescribed route, to get us there.

But what if we concentrated not on the whole race but on one small piece of it: this two weeks' worth of development rather than a whole year? This way, like a long-distance runner, we can respond to that small section of the race, measuring as we go like an athlete might time a single lap. How far off pace are we? Do we need to work faster or reforecast? Can we start to believe we can finish early?

Much of what you'll see in Part II, *Nine Practices to Extend the Life (and Value) of Your Software*, on page 43 is derived from the Agile movement. These ideas were pioneered by some of those smart people who long ago saw the weaknesses inherent in Waterfall, and the serious negative effects it was having

---

1. http://agilemanifesto.org/

on this developing profession. But as smart as the people behind Agile are, and how good their ideas, we still have a long way to go.

Implementing Agile

Agile has been around since 2001, but it still isn't well understood in the industry. Many organizations do one or a few of the easier Agile practices like stand-up meetings and two-week sprints, and claim they're doing Agile. Most Scrum teams know there's a Product Owner and work in fixed time horizons called *time boxes*. These are important practices, but are valuable only if adopted properly, fully, and in conjunction with other important practices.

It's not about Waterfall versus Agile. It's common for many of the Waterfall processes to seep into the Agile practices. For example, when requirements gathering becomes so complex that requirements have to be written down to later be read and interpreted, it can introduce major inefficiencies and bugs.

And keeping a separate QA process where developers pass software to testers for verification is expensive and inefficient. Retaining these practices and adopting two-week sprints and stand-up meetings won't get you much improvement.

I prefer to focus on practices that address the specific forces of developing software rather than on labels like Waterfall or Agile. This book is not saying that Waterfall is bad and Agile is good. That's far too simplistic to address the core issues.

In my experience, one of the main benefits of developing software in an Agile environment is that it supports making development a discovery process; the team constantly receives feedback and learns from it. Agile requirements—or as Agile calls them, stories—do not by themselves replace the sort of lengthy, detailed specifications that Waterfall demands. Stories are supposed to spark conversations—requiring and encouraging meaningful interaction between software developers and the Product Owner. It's from this interaction that developers learn enough about what's needed to build it.

Just removing specifications without replacing them with conversations between developers and the Product Owner is not the intent of Agile. And if all the Product Owner is doing is taking specifications from the customer and creating detailed requirements, then maintaining documentation along the way—that's just Waterfall with a Product Owner. It's not Agile.

We need to look deeper to find the hidden essence of Agile, which is not just having a Product Owner and getting rid of specifications but really changing the conversation to the *what* and the *why* instead of the *how*.

For example, a central purpose behind the practice *Build in Small Batches* is to take tasks from start to finish as quickly as possible, and smaller tasks can be taken to completion quicker. Many teams do iterative development, but then their work waits in a queue to be validated by a QA team right before release. They take their work to 99% completion, but that's not good enough. Their code harbors an unknown amount of risk that is revealed only *after* integration and testing.

When people understand that the purpose of building in small batches is to take tasks to completion as quickly as possible and to limit work-in-progress, they apply the practices more advantageously and begin to see bigger benefits.

Likewise, time boxing can be misunderstood and misapplied. The practice of breaking big problems down into smaller problems using time boxes in Extreme Programming is called *iterations*, and the term in Scrum is *sprints*. But I'm not a big fan of either of those terms. They tend to give the wrong connotation.

Agile and Scrum are not about rushing through work but working in small chunks. Agile is really all about *scope boxing*—limiting the scope of what we're working on—and we really only time box in order to get people familiar with scope boxing.

Time boxing is simply saying, "We're going to work on this for a fixed amount of time," and usually that's a very short horizon—in Scrum they say one to four weeks—and typically the cadence is every two weeks for an iteration or sprint.

The key, though, is that we should be trying to think smaller in terms of *scope* or units of *work*, rather than units of time. We break down big tasks into smaller units of work that still produce an observable result. And the smaller the unit of work the better—smaller tasks are easier to estimate, implement, and verify.

Scrum caught on as a methodology to manage software development and all but forgot about supporting the technical practices of Extreme Programming. Scrum encourages teams to self-organize, which sounds like a great idea, but just telling developers to self-organize doesn't provide enough guidance to have them adopt practices that help them focus on code quality and write maintainable software.

Just having to go back to code written a few weeks ago and add features can be enough to drive many developers to start writing more maintainable code. But when the technical practices are ignored, improperly adopted, or just generally misunderstood, we end up with teams saying "We do Scrum" while they're really still operating in a requirements-heavy, test-last Waterfall environment. They're just writing smaller batches of code, but it's still full of dependencies that make it hard to work with and bugs that aren't discovered until much later.

I've seen Scrum teams improve their immediate productivity only to find, four or five years into a project, that they've accumulated so much technical debt and their code is so poor that it's nearly impossible to work with. Ultimately, they end up having to address their poor development practices and dig themselves out of the hole they created with poor-quality code before they can become productive again.

I've seen teams adopt Scrum and Extreme Programming but utterly fail. I've seen teams do Waterfall and succeed. Every approach has benefits and drawbacks. We must understand the purpose of every practice to use them correctly.

We've seen how the forces of software engineering are very different from anything in our previous experience. Even electrical engineering and mechanical engineering are based on physics. But software does not obey physical laws, and we sometimes have a difficult time relating to it and really understanding it in a detailed way.

Nearly everything in the physical world is fault-tolerant. Living and non-living systems have enormous resiliency. But software is by far the most fragile thing in our world. One incorrect bit can cause a catastrophic systems failure. Because of this single fact, we must build software in a verifiable way.

To many, software development is counterintuitive. Quality control standards that revolutionized manufacturing utterly fail when applied to software projects. Much of what we learned in the Industrial Revolution is meaningless when it comes to software. It's an entirely different animal.

Balancing Art and Craft

Software development is a complex and varying field that encompasses many skills and abilities. Developers must draw on a variety of techniques because the problems they'll face one day are entirely different from the problems they face the next day, and the next day, and so on. As such, developers need a range of skills that can address these varying problems. Like a carpenter's tool belt that keeps his most-used tools handy, developers need a range of *intellectual* tools at their disposal for addressing an unpredictable range of software problems.

The fact is, anyone can write a simple program to make a computer do something—it's actually an easily learned skill. This is the *craft* of software development: the set of skills that can be learned, then perfected through practice. Craft is a discipline. It's what they teach you in school. You might have learned everything you need to know about sentence structure in middle school, but that doesn't make you Hermann Hesse, J. D. Salinger, or Stephenie Meyer. You need to have a basic expertise in the craft of software development, but that's just the beginning.

Unfortunately, many of the skills developers learned in school are outdated and promote the creation of code that's difficult to maintain and extend. Developers may get a program up and running, but going back into the code and enhancing it can be a difficult and risky proposition.

In Agile software development, developers are constantly going back into their code and extending behavior. This calls for a range of technical practices and ways of thinking about software that most developers are unfamiliar with.

In any reasonably long career in software, a developer might have a chance to learn about fields as diverse as video compression, foreign exchange banking, auto-piloting boats, econometrics, image and graphical processing, remote sensing, signal processing, big data, and much more. Every project is an opportunity to learn about another industry and solve a unique set of problems. And those unique problems will require unique solutions.

Developing software requires a range of skills and abilities—the craft—but no set of learned skills can hope to tackle *every* problem. Software development is one of the few fields that uses both the left (objective, logical...*craft*) and the right (subjective, creative...*art*) sides of our brains. Many people are surprised when I say this. Their image of programming is totally analytical—all about the algorithm—but those of us who code are aware that there's a lot of creativity and imagination needed to write good code.

But the software development profession is still young and the software industry is still in the process of being adopted by other industries.

Agile Crosses the Chasm

In his book *Crossing the Chasm,*[2] Geoffrey A. Moore writes about the *Technology Adoption Life Cycles* for new products. He describes five distinct groups of adopters for any innovative new product:

- *Innovators* are the first to adopt new technologies.
- Inspired by the success of innovators, *early adopters* are next to adopt new technologies.
- Once a lot of the kinks are worked out and it's easier to use, the *early majority* gets involved.
- With the help of the early majority it becomes mainstream and the *late majority* gets involved.
- Finally, the *laggards* are forced to get involved once the other alternatives are no longer available.

We can see the Technology Adoption Life Cycle play out as each new and innovative product is introduced, but this same adoption life cycle plays out when any innovation is introduced. Moore describes the midpoint, as an innovation makes its way through the early adopters into the early majority, as "crossing the chasm."

Agile has hit the early adopters and is penetrating the early majority. It's *crossing* the chasm. But even fifteen years on or so, it hasn't fully *crossed* the chasm, and even when you cross the chasm there are still challenges ahead.

But there are aspects of Agile, like the technical practices of Extreme Programming, that are still in the innovators stage. It's not unusual for *discontinuous innovation* to be adopted *discontinuously.* Adoption usually happens along a path adopters feel is safest. This is why some of the easier and more familiar—but less valuable—practices tend to get adopted first. And as we'll see in the next chapter, Agile won't be "the norm" until we really understand the principles behind the practices.

Demand Technical Excellence

It's no secret what at least some of the original authors of the Agile Manifesto think about Agile adoption. During the ten-year reunion of the Agile Manifesto, Jeff Sutherland said the number one key success factor for Agile adoption is to *demand technical excellence.*

---

2.   Moore, Geoffrey A. Crossing the Chasm. New York: HarperBusiness (1991)

Although the Agile Manifesto states, "Continuous attention to technical excellence and good design enhances agility," in retrospect many of the Agile Manifesto authors felt technical excellence wasn't stressed strongly enough and that "demanding technical excellence is the top priority for the next ten years."[3]

But what exactly do they mean by "technical excellence"? Given that the vast majority of software written today is difficult to work with, it's fair to assume that most developers don't really know what "technical excellence" is.

Because software is virtual, it can be difficult to think about correctly, especially for people who don't write code every day. Most fundamentally, software is a model or representation of something, like a painting. To a painter, technical excellence might involve an understanding of the materials he uses, when to apply various techniques, but above and beyond any of that it's to be consistent with the purpose of the piece.

The same is true in software. In software, technical excellence involves many things that take years of study and a great deal of focus to master. Yet time and focus don't guarantee a person will become a great developer.

In Part II, *Nine Practices to Extend the Life (and Value) of Your Software*, on page 43 we'll cover essential technical practices and why they're important. We'll focus on how to apply these practices for their best use by understanding why they work. By the end of this book you'll understand how to use these nine practices for successfully building software.

Retrospective

Smart People, New Ideas, and our first taste of a growing community of other developers who have recognized a problem and are trying to find ways to address that. But is this the "silver bullet" we're hoping for? Or are we better off looking for guiding lights?

In this chapter, we discovered…

- Though there are significant challenges facing us, some smart people have brought forward new ideas to start moving the software industry in the right direction.

- Agile methodologies offer an alternative to traditional Waterfall development for building software in iterations that help drop the cost of development.

---

3. http://www.infoq.com/news/2012/04/Agile-Resources-Microsoft

- Software developers need to learn to balance the objective craft of writing software with the subjective art that the unique demands of software development require.

- Despite its fifteen years or so, Agile is still "crossing the chasm" from radical new innovation to the mainstream.

- Software developers and managers need to demand technical excellence and create quality software *on purpose.*

Agile software development directly addresses the challenges of a process-heavy methodology, like Waterfall, by offering a lightweight process based on technical practices for creating maintainable code. But many Agile teams aren't aware of these technical practices or misapply them and end up not getting the benefits they hoped for. We must understand the principles behind the practices in order to apply them properly.

Part II

Nine Practices to Extend the Life (and Value) of Your Software

How do we really make something new into a common practice? How do we not just learn new practices but gain proficiency with them? And then go past that to where those new ideas become positive habits?

Some developers are more effective than others, and I've spent most of my life trying to discover what makes these extraordinary developers so good. What I've learned is that these people weren't born that way. They simply make a few distinctions that the rest of us don't. If we understand what they understand, learn some principles and practices, then we can achieve similar extraordinary results.

CHAPTER 4

The Nine Practices

Building software is complex—perhaps the most complex activity that humans can engage in. Writing software is a discipline that requires a range of skills and practices to accomplish successfully.

It's easy to get it wrong—the virtual world is so different from the physical world. In the physical world, we can easily understand what it takes to build something, but in the virtual world this can be much more difficult to see and understand. The software development profession is just starting to figure things out, much like the medical profession a few hundred years ago.

It was less than two hundred years ago that the medical community laughed at Ignaz Semmelweis for proposing that microscopic creatures could cause disease. How could something as trivial as washing your hands before surgery make the difference between life and death to your patient?

The medical community held this view in part because germ theory did not exist yet and partly because they were at that time actively trying to dispel the myth that invisible spirits caused disease (often truth and myth share a lot in common). Therefore, the practice of washing your hands before performing surgery wasn't considered essential.

Battlefield surgeons in the Civil War knew about germ theory, but they argued they had no time to sterilize their instruments. If a soldier needed an amputation they didn't have time to wash the saw. But when the medical community looked at the success rates of battlefield surgery they discovered that, in the Civil War, many more men died of infection and disease than died on the battlefield, so medicine had to rethink its position.

When we understand germ theory, we understand *why* we have to wash *all* the instruments. This is the difference between following a practice (the *act of* sterilizing a specific instrument) and following a principle (the *reason for* sterilizing all instruments).

And the thing about the following software development practices, just like sterilization, is that we have to get it *all* right for *any* of it to work. If we happen to miss one of those things…one germ can kill your patient, and one bug can kill your application. And in this we require discipline.

I don't believe there is one right way to develop software just as there's no one right way to heal a patient, create art, or build a bridge. I don't believe in the "one true way" of anything, but especially not for programming.

Still, having worked with thousands of developers, I've seen firsthand how we constantly reinvent the wheel. Software development has attracted a range of people from all backgrounds, and that has brought many fresh perspectives to creating software. At the same time, the huge diversity among developers can be a real problem. Enterprise software development involves enormous attention to detail and a lot of coordination among those involved. We must have some shared understanding, a common set of practices, along with a shared vocabulary. We must arrive at a common set of goals and be clear that we value quality and maintainability.

Some developers are more effective than others, and I've spent most of my life trying to discover what makes these extraordinary developers so good. If we understand what they understand, and learn some principles and practices, then we can achieve similar extraordinary results.

But where to begin?

Software design is a deep and complex subject and to do it justice requires a great deal of background theory that would need several books to explain. Furthermore, some key concepts are not yet well understood among all developers and many of us are still struggling to figure out the context for software development.

In many ways, legacy code has come about because we've carried the notion that the quality of our code doesn't matter—all that matters is that software does what it's supposed to do.

But this is a false notion. If software is to be used it will need to be changed, so it must be written to be changeable. This is not how most software has been written. Most code is intertwined with itself so it's not independently deployable or extendable, and that makes it expensive to maintain. It works for the purpose it was intended for, but because of the way it was written it's hard to change, so people hack away at it, making it even harder and more costly to work with in the future.

We want to drop the cost of ownership of software. According to Barry Boehm[1] of the University of Southern California, it often costs 100 times more to find and fix a bug after delivery than it would cost during requirements and design. We have to find ways to drop the cost of supportability by making code easier to work with. If we want to reduce the cost of ownership for software, we must pay attention to how we build it.

What Experts Know

Experts organize their knowledge in specific ways. They often have their own vocabulary to describe their key distinctions. They use metaphor and analogy, and have formed key beliefs around their experiences. Their *context for understanding* is different from the rest of us.

All of the techniques experts use are learnable skills—when you understand what experts do and do what they do, you're likely to get the same results.

Expert software developers, the ones who are getting not just incrementally better but hugely better results, think about software development differently than the rest of us. They pay attention to technical practices and code quality. They understand what's important and what's not.

Most importantly, expert software developers hold themselves to higher standards than the rest of us.

I was surprised to find that the best developers I know are also the neatest. I figured fast coders had to be sloppy coders, but what I discovered was just the opposite. The fastest programmers I've met paid particular attention to keeping their code easy to work with. They don't just declare *instance variables* at the top of their classes; they list them in alphabetical order (or however else it makes sense), they constantly rename methods and move them around until their right home is found, and they immediately delete dead code that's not being used.

Even after noticing this correlation between these fast coders and how neat and tidy their code was, it took me a while to recognize the causal relationship between these two things. These people weren't faster *in spite* of keeping code quality high; they were faster *because* they kept their code quality high. Realizing this affects how we think about developing software.

1.	Boehm, Barry, and Basili, Victor R. "Software Defect Reduction Top 10 List." *Computer*, Vol. 34, Issue 1, January 2001. https://www.cs.umd.edu/projects/SoftEng/ESEG/papers/82.78.pdf

Most people recognize that a well-thought-out approach to solving a problem can pay back over the long term. What most people don't realize is the payback is usually much faster than expected. In the physical world we recognize quality as a desirable attribute that we're willing to pay more for. Higher-quality physical things tend to last longer and are therefore more expensive. But the virtual world is different.

In the virtual world, a focus on quality is always less costly to execute in the long term and often also in the short term. This doesn't mean developers shouldn't make compromises at times, but when they do they should also recognize the price they'll pay every time they'll have to go back and work with poor code. If that price is high, then they may want to go back and clean up the code before making further enhancements.

Business takes a cost-benefit approach. Software should be no different. Like any asset, software must be maintained so that it doesn't become a liability.

Shu-Ha-Ri

Mastery involves more than skill and ability. The Japanese martial art Aikido defines three stages of mastery: *Shu, Ha,* and *Ri.*

Shu is the form, the explicit knowledge. "Wax-on, wax-off" from the movie *The Karate Kid* is an example of the Shu stage of learning. Daniel, the young disciple in that movie, was told to wax cars with a circular movement. He wasn't told why or how it would prepare him to reach his goals. Once he mastered the form he was shown why.

Often, people learn Agile as a set of rules, as do's and don'ts. That is just the first stage of learning, yet many people feel that once they learn some rules they're ready to do Agile.

But complex activities, like developing software, are hard to pin down with rules. There's a lot of contraindications in software where the best approach in one situation could be a bad approach in another situation. As a result, becoming a software developer typically involves a long learning curve.

The reason one starts with Shu is that the theory behind the practices isn't obvious. In martial arts, to defeat your opponent you must do more than understand theory; you must put theory into practice. In Aikido, this is called *Ha.* The same thing is true in software development. To be successful, we must know the theories—the principles underlying the practices—in order to put the practices to good use.

You can't learn Ha prescriptively, as a set of rules. It has to come from experience, but it is possible to learn some from other people's experiences.

Once you've used the practices, understand the underlying theory at a deep level, then practice and theory begin to dissolve and we approach the highest level of mastery in Aikido, *Ri*. This is the realm of true mastery that can only be obtained through ongoing study.

In his book *Outliers [Gla08]*, Malcolm Gladwell suggests that after 10,000 hours of practice we become natural in a domain that requires intellectual rigor. We no longer have to think about it because it's almost second nature. If truly mastering any complex activity takes about 10,000 hours, then software development is no exception.

Pablo Picasso understood this. He learned the rules of painting so he could break them. He created paintings unlike anyone who came before him, but few people know that Picasso was trained as a classical painter. He could paint a painting in the style of the classical masters and spent most of his life acquiring those skills. But he wasn't satisfied. He went on to transcend those skills and arrive at something else. To break the rules and break new ground, we first have to master the rules.

The same is true with software development. There are a lot of rules and constraints when building software and there's also technique. Like any other human creation, a computer program is a model of something. We're used to *physical* models, but programs can also be *behavioral* models.

In order to accurately model something we must first understand what it is we're modeling, and we must also understand what modeling skills or techniques are available to us. I find it useful to break out these techniques into two categories: principles and practices.

First Principles

First principles were originally described by Marcus Aurelius, when he discussed the Golden Rule, which states, "Do unto others as you'd have them do unto you." The reason the Golden Rule is a first principle is that much of our law, our society, even our culture is based on that one simple statement. You can infer other principles from first principles.

The Golden Rule is an overarching first principle in the law. It's foundational to the pursuit of justice. Consider what the law would be like without the Golden Rule, if it were every person for themselves. Understanding and agreeing to the right principles is central to the success of any discipline.

Software development doesn't yet have the equivalent of the Golden Rule or the Hippocratic Oath. We're still figuring out what's important and what's unimportant, what we should pay attention to and what we can safely ignore. This is to be expected from such a young field and one so different from every other field of study. But we are starting to establish some principles for developing software.

An example of a first principle in software development is the *Single Responsibility Principle*[2], which states, "there should never be more than one reason for a class to change."

While this seems like a simple statement, it carries with it a great deal of weight. Since classes act as templates for the objects in a system, it means that we should design our classes so that they represent a single *thing*. This implies a lot. It implies we'll have lots of little classes in the system and each one will be focused on fulfilling a single responsibility.

By narrowly focusing a single responsibility for a class, we limit how that responsibility can interact with other classes in the system. This makes it easier to test, find bugs, and extend in the future. The Single Responsibility Principle guides developers to design systems that are well partitioned and modular.

Another example of a first principle in software development is the *Open-Closed Principle* stated by Bertrand Meyer in his book *Object-Oriented Software Construction [Mey97]*: "software entities (classes, modules, functions, etc.) should be open for extension, but closed for modification."

This means we should design systems so they can easily be extended without changing much existing code. When I ask developers why the Open-Closed Principle is important they immediately know why: because changing existing code is often harder and more error-prone than writing new code. When developers understand and value the Open-Closed Principle they tend to write more maintainable code that costs less to extend later.

Principles are very powerful but they're not actionable. Principles tell you what to do but not how to do it. In software, there are many ways to achieve "Open-Closed-ness" in code. It would drive us toward cohesively building objects, programming to abstractions, and keeping behaviors decoupled. It's important to note that these characteristics are side effects of trying to achieve the principle.

---

2.   http://www.butunclebob.com/ArticleS.UncleBob.PrinciplesOfOod

Likewise, there are many ways to achieve the Single Responsibility Principle. Following this principle would drive developers to do things like calling out more of the entities in the problem domain, isolating behaviors, and making the system more modular. All of these things help build more resilient architectures.

Principles often go unstated. Developers may have a vague awareness of what they're striving for, but often don't have it clearly articulated in their own minds. It's helpful to think about principles as the overarching wisdom that helps guide us to do the right things.

To Be a Principle

Principles can be crisp and clearly defined, or they can be vague and unarticulated. Whether stated elegantly or not, principles point us in the right direction and take us closer to the true nature of what the principle applies to. Principles may give us insight or just be good advice. And by "us" I mean not just software developers but everyone those developers might come in contact with—everyone on and around a software development team.

Principles help us generalize about a thing. They help us organize our knowledge. Not all principles are equal. Some are purer, more basic than others, and as we saw, principles from which you can infer other principles are called *first principles*.

I think of principles as lofty goals. They're things that we want to strive for because we know they're good and virtuous. We also know that while principles present worthy goals, they're not always achievable. In software, principles represent overarching advice that helps developers build better software.

To Be a Practice

Principles are important, but principles alone are not enough. We also need ways of achieving principles in practical situations and that's what practices are for.

I use strict criteria for defining a practice. In order for something to be a practice it must

- provide value at least most of the time,
- be easy to learn and easy to teach others,
- be simple to do—so simple, in fact, that you can do it *without thinking about it.*

When a practice fulfills these three conditions, then it can easily propagate among a team and its benefits compound. You can just *do* the practice and it automatically saves time and effort on an ongoing basis.

The nine practices in this book represent a core set of high-value practices that are often misunderstood and misapplied but hold the key to sustainable productivity. And all of them are huge time-savers. I'm not about giving developers more work to do. They're already too busy as it is. The practices I advocate developers adopt save them time both in the short term and the long term. They help developers build focused, testable behaviors.

Principles Guide Practices

Developing software is a seemingly endless set of questions and choices. Questioning is a powerful but tiresome process. Should I do one thing or another? Evaluation is important; it's how we come up with new ideas and innovate.

But questioning ourselves all the time is exhausting. I'm not advocating that developers go fully on automatic, but it can be helpful to have some general practices that can quickly be applied without thinking about whether you should do them or not and that bring you closer to achieving a principle. For example, the simple practice of eliminating duplication in code can lead to unifying and defining classes, each with a single responsibility, which gets you closer to achieving the Single Responsibility Principle. I've trained myself to quickly spot and eliminate duplication in code. I don't have to ask myself if I should get rid of it; I just do it out of habit, and having that habit makes it easier for me to do good work.

When you understand the purpose behind the practice, all of the practices I'm recommending can be done without too much thought. This gives you tools to better define and build software. Practices replace questions and uncertainty with action.

Principles tell us how to apply practices to maximal effect. They help us use practices to their fullest. Principles are like guiding lights. They help show us how to use our practices correctly.

An example of a principle in investing is "Buy low, sell high." That's really good advice for investing but it's also really crappy advice because I haven't told you *how* to do what I told you to do.

Principles are the things we want to drive toward, and practices tell us how to get there. We can actually *do* practices, so an example of a practice in investing would be *dollar cost averaging*. If every pay period, or every month—a fixed period of time—I take a certain percentage of my income and invest it, when prices are low I'm buying more stock with that same fixed investment. With the fundamental assumption that the market will continue to go up, I will have "bought low" most of the time. Then if I hold on to those investments until I'm ready to retire, and the price of a share of stock is higher than the average price I've paid over those years of automatic investments, I'll "sell high"—principles (buy low, sell high) and practices (dollar cost averaging) go together.

Practices help us get closer to principles, but principles help us use practices correctly. We get lost unless we keep our eyes on both of them. Either we're great theoreticians but have no clue how to get there, or we're very pragmatic with daily tasks but don't work toward any specific end. We need to balance both.

Each of the nine practices in this book has an important purpose. When you understand the purpose behind the practice, you'll know how to apply the practice correctly, when to not apply the practice, and what the alternatives are. Practices apply principles; they are practical embodiments of principles.

Anticipate or Accommodate

Without the right set of practices that support creating changeable code we are unable to easily accommodate change when it happens and we pay a big price. This leaves us in a position where we have to anticipate change before it happens in order to accommodate it later. And this can be stressful.

There's a lot of stress when the team has been working on a big feature thinking, *Okay, it's now all been compiled and oh, boy, I hope it works. I wonder what I'm going to see at the end of this.*

The bottom line is *stress doesn't help build a better product*. And when developers realize that fundamentally the software development industry is built around anticipating change rather than having a time-tested set of principles and practices to accommodate change when it happens, we can see that this still young industry has a long way to go.

That's the dichotomy: anticipate or accommodate, and most developers don't yet know how to accommodate change in software. Imagine if every actor always had to get it right on the first take. Making a movie would be so stressful that it would be hell. Just knowing that you don't have to be perfect on the first and only pass makes anything so much easier, and by eliminating (or at least dramatically reducing) the stress of performance anxiety, developers find they can pretty much get it right on the first take most of the time, or discover a new idea or way of doing things, and take on more challenges because now they know if they fail the first time they can still recover.

Most of us can't accurately predict the future. What the user might want after the team delivers what was asked for is really anyone's guess. Anticipating future needs can be exhausting and you're probably going to be wrong most of the time anyway. Yet I find a lot of developers engage in anticipating future needs for their code, even though what they're anticipating is not a requirement today. This can cause developers to waste time worrying about features and functionality that are not currently needed and robs them of valuable time to deal with things that are needed right now.

Rather than try to anticipate what the user might want in the future, what if developers could find ways of accommodating change once it's asked for? What if there were a series of principles and practices that developers could follow, without even thinking about it, that would make changing code easier? Then when the inevitable happens and the customer wants a new feature, the code can accommodate it.

This is not just wishful thinking. I believe developers must and can have a series of standards and practices they can share to help deal with change. We'll discover many of these practices together in the rest of this book and with this knowledge you'll be able to discover many others on your own. But before we can look at these practices we must arrive at agreement for what "good" software is so we understand the principle—the reason for using the practice—in the first place.

Defining "Good" in Software

What makes software "good"? When developers look at a design or a piece of code, how do they determine if it's well written? What are the things they look for?

When I ask developers these questions, I rarely get a consistent answer. For some people, "good code" must be fast and efficient. For others, it must be easy to read and understand. Still others say it must be bug free.

These are all good things, but how do we achieve them? And when we have to trade one thing for another, where do we draw the line? These can be hard questions that don't often get asked, but they can affect how managers and software developers alike work on a daily basis.

The external qualities that the customer experiences—usability, lack of defects, timely updates, and so forth—are symptoms of the software's internal qualities. Even though users don't directly experience these internal qualities, they are affected by them. Software with poor internal quality can be difficult for developers to work with.

Back in the early 1980s, I used a dBase III compiler called Clipper.[3] It was an enormously successful product that made Nantucket Software tens of millions of dollars. But as bright as the developers were, they were unable to come out with any significant upgrades due to the complexity of the code. Eventually, they lost their market opportunity and went out of business.

For too long developers have operated under the assumption that software doesn't need to be changed, that developing software is a *write-once* activity. But the truth is that if software is used then it will likely need to be changed. And this is a good thing. It means that users are finding better ways to gain value from software. Developers want to accommodate users by making their software easily changeable.

Software that people find valuable and use will likely need to be changed in the future. For this reason developers must focus on standards and practices that support the internal code qualities which make software easier to work with. When I ask developers what internal qualities they should strive for in the code they write, I don't get a consistent answer. We're a young industry and we haven't yet arrived at a strong universal consensus for development standards.

We must forge a common understanding of what "good" is, not just to one person but also to our industry at large. When we do this, we will be able to gain consensus on the fundamental goals of professional software development.

Given the costs involved in fixing bugs and adding features to existing software, I'd say above and beyond all else that good software does what it's supposed to do *and* is changeable so it's straightforward to address future needs. Making software changeable extends the return on investment (ROI) of the initial effort to create it.

Software is an asset and the value of that asset depends not only on the value we can derive from it today but also into the future. Life-cycle management has become an important part of building architecture and product design, so it should be no surprise that it's an integral part of software development.

---

3.   http://en.m.wikipedia.org/wiki/Clipper_(programming_language)

Of course, developers often don't know up front what part of their code might need to change. Therefore, they have to write *all* their code to be changeable. Developers achieve changeability by understanding what quality software is and how software needs to be changed over time and building habits from the principles and practices that support this.

Many people characterize quality in software by external criteria, such as it does the right thing, it's bug free, it runs fast, and so on. But these are effects of a deeper cause. The kind of software quality we'll be discussing in this book is *internal quality,* and as a result of building in that internal quality, we'll get closer to those things we recognize as external quality—they are causes rather than effects, and they underlie good software.

They are sometimes subtle and small, but they add up and are at the core of all good software development principles and practices. It's not enough to say you're "doing Agile." Agile methodologies encompass management practices, but the technical practices of XP are at the core of Agile. To really see the benefits of these smart new ideas, we have to understand the principles behind the Agile practices we employ.

For this book, the principles—the reasons for changing how you develop software using the nine practices to follow—are going to sound pretty obvious, but then so does "buy low/sell high." What the nine practices in this book help you do is build bug-free software that is simpler (and therefore cheaper) to maintain and extend: Build better/risk less.

Why Nine Practices

Scrum provided a minimal framework to support Agile development and Extreme Programming initially proposed twelve core practices.

I've distilled that down further into nine essential practices. The first two are what most people think of when they think of Scrum, and the last seven are specific technical practices. These nine practices are designed to help us think about software development in the right way, so we can break the cycle of big releases, which is very much against conventional wisdom.

The nine practices are as follows:

1. Say What, Why, and for Whom Before How
2. Build in Small Batches
3. Integrate Continuously
4. Collaborate
5. Create CLEAN Code

6. Write the Test First
7. Specify Behaviors with Tests
8. Implement the Design Last
9. Refactor Legacy Code

They say people can hold in their heads seven, plus or minus two things at one time, so nine things are about the most anyone can remember. Nine things are also about as much room as I have in this book. These nine practices are the ones I've found to be of the highest value but are also the most poorly understood and often misapplied.

You don't have to adopt all nine practices, but you do have to understand their purpose. If you have other ways to mitigate the issues one of these practice addresses, then you can safely replace that practice. But just like Picasso, you must understand the rules before you can safely break them.

You may notice a common theme throughout these nine practices that suggests building out verifiable behaviors. This helps keep development focused on building the right things and on doing it in a way that's easily verifiable and supports changeability in the future.

These nine practices help streamline the software development process while still supporting the creation of changeable code. Of course, there are many other practices that support writing changeable code, but these nine provide a solid foundation and a good start for dropping the cost of building and maintaining software.

My goal for this book is to help you think effectively about building software so you can build it more efficiently and your software will be easier to extend later.

Retrospective

The Nine Practices are at the core of good software development. They help keep development focused on writing maintainable software.

In this chapter, we discovered...

- If software is to be used it will need to be changed, so it must be written to be changeable.

- In order to accurately model something we must first understand it.

- All the things needed to become an outstanding developer are learnable skills.

- Rather than trying to anticipate what changes will be needed, we'll develop engineering practices that support accommodating change when it's needed.

- Software development has its own set of unique challenges that are different from other disciplines, and to address these challenges we must understand the principles behind the practices.

The nine practices we'll cover in this book directly address many of the challenges in building software. The focus of these practices is not to make developers work faster. The emphasis is on building code that's more straightforward to maintain and extend. By focusing on building quality into code so it's easier to work with, developers can work faster, not just in the short term but also over the life of the software they create. This reduces the likelihood their software will become legacy code.

CHAPTER 5

Practice 1: Say What, Why, and for Whom Before How

Up to 50% of development time in a traditional software project is taken up by gathering requirements. It's a losing battle from the start. When teams are focused on gathering requirements, they're taking their least seasoned people—business analysts who don't have a technical orientation in terms of coding—and sending them in to talk to customers. Invariably they end up parroting what the customer says.

We all have a tendency to tell people what we think they want to hear, and some customer-facing professionals still fall into this trap. It's uncomfortable to try to find a way to tell your customer, "No, you don't want that, you want this," or "Let's not worry about how it works and instead trust our developers to get us there."

It's easier to list the features requested by the customer and tell them exactly what we think they want to hear: "Got it. We can do that." But can we?

More importantly, *should* we?

It's natural in spoken language to talk in terms of implementation. That's how people tend to speak, and it's hard to identify when we're doing that. I go from *my* specific understanding to a generalization. You hear that generalization and go back to *your* specific understanding. And in the end we have two different experiential understandings of what we think is common ground, but they're probably completely different.

Requirements have no form of validation and that's translated from the customer telling the analyst, the analyst writing it down, the developer reading it and translating it into code....It's the telephone game. There are all these different ways of reinterpreting stuff so when you finally give the released version to the customer they're apt to say, "That's not what I said. That's not what I wanted."

Don't Say How

Customers and customer service managers alike should get away from the whole idea of telling developers *how* to do something, and there are several reasons for that.

The way software is built is not terribly intuitive for people who don't know how to do it. It's not as if everyone can just sit down at a computer and figure it out. So considerable effort is put into trying to translate the software development process into something more understandable to the layperson, as a way to help the customer feel more confident that his or her needs are being heard and there's solid agreement as to what the project is and what it will do. That's perfectly reasonable, but unfortunately that effort tends to yield a rigid set of requirements.

Requirements sound like a good idea, but because of the way people tend to communicate in terms of *how*, they end up causing more problems than they solve. And by the way, this is a problem in spoken language. It's systematic of the way self-consciousness works and not exclusive to software requirements.

As soon as a team of developers hears or sees a requirement that says *how* to do it, it's as if their hands had been tied behind their backs. It's effectively saying, "Do it this way." And that's what the developers code up, and by default they code it up procedurally rather than stepping back and saying, "Now, how could I create a cacophony of objects to interact and create this behavior?"

Software development is no longer about telling the computer to do this, do that, do this. It's about creating a *world* in which the computer is compelled to do these things based on the interaction of the objects involved.

That sounds a little like the movie *Tron*, and I don't want to be anthropomorphic about it—obviously there's no consciousness inside a computer—but if you make a hill object and a ball object and if you model them well, the ball should roll down the hill.

And something similar should be done with our business rules.

Business rules are the rules of the system, the bits of code inside the *if* statements. Business rules tell the system when to take action.

Software developers want to express these rules in terms of the domain we're modeling. Whatever domain or business our software is modeling, we want to use *their* terminology and draw on that domain knowledge. We want our business rules to naturally follow from the objects in our software models, or what I refer to as the *problem domain*.

This shouldn't be too strange to consider. Think about it manually—in terms of real-world objects and things. Builders follow a blueprint, clerks organize files in a filing cabinet, but they do those things in a way that makes sense. Builders don't look at the blueprint upside down or backward or draw blueprints that aren't to scale, and no one would file the folder marked "Bernstein, David" under P for "person," or R for "one of the letters in his last name."

Software developers want to do the same thing with software objects.

The objects in the virtual world of a program should mirror the relevant aspects of the objects in the real world that they represent.

Turn "How" Into "What"

What we should all be going for is a collaborative relationship with the customer. But the problem continues to be the spoken language. It's simply too easy to fall into a pattern of saying how to do something. And the domain of the how is exclusively the domain of the software developer.

As software developers, we want to know from the Product Owners and customers *what* they want and *why* they want it, and we want to know *who* it's for—we don't want them to tell us *how* to do it, because that's our job. That's the world software developers live in. We straddle the *what* and the *how*. We're the only ones who get to know *how*.

If I wanted to have a house built for myself, I'd hire an architect, a contractor, a plumber, an electrician...and I'd tell them I want a kitchen with lots of counter space and a gas range, I want this many bedrooms, a Jacuzzi tub, and so on.

What if the architect then asked me what angle the roof should be, the contractor wanted me to tell him which nails to use, the plumber waited for me to tell him how many feet of pipe to order? My response to all of them would be "Make it according to code, and make it good." If the architect then asked me what a building code was, I'd get another architect. I don't know what the code says, but I'm willing—and happy—to hire a trained and experienced professional who does. We trust those codes, even if we don't know what they are, and we trust professionals to do the right thing.

And even if there are no "building codes" for software, there are trained and experienced professionals who can not only handle the "how" but can offer new features, new ideas, and new approaches to make the end result something much better than first described.

Software developers are experts in implementation as well as abstraction. In the development process, developers come up with all sorts of alternatives that may not make sense to nondevelopers, because a good developer's primary concern is maintainability.

And there's far more than one way to do anything.

It's almost impossible for different teams to build software that is exactly the same. I could give a thousand developers the same requirements—and I've done this—and I see a thousand different approaches. The end result may look the same—indeed, they probably *do* look the same—but how they're implemented is different in subtle ways, and sometimes in very big ways. And that's good—that's where new and better ideas come from. But there needs to be some common ground, some standards and practices where the context is set first so the software can be built correctly, without a lot of dependencies on implementation.

As of this writing, I've trained more than 8,000 developers in classes that usually include some form of programming lab. So far about 500 developers have done one of my programming labs that involves writing the guts of an online auction system. No trivial task.

What I've found is a startlingly diverse range of solutions.

Most will have a lot of similarities and they'll generally call out most of the same entities—such as auctions, sellers, and bids—but there'll be subtle differences in implementation. Some will keep a list of logged-in customers, whereas others simply have the user object keep track of whether it's logged in or not.

There's no right answer for these kinds of things. I don't care how one developer implements a feature; what I care about is that all developers understand the trade-offs of their decisions and the other paths they didn't take.

Software developers don't have to "standardize" implementation beyond a set of core principles, patterns, and practices developers should be aware of. But they do want to "standardize" how they define behavior and what tests to write. If developers can agree on what tests to write to specify behaviors, then they suddenly arrive at a great deal of common ground.

Have a Product Owner

In every *great* software development project I've ever worked on, we've had a Product Owner. Typical names for this role include product champion, customer representative or onsite customer, or project manager; sometimes it's even team manager, or team leader. Whatever you want to call this person, I'll continue to refer to him or her the way Scrum does, as the Product Owner or PO: any individual who is mostly responsible for the product, who's *most* in touch with the customer, and who best understands what the product really is. The Product Owner becomes the authoritative source, and this role is absolutely critical.

Having worked at IBM for many years and built on projects/products designed by committee, I can tell you it absolutely doesn't work.

After all, *most* things designed by a committee don't actually work.

The Product Owner not only guides but drives the development process, though this is *not* necessarily a technical role. In fact, it tends to work better if the PO is not a technical person but has an intimate knowledge of what the product is—this person is *really* familiar with his or her domain.

And is prepared to take the heat…

On one hand, the PO is a superstar. On the other hand, the buck stops there. The PO is sometimes referred to as *the single wring-able neck*. That person must be the final authority. Even if the Product Owner is wrong sometimes, software developers need to have clear and direct answers to questions. Developers are in the midst of details that most people don't ever think about and few really understand.

The Product Owner is the relationship hub. Everybody goes to that person with updates and questions, and he or she filters that information. The Product Owner holds the vision for the product, defining what is to be built next, though defining *the product itself* is a collaborative effort within the whole team—of course driven by the PO and any subject matter experts (SMEs) with a stake in it.

The Product Owner is the person who says, "This is the next most important feature to build."

The Product Owner orders the backlog and the features to be built, ensuring that the most important stuff gets built and the least important doesn't, at least not right away. One of the main benefits of an ordered backlog isn't so much to do the most important stuff first, but to let the least important stuff fall off the edge so we don't waste time on it.

This is the part of our industry that hasn't yet been figured out well.

On a film crew everyone does his or her job and does it well, and the film couldn't be made without the contributions of each of them. But to make a great story, to make a really great picture, it's the director who knows the flow, the pacing, and everything that makes it come alive. The Product Owner is like a film director—both have to take responsibility for the whole project.

Developers are particularly good at coming up with questions no one has ever considered. They have to ask those questions, in an enormous level of detail, to code software that does what they want it to do. If they don't, and if they fail to take into account one possible condition or one potential problem, there's no guarantee what the computer will do, and the program usually crashes.

Sometimes developers get it wrong—not the code, but *what the code is actually supposed to do*—and that's why we need the Product Owner there to answer questions and research the right outcome—even if many times it's not an absolute answer.

We need to carry forward the intent of the user and not get caught up in minutiae or details or politics.

Still, the idea of working without specifications makes some developers skittish. Asking developers to write software before they have all the requirements, before they *know* what to do, seems inefficient, even reckless. But developers can actually start building without all the requirements, adding as they go, and do it efficiently and with a considerable increase in quality.

This goes back to the idea of asking "What?" and not "How?"

So then, what is the alternative to specifications?

Stories Tell What, Why, and for Whom

A story is a one-sentence statement that describes

- what it is...
- why it's there...
- and who it's for.

Let's say we're tasked with creating software for online movie ticket sales. One story might read:

> As a moviegoer, I'd like to purchase tickets online so that I don't have to wait in line at the theater.

That one sentence tells me who it's for (moviegoers/consumers), what they want (to buy movie tickets online), and why they want it (to avoid long lines at the box office). That's a great start, but it's just a start; there's not enough information here to start coding. So stories alone don't replace specifications, but they focus on the context: the *what* rather than the *how*.

There's a lot more to writing a good story that's beyond the scope of this book. A good book on story writing is Mike Cohn's *User Stories Applied: For Agile Software Development [Coh04]*.

Alistair Cockburn says that stories are "a promise for a conversation."[1] We don't have enough information to build the feature, but we do have enough information to start a conversation about that feature.

Requirements are replaced not by stories but by the interaction between the Product Owner and the developers, and the interaction between the Product Owner and the customer. Those interactions are where the rich understanding comes from to build the software.

And by the way, stories are typically written on 3x5 cards so there isn't a lot of room. I usually give the team big markers, too, so they have to write in big block letters. We don't want that much detail, and it's okay to look for ways to try to make adding detail—adding "how"—as difficult as possible.

The long and complex process of writing everything down in English is inaccurate when it comes to code. Rather than just building a set of instructions the developers not only don't need but will work better without, stories allow us to focus on the work, so developers are building in a way that's rich with discovery, and that really is exciting.

Exciting *and* efficient.

In a traditional Waterfall process the plan itself often takes on a life of its own, so there's a palpable sense of completion at the end of the planning session. The people involved in creating the requirements can feel that they've

---

1. Cockburn, Alistair. "A user story is the title of one scenario whereas a use case is the contents of multiple scenarios." http://alistair.cockburn.us/A+user+story+is+the+title+of+one+scenario+whereas+a+use+case+is+the+contents+of+multiple+scenarios/v/slim

finished the project, but all they've done is get to where we *think* we've agreed on what this thing should look like once somebody actually does any work.

Then developers sit down to code it and realize that maybe 25% of the questions they needed answered actually have been answered: have we thought about this or that or this—and how do we handle that?

Stories are about making sure the focus remains on *the development of the software itself* rather than on the plan for the development of the software.

In Agile we say, "Barely sufficient documentation."

Many teams spend so much time with specifications and design documents that they forget software development is all about coding. They end up with all these disjointed documents apart from the code. Instead, the code itself should *embody* all that knowledge. They're so busy working on all those artifacts to document the system that they have no time to make the code itself expressive and easier to work with.

It's the conversation that makes the development process work, and by far the most efficient way to build software is that collaboration between Product Owner and developers.

A story is finite and speaks of a single feature for a specific type of user and for a single reason, whereas requirements can be pretty open ended. When a story is finite it means it's testable, and when a story is testable, you know when you're done. This is absolutely critical for software developers because when we don't know how a feature is going to be used, we overbuild it. This is why nearly half of all the features in software are never used.

Software developers overbuild because we're *scared* that this feature is going to be used in a way we didn't anticipate. If I know how it's going to be used, I can build it right and build it for that need, and then I can move on.

A lot of "what-iffing" occurs in software development. That's where the sorrow and unhappiness comes into our industry—that anticipation. Any time you have to *anticipate* is a recipe for misery, because you never know if you've done too much. You never know if you're doing enough. You never get that feedback either.

No wonder developers age quickly.

So that whole idea of "let's let development become a discovery process" is a very exciting thing, and a powerful way to build software. And then, of course, developers start doing things like prototyping and showing their work in progress that inspires, from the customer, all sorts of new ideas for features and functionality.

Software developers do still like to be definitive, and I don't mean to imply that this sense of discovery is a slow, meandering journey. We can and should build acceptance tests—and there are automated tools to do this for us—and when that tool says "Yes, it passes," okay, *great!* And we can move on.

We don't have to stay up at night wondering, "Did I cover that case or this case?"

Set Clear Criteria for Acceptance Tests

Working from *barely sufficient documentation*, the team will need to know a few things before starting to build a feature. Rather than working from step-by-step requirements, Product Owners need to know

- What are their criteria for acceptance?
- How much detail do they need in order to engage in a conversation with developers?

And developers usually need to know a fair amount about what is to be built.

No one should try to automate conversations between the Product Owner and the developers, but we can automate the criteria for acceptance:

- what it should do
- when it's working
- and when we're ready to move on

This allows developers to then focus on edge cases—on problems or situations that occur at extreme operating parameters.

Customers are often surprised when those kinds of questions come up. They hadn't thought of those issues in the process of building requirements, even if they experienced those problems in the course of doing business. But those are the things developers have to put in the software to make it actually work *all the time*, not just when everything else is working perfectly—what we call the *happy path.*

The happy path assumes that nothing will ever go wrong. But developers, of course, have to deal with the alternate paths, error paths, and exceptional paths, as well. There's only one or a few happy paths in a feature, but there may be several exceptional paths, so dealing with those exceptions in a systematic way can be very helpful in simplifying the software.

Corner cases are divergent from the happy path. As a developer, maybe I get inputs that are out of bounds, or encounter an error because I go to access some service online but that service is down at the moment. How do I handle that? How do I respond?

Certainly, I don't want to crash the computer. I want to do something more meaningful. Maybe I put a message up to the user or try an alternate path. Developers need to flesh out alternate processing, the unhappy paths, error conditions...all of those things. This means asking: *What could go wrong with the story?*

Put those divergences in your acceptance tests. You really have to define all the edge cases in order for your story to be complete. When you make a mistake, or fail to handle an edge case, the computer has free reign to simply crash. I used to call it "the blue screen of death."

Whatever you call it, it's not a pretty sight.

Automate Acceptance Criteria

Being able to express requirements as acceptance tests creates another venue for a whole different, rich set of information. It helps developers understand the customer's real business needs so we can write the right code, and it lays it out in a way that's very readable. Acceptance tests aid in defining a system behavior and provide real examples as input and expected output. We're no longer talking in the theoretical. Now we can say, "Given these specific inputs, I should produce this output." It becomes tangible.

Concretizing the abstract is a critical skill for software development and the reverse, abstracting the concrete, is just as critical. Using acceptance tests to flesh out behavior and implementation gives developers the ability to go back and forth more easily. Usually, two—or at the most three—examples of behavior are enough to start coding, enough to help us understand and generalize. Using automated acceptance tests to help formalize that definition of behavior means everyone is on the same page. The Product Owner has the same expectations as the developers.

Whether or not you use automated tests, it's good to jot down acceptance criteria and corner cases on story cards to remind yourself what exceptions you'll need to handle. Knowing a feature will be done when it satisfies specific acceptance criteria helps focus development and keep us on task. Developers sometimes tend to overbuild, or what we call in the industry "gold plate," because we're unclear on how our software is going to be used or if it's robust enough. Again, having well-defined acceptance criteria eliminates that problem.

All projects need a superstar Product Owner to really be successful, just like the most successful movies are ones that have great directors. With automated acceptance criteria there's no ambiguity. It's a discipline that helps both the Product Owner and the developer focus on the things that matter most in bringing the project to successful completion.

Let's Get Practical

Here are some ways to put these ideas into practice.

Seven Strategies for Product Owners

At the core of a great product is a great Product Owner (PO). The Product Owner holds the vision for the product and prioritizes the work to be done. Here are seven strategies for the effective Product Owner.

Be the SME
> The PO must be the subject matter expert (SME) and have a deep understanding of what the product is to be. POs must spend time visualizing the system and working through examples before it's built so they understand it as much as possible.

Use development for discovery
> While POs must hold the product vision, they must also keep an open mind to discovering better solutions in the process of building it. Iterative development provides many opportunities for feedback, and POs should take these opportunities to get features that are in the process of being built into the hands of users to make sure development is on track.

Help developers understand why and for whom
> Understanding why a feature is being requested and who it is for gives developers a context for what's being requested. Developers can often come up with better, more maintainable implementations that get the same job done but that are also more generalized, flexible, and extendable.

Describe what you want, not how to get it
> One of the many benefits of stories over specifications or use cases is the focus on what to build and not how to build it. Developers often interpret specifications or use case descriptions literally into code, making it difficult to generalize a solution later. POs must be careful not to tell developers how to do something and instead focus on what they want done. This can give developers the freedom to come up with solutions that are more maintainable.

Answer questions quickly

Single-sentence stories can't replace a specification. Stories are meant to be a starting point for a conversation between the PO and the developers. The PO must be always available to answer questions that come up throughout development. Often, answering developer questions becomes the bottleneck during development, and when the PO is not available, development slows down and developers must make assumptions that may turn out not to be true.

Remove dependencies

POs typically don't code but they can help the team by working with other teams their developers depend on to ensure the dependencies don't hold anyone up. They order the backlog and must ensure that any dependencies across teams have enough lead time.

Support refactoring

It's the PO's job to request features, but a PO must also be sensitive to the quality of the code being produced so it remains maintainable and extendable. This often means supporting the team when they feel that refactoring can help.

The Product Owner is a critical role in driving product development with Scrum. It is not a technical role, but it requires great talent and communication skill. When a PO is available to the team to quickly answer questions and provide direction, software development can rapidly move forward.

Seven Strategies for Writing Better Stories

It helps to focus on what we want to build and for whom. Here are seven strategies for writing better stories.

See it as a placeholder

Stories alone are not meant to replace requirements. They are supposed to help start a conversation between the Product Owner and developer. It is those conversations that replace requirements; stories are just placeholders. Use stories to capture the main ideas you want to bring to sprint planning for further discussion.

Focus on the "what"

Stories focus on what a feature does, not how it does it. Developers should determine how to build a feature as they're coding it but first figure out what the feature will do and how it will be used. This helps developers hide implementation, making software more decoupled and easier to extend.

Personify the "who"

Knowing who a feature is for helps developers better understand how the feature is likely to be used, which gives insight into improving the design. It also helps developers cluster features around user needs or scenarios to build a more complete set of features for a type of user. Give your imagined ideal user a backstory—what is his or her name, desires, interests, and so forth? This will help you better visualize and understand the people who'll be using the features you're building.

Know why a feature is wanted

Understanding why a feature is wanted and what it's trying to achieve can often lead us to better options. The "so that" clause of a story specifies why a feature is desirable by stating the benefits of the feature. This can give us options for developing a feature as long as it's consistent with why that feature is desired.

Start simple and add enhancements later

Incremental design and development is not only the most efficient way to build software, it also offers the best results. Designs that are allowed to emerge are often more accurate, maintainable, and extendable. Understanding refactoring and emergent design helps us build higher-quality software faster and gives us avenues to change designs with minimal rework.

Think about edge cases

Stories state the *happy path* but there are often other paths we have to take, including alternate paths and exception/error handling. I typically jot down edge cases on the back of the story card to keep track of them, and later I'll write tests for them to drive their implementation.

Use acceptance criteria

Before embarking on implementing a story it's important to have clearly defined acceptance criteria. This is best expressed as a set of acceptance tests, either using an acceptance testing tool such as SpecFlow, FIT, or Cucumber, or you can just jot it down on the story card. Acceptance tests tell developers when they'll be done implementing a story—when all the acceptance tests pass. This helps keep them from gold plating and over-implementing.

Stories are fundamentally different from other requirements documents in that they're a minimal description of what, why, and for whom a feature is intended. This is enough to start the conversation between Product Owner and developer so development becomes a discovery process instead of developers blindly following requirements.

Retrospective

Say What, Why, and for Whom Before How in order to describe goals and constraints, not implementation details. Say what to build but don't say how to build it; let developers discover the how and abstract the how with the what. This helps hide implementation details so code is simpler to work with and less costly to extend. When stories replace requirements and development becomes discovery, we build a better product than if we'd tried to figure it out up front.

In this chapter, we discovered…

- By focusing on *what* the software should do instead of *how* it should be done, developers are free to discover the best implementations.

- To build better-quality software, you need to know how to communicate with the people around you.

- Shifting the crucial conversation for defining features from describing implementation details to describing *what*, *why*, and for *whom* helps development become a discovery process.

- Effective Product Owners write good stories with clearly defined acceptance criteria.

- Build features more effectively to reclaim up to a third of all time spent in development, eliminating written requirements and building a creative collaboration between the Product Owner and the development team.

Teams that change the way they define features from describing implementation details to saying what, why, and for whom the feature is can reclaim up to a third of development time by eliminating written requirements and starting a creative collaboration between the Product Owner and the development team.

CHAPTER 6

Practice 2: Build in Small Batches

The Scrum practice of time boxing forces developers to break down big features into smaller tasks, and though this may sound simple, it can be a challenge to implement. Accustomed to trying to build several features at once and focusing on the release instead of the feature or tasks, developers can end up overwhelmed, behind, and in a rush to finish.

Filmmakers don't make a whole movie in one two-hour take; they shoot it not even, necessarily, a scene at a time but a *shot* at a time. When they have that shot, only then do they move on to the next. Though a director will always be keeping an eye on the movie as a whole, all efforts that day—or that part of a day—are on getting that *one shot.*

There are instances in which filmmakers will bring in multiple cameras and use other techniques to try to get a whole scene in one take. In the same way one task in a software project may be much bigger and complex than another, so everyone involved in software development has to start getting better at understanding that granularity so we can distinguish which task is a "shot" and which task is a "scene."

In software development, there are forces that drive the actual size of an individual unit of work, and "small" alone isn't the only criterion. That unit of work should also show *measurable results*. It should be something from which you can see some observable behavior.

Sometimes it takes a little more of a chunk of work to be able to show some observable behavior. We have forces that are pushing us to make things bigger and we have forces pushing us to make things smaller, and it's up to us to try to find the proper balance between the two so that we're going for the *right size*, not just "smaller."

When the team commits to building software that provides value over a short cadence, like every few weeks, it forces them to break down big problems into smaller, more manageable ones. Skills are involved in doing this, and when a team gets good at those skills they may find they no longer need to strictly adhere to iterations; development can be more of a flow.

Time boxing is the practice of working on tasks for a fixed period of time. Scope boxing disregards time in favor of completing easily described units of work: a single story or feature. Choosing between time boxing or scope boxing really depends on the type of work being done. If the sizes of the tasks are all uniform and small, then scope boxing may be preferred. Managing scope requires more discipline than managing time, so it's generally preferred to start with time boxing until you get really good at breaking down features into small tasks.

We can use different ways to find the right size for a batch of work, but we should always start by being honest with ourselves.

Tell Smaller Lies

The truth is we can't help but lie to ourselves, and this is actually a good thing. It helps to walk through life with certainty because the truth is that there is no certainty and if we really, truly embrace that as human beings we would never get out of bed in the morning. Survival calls for us to walk around with certainty...but not *always*.

If we need to tell ourselves lies to do things—and I mean "lies" in the most positive sense of the word—then let's let those lies be small lies so we won't suffer the full agony of the truth when it comes out. That's really what Agile is. We set up horizons that are shorter; we build in smaller pieces so that when we feel we're off course we know it sooner and we can do something about it. And that's the important part: *to do something about it*.

Just knowing what to do—the right thing to do—is not enough. A lot of us know what to do and for whatever reason we just don't do it.

Rather than building software in the discrete phases of analysis, design, code, test, and deploy, it's far simpler and less risky to build a system feature by feature—every few weeks more features are added to a functioning system. This is simpler since smaller tasks are easier to work with than larger ones, and less risky because as features are built they're integrated into a working system so there are no surprises later.

Rather than the big lies developers told themselves in an annual development cycle, they can tell smaller ones when they build in two-week iterations.

Be Willing to Flex

Project management isn't necessarily known for its flexibility, but reality sometimes forces that necessity on us all. We can either be ready for change or be thrown by it.

Maybe you're willing to flex on scope. Or maybe you're willing to flex some on release dates. But in fact we have to be able to flex on *both of them*. Notice we say "scope" and "dates" because the word "resources" does not apply to people.

People are not scalable.

Frederick P. Brooks, Jr. elaborated on the sanctity of the critical path in his book *The Mythical Man-Month [Bro95]* in which he wrote, "The bearing of a child takes nine months, no matter how many women are assigned." You can have one baby produced in nine months by one woman, but you cannot have one baby produced in one month by nine women.

If you manufacture toasters and get a big order and want to double production, you can double your employees, create a new assembly line, and double output...and that works!

But if you're building software and have a big set of requirements come in and need to double your productivity, if you double your staff...what happens?

Things slow down or even stop completely.

This is another clue that building software is not like manufacturing.

There are rules of parallelism in manufacturing—two completely independent assembly lines can double productivity—but in software there's so much interaction between people that when we add more people there's more interaction, and things get slower. Rote tasks on an assembly line can be completed independently of each other, but software development doesn't involve rote tasks. Often when we add more people to a project, it requires more communication and coordination, which can slow a project down instead of speed it up.

In fact, one of the great secrets in the top teams in software is that they're very small. And they do that because the human interaction takes a lot of time.

So if you can't add more people, and you can't have more time because you've committed to a delivery date, and if you have to ship with these features because marketing says so, then what gets forsaken?

Developers know what that is. It's the only thing that's under our control:

The quality of our own work. And quality is the one thing we never want to sacrifice.

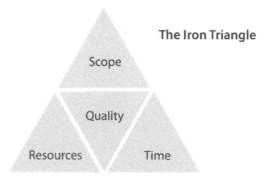

The Iron Triangle

Scope

Quality

Resources   Time

This is the so-called *Iron Triangle:*[1] scope, time, and resources (STR). In manufacturing they say pick two and the third must be fixed. The STR assumes the following relationship:

Scope = Time * Resources

But this is the wrong formula when applied to building software. In building construction, scope is fixed. You can't "release" a building without finishing the roof, even if that's the last thing on your to-do list.

In software scope is the *easiest* to flex. Developers often build the wrong thing or overbuild the right thing so flexing scope should be the first place we look. Understanding how to scope using techniques like *minimal marketable feature sets (MMFs), story splitting,* and other techniques can be helpful in "right-sizing" feature sets.

The most valuable features should be created first, and possibly released early to customers, if they would get some value from having it. That way, if development isn't as far along as expected when the release date arrives, the software will still provide some value. Given that nearly half of the features delivered are never used, giving the user something instead of nothing can mean the difference between success and failure.

---

1. Also referred to as the Project Management Triangle; see http://en.wikipedia.org/wiki/Project_management_triangle

All this leads to shorter feedback cycles. The more feedback you get the more likely you'll be to identify a problem, and the sooner you get that data the more likely you'll be able to do something about it.

By working in smaller batches, we're seeking validations over assumptions.

This also shifts the mind-set a bit so that now you're starting to think about what it is you *don't* know as you're developing.

Cadence Dictates Process

In "How Cadence Predicts Process,"[2] Mary Poppendieck discussed how the rhythm of release cycles affects the efficiency of your system. She used the example of a six-month release cycle. If you spend six months in a release cycle you're probably going to spend the first month at least on requirements, identifying what it is we need to build. So we're doing that instead of coding. We're probably going to be spending—and this is almost universally true—the last two months, a third of our time, on testing and integration.

This means that more than half of a software developer's time is spent *not writing software*.

Say you've built twenty-five features in one six-month release cycle, essentially a feature a week. Assuming requests for features come in randomly, the average wait time before the next release cycle begins is three months (half the cycle time) plus an additional six months to complete the release. That means that the average wait time for a feature is *nine months* and it means your process efficiency is on the order of 2.6%. Batching is unbelievably inefficient.

Assuming all tasks take one week to complete, the shorter the release cycle the higher the process efficiency.

Release Cycle	Average Wait	Efficiency
1 week	1.5 weeks	100%
2 weeks	3 weeks	50%
1 month	1.5 months	23%
2 months	3 months	12%
3 months	4.5 months	7.7%
4 months	6 months	5.8%
6 months	9 months	2.6%

---

2. Poppendieck, Mary. How Cadence Predicts Process (blog). http://www.leanessays.com/2011/07/how-cadence-determines-process.html

Of course, not all tasks are a week long and the more variance in task size the longer our release cycle will have to be. The word "efficiency" may be a bit misleading here. This shows how much of a software development process is devoted to a single task. The more work-in-progress we have, the less efficient the system is overall and the more task switching is required.

These inefficiencies are compounded by much greater inefficiencies as release cycles get longer. It requires written requirements—a major inefficiency. It imposes a formal test/integrate phase.

It forces us into Waterfall.

The longer the release cycle, the more work tends to be batched by task type (design, code, test, integrate) instead of taking each task from start to finish—from story to fully integrated implementation—as quickly and efficiently as possible.

Batching features and long release cycles demand written requirements, and that adds a whole slew of errors and inefficiencies into the process. According to IAG Consulting's 2009 Business Analysis Benchmark,[3] over 41% of new project development resources were consumed by unnecessary or poorly specified requirements.

Agile replaces requirements with stories, and we've established that stories are *promises for a conversation*, so what Agile is really saying is that we need to replace requirements with conversations. You still know that you're building this and not that, that the customer wants a particular thing that does something, which is what requirements really should be. But then the conversation needs to continue in an *informed* manner—a conversation you've done your homework for before you arrive so you can really focus on what to build.

Talking to someone, seeing each other face to face and asking, "Should I return true or false in this situation?" and then having that person answer, "Well, let's figure it out," is much more efficient than coding based on requirements that would never even have that question in the first place. That leaves developers to guess, and as a developer I'm lucky to be right *half the time*.

How much money would you bet on a coin toss?

---

3.   IAG Consulting. "Business Analysis Benchmark." http://www.iag.biz/resources/library/business-analysis-benchmark.html

Smaller Is Better

Breaking down big tasks into smaller tasks requires the skill to decompose but still make code modular.

But let me be clear: When I say "smaller tasks," I don't mean blindly lopping off different pieces of a task so that when stories are integrated back together to build a bigger feature, it won't work. Knowing how to break big tasks out is an absolutely critical skill all developers and Product Owners must learn.

When teams focus on features they're saying, "We want to see a specific behavior out of a system and we want to see enough of a behavior that it can be observed, but not too much that it would be difficult to test. What can we do in the next *two weeks*?"

But in Waterfall, teams are left to cast about for what they're being "graded on," for lack of a better term. What's my workload for a week, and how am I being evaluated on the results? My workload in a Waterfall environment is typically, "I'm coding a bunch of stuff." So there is decomposition, but what we've done is decompose our features into functions.

Typically this is not done by the developers; it's done by the architect or somebody in charge, and the developer then gets a task: "Write these functions." And he writes those functions, and compiles it, and maybe steps through it in a debugger, then it sits in the queue and waits till the end of the project to integrate. So he's evaluated on lines of code—but the customer couldn't care less. Customers don't evaluate software based on lines of code; it doesn't do anything for the customer, and there isn't any intrinsic *value* of giving the customer more lines of code.

What is our goal? What is the thing we should measure ourselves by?

Think back to the lessons of W. Edwards Deming and Lean. We should measure ourselves on *what is valuable to the customer*. This is one of the few metrics I subscribe to as it discourages local optimization. Pretty much every other metric—lines of code, velocity, that kind of stuff—is a local optimization. If everything else slows down around you, it's worthless; it's not useful.

Smaller is better for four essential reasons:

- It's easier to understand.
- It's easier to estimate.
- It's easier to implement.
- It's easier to test.

Smaller tasks are also far less risky because they give us more opportunity for feedback.

Divide and Conquer

This concept—*divide et imperia*—worked for King Philip II of Macedonia. Keep the rival city-states bickering with each other and you never have to fight more than a few—or one—at a time rather than having to face a united front. We'll use this concept to show that big problems are just a bunch of smaller problems, and smaller problems are far easier to solve than big problems. So it's really a matter of *decomposition*, and this is one skill—not the only skill by any means—but one of the key skills we need to develop in order to move software development from vocation to profession.

There's a Haitian proverb: *Little snakes need to grow in hiding.*

If you want to get rid of a snake that lives under your house, do it when it's young. Don't wait for it to get big, or it'll take the whole village to pull it out. Let it be a baby snake.

So many problems, if you deal with them early on, are simple problems. This is not rocket science. Everything we're talking about here is basically just common sense. But common sense and conventional wisdom are often at odds with each other.

Typically stories, features, tasks—things that we have to do—are big because of two reasons: either they're *complex* or they're *compound*.

Take compound stories and break them up into their components. If it's a compound story, you obviously know what their components are. Make each of those components its own story.

A story is complex, most of the time, for only one reason: there are unknowns. The way we deal with complex stories is to *separate the known from the unknown*. We iterate on the unknowns until we make that domain, the domain of the unknowns, smaller and smaller until it simply disappears.

Again, the Agile approach of time boxing can be very valuable here. It says: I will take this next iteration to look at this issue and figure out what options are open to me in solving it. Are there libraries that can help me? Can I break it out smaller? What are the key things that I *need* to know? What do I *not* know? And so on.

When we're researching unknowns we want to do one of two things:

- *Turn what is unknown into what is known*, so if there is a big unknown we know how to deal with it, or...

- *Encapsulate it.* If there is a big unknown that we can *hide*, then hide it so we can deal with it later.

If we're working on too much at once, we've got a lot of waste because there's a lot of in-process work. This is the concept behind queuing theory, which Swedish Agile consultant Hakan Forss compared to managing highway traffic patterns. Just as lowering the speed limit in certain traffic bottlenecks allows more cars to pass through, "by lowering the amount of work you have in the process, you will stabilize the system."[4]

Forss used this variant of Little's Law:

Cycle Time=Work-in-Progress/Throughput

Work-in-Progress—the number of items on our "to-do list"—divided by the time necessary to complete each item equals our cycle time.

By reducing the number of items on your to-do list, your cycle time decreases accordingly, providing faster feedback and revealing issues while they're still small problems more easily fixed.

In traditional requirements-based development, *everything* is front-loaded onto that "to-do list," which is precisely what a set of requirements is. That makes for a huge number for work-in-progress, which then makes cycle times jump up into months, even years, leaving small problems time to fester and multiply into system-crashing bugs.

This isn't only true in Waterfall software development; it's also true in many organizations claiming to do Agile. Whenever you put off integration and testing until later, you're keeping your work-in-progress high. Taking a task to 99% completion isn't good enough because the amount of risk is still unknown. The *only* way to eliminate the risk associated with adding a new feature is to fully integrate that feature into the system *as it is being developed.*

The solution, as we will see, is to integrate continuously, which provides instant feedback as to whether or not bugs have been introduced. This kind of instant feedback helps developers fix defects when they're small so they can move on without much effort.

---

4. YouTube. "Hakan Forss 'Queuing theory in software development.'" Uploaded July 1, 2011. https://www.youtube.com/watch?v=tt4vnCzHAZk

Shorten Feedback Cycles

I prefer smaller batches when I look at feedback cycles—and I mean *all* software development feedback cycles—and there should be *many* ot them.

Talking to the customer is an example of a feedback cycle; demoing at the end of an iteration or feature that you're building is another. One of the feedback cycles we get as developers is from our compiler. We write some code and then compile it, and the compiler tells us we have some syntax issues, or whatever—and this is a fundamental form of feedback for developers. The next step is the feedback from an automated test suite that immediately notifies us if code is broken, and so on.

But it's not enough to break tasks down and get more feedback. Developers need *constructive* feedback that they can take *action* on.

Feedback is either good news or bad news, depending on whether or not you can do anything about it. We need to find ways of assimilating and incorporating feedback. Agile uses techniques like retrospectives, reviews, check-ins...there are all sorts of ways of getting feedback. But perhaps most importantly for developers is having a fast automated build that we can depend on for catching errors as we go.

Some of the top developers I know run their tests *every twenty seconds*—three times every minute—as they're writing code. This is a kind of a support that good developers learn to embrace.

Software development is a mentally taxing profession, and once we start getting into our forties, we know we're not as quick anymore, and so we have to start relying on other skills. I have no qualms about saying that I want to teach developers how to be lazier. The lazier we are, the more *thoughtful* we'll become. And when we do that we get far better results, with far less stress.

When I teach a class I try not to use the word "wrong" because at the level we operate on as professional software developers there's no such thing as right and wrong—there are only trade-offs. But one student in a particular class said something I thought was just wrong. When I pointed it out to him he said, "Just tell me how to do it right the first time."

And I said, "With all due respect, this is the wrong question to ask because *we're setting ourselves up to fail.*"

Forcing ourselves to do it right the first time is actually doing it the hard way. If you give yourself the freedom to be able to make mistakes, but understand what it costs and mitigate those mistakes, it really is the fastest route. The fastest route between two points is not always a straight line.

I want to have customer questions answered as quickly as possible. We've all heard many times that the organization can't afford to have the customer on site with the team all the time. I say you can't afford *not* to. Otherwise developers start guessing, and as smart as developers are they're going to be wrong about half the time—back to *how much would you bet on the flip of a coin?*

But there's another feedback cycle that developers often don't recognize, and it's absolutely critical. It's the one feedback cycle to really focus on speeding up—that's easy and cheap, and provides tremendous value—the build.

Speed Up the Build

When I say "speed up the build" what I mean is *create a build environment that gives the results not in three hours, but in three seconds.*

In order to do that you have to understand what your dependencies are. Very often that process helps developers see whether their architecture is good.

My consulting clients expect me to give results quickly, so I've learned a whole lot of techniques to create value fast. I often give suggestions on how they should best spend their effort, so I spend a fair amount of time looking at their code. The build will tell me whether or not they have a good architecture.

I have a client that requires 24 gigs on every developer's machine, because even if you change the spelling of one little word of a message box you have to rebuild the entire enterprise system; nothing is hidden from anything else. And they had a brilliant architecture. The only problem was that the architecture was unencapsulated. A developer thought, *I'm not going to use this API. It's just going to change some data in a database. I'll do it myself.*

Because these developers broke the rules and there is no enforcement, everything became sprawled out. The result is 24 gigs on every machine to do a build.

But hey, memory is cheap. Just throw more hardware at the problem!

That may be the path of least resistance, but they now suffer a three-week release cycle—it takes them three weeks to validate that a release candidate is releasable with even the smallest change because they have to manually retest everything. And they want to go to a two-week iteration. If you do the math, it doesn't actually work, so they have to rewrite everything.

Let me repeat that: *They have to rewrite everything.*

There are very few examples where you have to actually rewrite the entire system, but they're there, and in this case it was because the behavior and the data have both been messed with at the same time. And, by the way, they're running nearly a billion dollars' worth of business every year, so this is not a small company. They struggled to transition all of their customers to the new system. They're in an incredibly bad situation.

Software developers don't have off-the-shelf components. We don't build software by buying a part and just plugging that part in, but we can build in parts. If your car doesn't start because the spark plugs aren't firing but the spark plugs have been welded in, are wired to a dozen other components, and are also helping hold the engine in the engine compartment, it may be easier and more cost effective to just buy a new car than to change your spark plugs. This is what we call "dependencies."

Good software development calls for building the parts and the whole together, but making each part as independent as possible.

We may find that there are still tendrils, things that connect things together, and those things should be a reflection of the real problem itself. There is a relationship between a customer and his or her street address, for instance. That's a good kind of connection. There may be a connection between the zip code of the customer and the zip code of the shipper, but maybe that's not the right kind of connection because if there's only one shipper, they'll have to deliver to any zip code. So understanding what can be decoupled—what can be separate from other elements—and what should be connected is of vital importance.

This makes total sense in the real world. We don't even give a second thought to the idea that the spark plug is not permanently attached to the engine. In the virtual world, it's not as obvious. In the virtual world, we don't tend to think in terms of parts.

Now, I'm not striving for no coupling at all; I'm striving for an appropriate level of coupling. And that often depends on your perspective. Very often when you think about a problem in different ways, you can come up with better solutions. The same thing is true in software. So you want to have a variety of techniques to think about software problems in different ways, then run through your tool box of techniques until you find the one that clicks.

It's the same thing a carpenter does. A carpenter has a whole bunch of tools on his tool belt, and a good carpenter knows when, how, and why to use each one. Software developers want to understand our tools and the scope of their usage in the same way other craftspeople, professionals, and artists do.

Respond to Feedback

I remember a team leader who was tasked with important, innovative decisions, and after an involved review of a client and a team, he was asked, "What is your number one key innovative decision?" And he said, "We're buying a coffee pot."

The coffee pot was on the fourth floor, and his team was on the third floor. Everyone on the team drank coffee. He did the math. It cost $40,000 a year to have the coffee pot one floor above them. They gave him twenty bucks to buy a coffee pot.

The more I work as a professional developer, the more I see things from a business perspective too. In business, there are two fundamental things that we have to focus on: value and risk. That's really what business is all about, and that's a solid vocabulary for a businessperson.

Software developers have a much bigger vocabulary. Developers just don't use the same words as businesspeople, so businesspeople don't always understand when developers are saying the same thing.

Having a system that provides frequent feedback is only good if the culture in which it exists supports responding to the feedback. In some organizations, budgets, delivery dates, and feature scope are locked at the beginning of a project. This is like saying, "If this train we're on is about to go off a cliff and there's nothing we can do, just don't tell me. I'd rather spend the last few seconds of my life in blissful ignorance."

But if there is both time and the willingness to respond, then I *do* want to know about it so I can do something about it! And that's the purpose of seeking feedback in the first place—to do something about it.

If you improve, let's say, 2% in every two-week iteration, at the end of the year you'll have improved by 50%. So look for any little way of improving.

The Lean Startup movement was created to figure out what the market for something really is. They say that using the Lean Startup approach companies can create order, not chaos, by "providing tools to test a vision continuously."[5] But it's not just about creating a better mousetrap. I have better mousetraps, and guess what?

Nobody cares because they aren't familiar.

---

5. The Lean Startup. "Methodology." Accessed November 12, 2014. http://theleanstartup.com/principles

In software, there are many ways to validate and test, and as in Lean Startup, we strive to test continuously. Working in the online world we learn two very profound things that are not intuitive. One is that you can get a true sampling of what's going on from surprisingly small numbers, like a thousand or ten thousand people—even a hundred or fewer people—and you can still clearly see trends. And not only can you see trends, you can find better alternatives. You can see if the people will actually buy your product. Sometimes we refer to this as A/B testing, where you have two versions of something with only one thing changed and you expose each version to different groups and measure the results. It's shocking how consistent this can be.

A developer from Google once told me that they A/B tested a one-pixel divider in a header against a two-pixel divider, and saw a relatively huge percentage—something like 17%—in the response rate from just a one-pixel difference.

Google A/B tests absolutely everything, and they have algorithms that combine all the data, figure it all out, and come out with the ideal solution. It's not that hard to do, but the results are phenomenal in that they're so consistent.

Build a Backlog

A backlog is basically the list of stories we want to build. Organize features—stories—in different ways. You can organize them by themes, by user type, by purpose, or any other way that makes sense to you. Essentially you're aggregating features to make a release. This is called the minimum marketable feature set (MMF) and it tells you what you *absolutely need* in this release in order for your product to be viable and usable.

If you know what your MMFs are, then you can add a few nonessential features to a release so if development finishes early there's something to work on. But if you run out of time, then you know what your drop dead is, and what capabilities you must include in order for the user to derive value from it.

Talk about *ordering* the backlog instead of *prioritizing* the backlog. The Product Owner is the one responsible for saying what is to be built next, and that's the next most important feature to build. But sometimes what's "most important" isn't as obvious as anyone would like it to be. Sometimes it's more efficient to build the second most important feature first because it'll also include capabilities that the more important feature will need, and it's a simpler path there.

Keep the ordering process flexible. That way, the team agrees on your MMFs and the order of the backlog items for the next few iterations, but then if someone gets a better idea, that idea can be exploited.

Here's the rule of thumb I try to adhere to: if a feature is in iteration I want to keep on task with that, but if this new idea is something that could be done in the next iteration or an upcoming iteration, then I do want to incorporate it—and there's no reason I can't. I just want to be careful not to stop developers mid-iteration, invalidating everything they were just doing. But then adding something to the order after that is why teams have the backlog in the first place; it's why we build in iterations, so that we *can* introduce something new when we realize it's better.

Break Stories Into Tasks

Stories describe an observable behavior in a system, but they may be too involved or too big to do within a two-week iteration. Break it down further into general work items called *tasks*.

The ideal task is something that takes about four hours to complete, but often, for a variety of reasons, tasks can take days or even weeks to complete.

People who live in the city know that most tasks, even trivial ones, take at least four hours. If you want to go buy a pair of shoes, if you want to go out and do whatever, it's always going to take at least four hours. And I always think about that when I think of a task.

Nearly every task in software development takes at least four hours—even the most trivial task— because you've got to check it out, you've got to test it, you've got to check it back in—you have to do all sorts of stuff.

We don't use hours for estimating; we talk about story points that some people treat as *ideal hours*. In an eight-hour workday we really get about four *ideal* hours. So if a task takes about four hours it's about a day's work. This is about as small as you can get a task.

After all, what is a freeway at 100% utilization? At 100% utilization a freeway looks like a parking lot. And that's the same with an employee. When you take an employee and try to utilize her for 100% of the day, she'll just stop. Somewhere around 50% is ideal. If you've got developers who are producing real value 50% of the time, that's pretty amazing. People aren't machines, after all. We need time for ongoing learning, we've got to stretch, we've got to eat, we've got to use the restroom.

We're human.

The most important question for any manager is: How much time are your developers spending *developing*?

It's common in most environments that developers spend about a third to a quarter of their time, sometimes a fifth of their time, actually writing code. But isn't writing code what software developers are being paid for? Isn't that what developers *love doing*?

Each task must take us a step closer to achieving the feature. Breaking tasks down by acceptance criteria gives us a way to measure or observe that we've accomplished the task, and if it brings us a step closer to finishing the whole story—the feature—then we know we're on the right track. There's a whole range of techniques around this, as long as, just like stories, tasks have measurable results.

Think Outside the Time Box

Scrum and other Agile methodologies have spread very quickly, which is good, but the essence of what they're really all about hasn't spread quite as far yet. Object-oriented programming (OO) was very popular starting in 1990 and almost everyone uses an OO language like Java, C++, or C#. But when you look at their code they're really not using OO; they're not really understanding the essence of the advantages OO languages have over procedural languages. They're not using objects to encapsulate behavior, to increase testability and decouple designs...It's just procedural code wrapped in a class statement.

Sort of the same thing is true with Agile. "The State of Scrum" came out in June 2013 and reported that 40% of the companies surveyed—and I think this is a good cross section of the whole industry—say that they're doing some form of Scrum. But when you ask them what it is they're doing you find they're doing stand-up meetings and iterations, and they're not even taking those iterations and bringing them to completion. Only 13% of those organizations are practicing continuous integration and only 37% of the organizations practicing continuous integration integrate daily or more frequently. In other words, fewer than 5% of the companies who say they are practicing Scrum actually integrate their code at least once a day. They're taking tasks to a point where they're not quite done and sticking them somewhere near the end of the cycle, and then they test it.

That's Waterfall.

You'll see some benefits, but you're not changing the game. Scrum isn't an all-or-nothing proposition. There are elements of Scrum methodology that you can do that will help in certain areas. But in terms of risk, it *is* all or nothing. It's binary. You either have risk or you don't have risk. When you have risk, it's unknown. That's why it's risky.

Manage Scope

If you have the potential for 1% of risk, you have a lot of risk. So the only way you can burn down risk is to take a story to its completion, which means we have to have a clear definition of "done." When you take an iteration to full completion, when it's fully integrated, then you know you have no risk. Until then you have a question mark.

This concept is reminiscent of Schrödinger's Cat.[6]

The Austrian physicist Erwin Schrödinger proposed a sort of thought experiment to illustrate quantum mechanics. He imagined (but did not actually build, mind you) a box in which he'd place a cat, but in the box is a device that, should the cat either purposely or accidently activate, it would release some kind of poison. His assertion was that, with the uncertainty as to whether or not that poison had been released, and with no direct observation of the condition of the cat, we have to accept that, while in that unknown state, the cat is both alive and dead. The only way to know is by opening the box.

In most development, we have our "cat" (the system) in a box with some unknown number of bugs. Until we actually take the program out of the box and see it run, like Schrödinger's Cat it's both alive and dead— it both works and doesn't work.

Risk tends to grow exponentially until one bug will knock the whole system out, so you want to make sure that you get to the point where each little piece of the system, in each iteration or feature, is risk free by having it fully integrated with the system.

But the truth is it's not always easy to know *how* to break tasks down. Scrum says to iterate every two weeks, but in order to do that a task has to be broken down into two-week increments. Splitting stories and breaking down tasks is a skill, like any other, and developers must get good at doing it.

If you start with the more rigid processes of time or scope boxing, learn them, make them a habit, understand the craft, build a set of principles and procedures, and then add to them and fix them, you can take the time boxes off and just build smaller tasks.

This is all about habits. If you're a smoker and you want to quit, you can use a nicotine patch to help break the nicotine habit. But if you keep using the patch for the rest of your life, you might not smell as bad, and your lungs

---

6.   http://en.wikipedia.org/wiki/Schr%C3%B6dinger%27s_cat

might start to heal, but you haven't actually broken the nicotine habit; you're still addicted to that drug.

Both Extreme Programming and Scrum are akin to nicotine patches. The real purpose of iterations is to try to get teams off the addiction of building in releases. Once off that addiction you won't need time boxes anymore—just like a smoker can eventually step off the patches and live a healthier, nicotine-free life. There's an Agile methodology that embraces that, and it's called Kanban.

Kanban demands that we limit the number of in progress items, the size of each queue (To Do, In Progress, and Done), but there are no sprints. Items can move from "To Do" to "In Progress," and then be completed and moved to "Done" or moved back to "To Do" in favor of a new priority.

But that item has to be moved back to free up space in the "In Progress" column. Otherwise, you end up with everything being worked on at the same time. All this is meant to help you work smarter, not harder, and trying to work on everything all at once is *much harder*. Work-in-progress (WIP) limits restrict the number of tasks the team can work on at any given time.

To Do	In Progress	Done
E F G	B D	A C

Kanban Board

Ultimately what we all have to focus on is managing scope, and we use time to do that. Even two-week iterations are artificial, and they're also somewhat inefficient. But it's one way to get to the point where you can say, "Oh, I have a task. I figure it's going to take four hours to do." Then you go off and do it, then ask, "Okay, what's my next task?" That's when you'll start to achieve a high level of efficiency.

That two-week iteration came from what feels most comfortable—what seems easiest to transition to. Remember, there's a lot of pressure pulling you into building bigger clumps. You want this feature to have this functionality. It's hard to break things down. Boeing can't build an airplane with only one wing and try to test it before adding the other wing. They have to build both wings together.

There needs to be a reportable period of time where teams can come together and sit down and see where they are. And this—like all meetings, frankly—can't simply be a meeting for meeting's sake. It's an opportunity to check in and see if you have impediments, to see how far you've gone, and to measure your progress. And when you start to get comfortable with doing that, you'll just do it naturally.

I would love to see teams simply flow and create, but in order to have that you need to establish a cadence. The other thing that's good about having two-week iterations is they're the beat of the drum. Other parts of the organization that need to sync up with development can sync up at those times. Even in a total flow environment, you still have to have synchronization points; otherwise the rest of the business won't be able to interact with development.

So our ultimate goal is smaller tasks. Disaggregate features into the smallest focused tasks we can, and take about four hours or so to complete it—the shorter the better—and it should have well-defined acceptance criteria: a clear definition of "done."

That's it.

Let's Get Practical

Here are some ways to put these ideas into practice.

Seven Strategies for Measuring Software Development

Software is different from tangible goods and it must be measured differently. The tasks that developers do are different from day to day, so productivity can't be directly measured in any meaningful, normalized way. I often advise teams not to measure velocity because it can send the wrong message and give management the wrong goals. Velocity can be raised at the expense of quality, which is a mistake. Here are seven strategies for measuring value in software development.

Measure time-to-value
> We produce software to fulfill some need or desire, and the time from when we start creating something valuable to when it's realized by users is a good measure of our effectiveness. Local optimizations are meaningless if they don't help to optimize the whole process. Measuring time-to-value keeps us focused on the big picture—something worth measuring.

Measure time spent coding

Developers love to develop but things can get in our way. Ironically, the time spent assuring quality in many organizations robs teams of valuable time they could have used to actually create quality. I know developers who spend less than 10 percent of their time developing. The rest of their time is taken up by meetings, reporting, and who knows what else that may not be contributing to the bottom line. A good development process is one where developers spend most of their time actually developing software.

Measure defect density

Most organizations track bugs, but this can have the adverse effect of increasing bug tolerance. Defects in code are often a symptom of a deeper cause: a defect in the development process. If defects are consistently showing up in production code, it means the development process may be broken. Look for the root cause and try to fix it. Defect density (bugs per thousand lines of code) is one of the few measurements that can be compared across teams and time, so it can be used for process calibration.

Measure time to detect defects

It's been shown that the cost of fixing defects increases exponentially as time elapses since the defect was created. The cheapest defects to fix are the ones that are detected and fixed immediately after creation. Finding defects faster not only decreases the cost of fixing them, but also helps developers become aware of things they may be doing that allowed the defect to be created in the first place.

Measure customer value of features

Not all features are equally valuable to customers. In fact, nearly half of all features created in software are never used. Backlogs are ordered so the highest-value features are created first, which lets less important features get put off or dropped. This leaves more time to focus on those higher value items. If developers are unsure of what features will provide the most value, they should ask the customer.

Measure cost of not delivering features

Sometimes the cost of *not* delivering a feature is the most compelling reason for building it. Ask your stakeholders how much the feature is worth and how much not having the feature will cost. The answer may surprise you.

Measure efficiency of feedback loops

The most powerful point of leverage for increasing efficiency is often in the process itself. A good development process has built-in feedback loops that can be used to tweak the process. The faster the feedback, the more efficient we can become. Find ways to fail fast and learn from failure. This is how teams rapidly improve.

Most teams who try to measure productivity end up sacrificing quality. Measuring productivity may not be possible and can certainly be disruptive. Instead, focus on producing and measuring value, both in the product delivered and in the process used to create it.

Seven Strategies for Splitting Stories

The shorter the story, the better. Short stories are easier to estimate, understand, and implement. Short stories help create cohesive, uncoupled code. Short stories are easier to test. So here are seven strategies for splitting big stories into smaller ones.

Break down compound stories into components

If a story is made up of sub-stories, break them out into multiple stories. This helps disaggregate components and makes a system more modular. It also yields smaller stories that are easier to work with.

Break down complex stories into knowns and unknowns

Stories are complex typically because they contain unknowns. We may not know exactly what the customer wants or exactly how to implement it. Separating what is known from what is not known is the first step to splitting stories with unknowns.

Iterate on unknowns until they're understood

Once something is identified as unknown, encapsulate it! Hide it behind an abstraction with a well-defined interface. Then you have the freedom to learn more without it being in your critical path. It's generally better to attack high-risk unknowns up front and defer low-risk unknowns until later.

Split on acceptance criteria

As we break stories down into tasks, we still want to have some kind of visible evidence when a task is complete. Splitting stories on acceptance criteria can help focus development while still providing some customer value within an iteration. It also helps clearly define when the story is done.

Minimize dependencies

We would rather stories not depend on other stories, but sometimes that can be difficult to avoid. Try to remove dependencies by creating well-defined interfaces between dependent components. If you must have dependencies, make future stories depend on previous stories and not the other way around.

Keep intentions singular

A story should be about fulfilling a single intention or a verifiable aspect of that single intention. Often, we think about a story as providing complete functionality to the user and we make them too big. Smaller stories are easier to work with. They don't have to be a full-blown feature; they just need to contain enough functionality for the user to derive value from it. Subsequent stories can enhance a feature to provide additional functionality.

Keep stories testable

Each story should have a series of acceptance tests defined as the criteria for acceptance. If stories are untestable or difficult to test, then we won't easily be able to verify them. Make each story have some demonstrable effect on the system so it's easy to verify. Automate acceptance criteria whenever possible.

Story writing is a skill that's honed over time. When stories are concise and disaggregated, systems are more focused and easier to build on. Keeping stories small, focused, and easy to verify helps to make systems clear and maintainable.

Retrospective

Build in Small Batches so every task can be completed in a short time (ideally about four hours) and make tasks fulfill acceptance criteria, or at the very least create an observable result. This helps simplify tasks and makes them easier to estimate, complete, and verify.

In this chapter, we discovered…

- Delivery cadence dictates the software development process.
- How to be more in control of your time.
- Smaller tasks are easier to estimate, test, and work with.
- How to break down features into observable behaviors.

- By developing the discipline of time-boxing we start to get good at scope-boxing—breaking down tasks into smaller tasks that are easier to work with.

The cadence of release cycles controls process. The shorter the interval for creating releasable software, the more efficient the software development process becomes. By building smaller, we make sure that tasks are easier to work with and drastically reduce overhead.

CHAPTER 7

Practice 3: Integrate Continuously

There are two ways to deal with pain: avoid it, or acclimate to it.

Integrating software into the build can be painful, exposing bugs and other issues that weren't visible before. Many software development teams try to avoid that pain by putting integration off until as late as possible only to find that integrating their code just before release is a lot more painful. Like the woodcutter who is too busy to sharpen his saw, these teams create situations that require more effort and risk than needed.

But what if instead of putting off the pain of integration, they tried to acclimate to it? What if they work on it a little bit at a time until it becomes a series of smaller problems— each less painful?

Continuous integration is the practice of integrating software as it's built rather than waiting until just before a release. Continuous integration is a critical practice because it not only helps eliminate bugs early but also helps developers learn how to build better code—code that can be integrated more easily. Until the feature is integrated, it's not guaranteed to work in the system.

But continuous integration is also incredibly valuable to developers as a feedback mechanism. When the build breaks it provides so much information it's sometimes hard to find the culprit. Broken builds must be fixed *immediately*, so developers don't want feedback to be overly verbose, forcing team members to parse through log files. Developers want it made clear what's broken so they know very quickly how to fix it.

Developers should be running continuous integration all the time and immediately seeing the results of their efforts on the system, seeing if bugs have been introduced or if their code plays well with the rest of the system.

Sophisticated tools exist to help us with continuous integration, but they all depend on working code. Compilers stop at the first error they encounter.

Unit tests run against *working code*. Even debuggers require working code to debug. Without working code developers are confined to running programs in their imaginations, which often doesn't match with reality.

Of all the key aspects of software development, continuous integration is the most important. It provides the framework and context for all other technical practices. Ironically, it's also the easiest to implement.

It's really a matter of infrastructure. All the tools needed to implement continuous integration are free and relatively simple to set up, and they provide a context for developing maintainable and extendable software.

Establish the Heartbeat of a Project

I think of continuous integration as the heartbeat of a project. It's something that happens in the background, and it never stops. It's automatic...or anyway, it should be.

It doesn't matter how big your team is, or even if you're a team of one. Go out and buy some kind of a computer. It can be any cheap machine. That becomes the *build server*.

The build server sits there and waits for new code to be added to the repository. When it sees new code come in, it goes about automatically rebuilding the whole system. It runs the automated tests, verifies that everything works, and gives you a result. That machine sits in the background and it's always running, it's always there, and always present...just like a beating heart.

Remove all human intervention from the build and release cycle so it can happen in the background—the same way we don't have to think about keeping our hearts beating in our chests.

Going from large releases to integrating continuously takes one of the biggest expenses in a Waterfall project—validating a release candidate—and makes it *free*.

Well, writing automated unit tests isn't free—it takes time and effort—but once you have them you can run them as many times as you want, over and over, without incurring additional expense. This means you can approach development entirely differently; you can use the system itself to give you feedback on how to modify the system. When developers discover how valuable that is, it becomes a key resource.

Know the Difference Between Done, Done-Done, and Done-Done-Done

One of the things any of us want to do when we determine our process is define what "done" really means. We typically have three different definitions of done:

> Done

...in a traditional Waterfall development environment, means that the developer who wrote a feature was able to get it to run, and got some kind of result on her machine. That's not good enough.

> Done-Done

...means that not only does it work on the developer's machine but it's also integrated into the build. We see it beating along with the heartbeat of the project and can quickly detect any potentially fatal arrhythmias.

The third definition of done is...

> Done-Done-Done

That means the code runs on the developer's machine, is integrated into the build, and is *clean and supportable*. This is an area that has always been missing in most of the software development world. We absolutely need to have supportability so we take the time to clean up the design and change the code to make it more readable, understandable, and simpler to work with. That's a very important step.

So *done-done-done* means that not only does it work, not only is it integrated into the build, but it's understandable, it's readable, and it's supportable. We all want our code to be all of those things because we want to drop the cost of ownership in software.

So when I say code is "done" I really mean it's done-done-done.

Practice Continuous Deployability

Continuous integration doesn't mean you have to deploy to production continuously. You don't have to *release* every time someone checks in new code or at the end of every iteration. Releases should be determined by market demand, by supportability issues, by deployability issues, by version management, and things like that—not by development. Continuous deployability means you *could* release to production at any time, if you wanted to. When you actually release to production is a business decision.

All code and other files needed to build the system must be maintained in a version repository so as software is being built, developers are checking new features into version control and everybody works from a single branch. This ensures that all team members are sharing the same codebase and working from the same source code.

Developers on the system can check out a working copy of the system and be able to build and run it on their local machine, but then they'll push any changes they want to make to the system back up to version control. By versioning all files, we gain the ability to roll any file back in time and see what was changed along the way.

In addition to the source code, a version control system should version everything else needed to build the system. This includes technical elements like configuration files, database layouts, test code and test scripts, third-party libraries, installation scripts, documentation, design diagrams, use case scenarios, UML diagrams, and so on.

I taught a course to a group of developers at one of the largest Internet properties in the world, and this little team was having trouble making consistent builds. They told me earlier that they would manually test a system but then when they deployed into production they got different results and found bugs they hadn't seen in their tests. I asked them if they were using version control and they said, "Absolutely! We version everything—all of our source code."

And I said, "Well, you also version your build scripts, your stored procedures, your database layouts, and so on, right?"

As I said that, about four people got up and walked out of the room. I thought perhaps I'd offended somebody, but at the next break I saw one of the people who'd left. When I asked him what the problem was, he said they wanted to verify with their team that they were versioning all the build scripts needed, and their database layouts…and they found that they weren't.

A few months later, he sent me an email and told me that this was the reason for their inconsistent builds in production, and now they were able to fully replicate their production environment on their test system.

They used to test and release in a three-week manual testing cycle, and then they would deploy to one of two datacenters. They would take about 1% of their traffic and push it to the datacenter that had the newly released code. If that worked well, they added another 1% and another and another until they bled off the second datacenter and got all of the users on the first datacenter with the new code. Then, three weeks later, they'd start the process again, with the second datacenter bleeding off all of the users from the first datacenter.

That seemed like a pretty inefficient way to deploy code.

Automate the Build

I want you to make it so easy to build software that it becomes invisible to you. You should be able to launch the build with a single click of the mouse.

Slow tests are the number one reason builds are slow, but there are techniques to make tests run much, much faster. Builds should take less than ten minutes to run. This is actually something James Shore and Shane Warden say in their book *The Art of Agile Development [SW07]*. But I think even ten minutes is pushing it.

For local builds, I like to see them run in just a second or two and when I promote to the build server I like builds to happen in just a few minutes, though it depends on the nature of what I'm building and how big it is. Some builds actually do require several hours. But you don't always have to do a full build of your entire system when you make one small change if your system is correctly decoupled.

When builds take over ten minutes to run, they're run less frequently. If that's happening, find the dependencies for the specific modules that are being worked on and *only test those modules*.

This will speed up builds, but what will *really* speed up builds is to *write good unit tests* and only test code that *needs* to be tested, not other code that code might use—and fear not, we'll talk about this in Chapter 10, *Practice 6: Write the Test First*, on page 147 and Chapter 11, *Practice 7: Specify Behaviors with Tests*, on page 165.

Understanding the dependencies related to making changes into a system is very helpful not only for identifying what module should be compiled and what test should be run but also because it helps segregate the system, making it easier to deploy and extend. The build should happen on the developer's local machine first. When everything works there, it gets promoted up to the build server. The build should be able to work even when the Internet connection goes down so that developers can continue to be productive even while there are problems with the network.

There are tools for Java, .NET, and other environments designed to automate builds. When a local build on a developer's machine is successful, and all the tests pass, it should automatically get committed to version control. This triggers the build server to run. Once the new code is compiled, tests should automatically be run to verify that those changes don't affect other parts of the system. Tests that take too long to run can move to a nightly build.

When code is simple its tests are also simple. We want to test as much as we can against simple units of behavior rather than complex ones so we can have as few bigger integration tests as possible.

With all the various techniques for speeding up unit tests, if we're testing our code in the correct way we can have thousands of unit tests run in under a second.

If the build breaks it not only holds up the developer who broke it but everyone else working on the project, so it's imperative that broken builds be fixed immediately. It's typically the responsibility of the developer who introduced the code that broke the build to either roll back the code or fix it.

Several years ago, I went to visit a friend of mine who works at a development shop that practiced Extreme Programming. Their walls are covered with team agreements and task boards and every station has two monitors, two keyboards, two mice, and one computer so two developers can work together and pair program. The sight almost brought tears to my eyes, especially since I knew the team was wildly successful. Then I noticed some pretty heavy-duty hardware in the corner with one of those red flashing lights and a firefighter's helmet sitting on top of it. I asked my friend what that was and he said it was the build server for the team. Then he grabbed the keyboard and said, "Let me show you what happens when the build breaks."

He went in and changed some code in the system to force the build to break—and all the fluorescent lights went out in the building, a siren started to go off, and the red light started to flash.

He said, "Broken builds are not allowed in our shop."

The moment a build breaks everyone is aware of it, and the developer who broke the build has to go to the build server, put on the firefighter's helmet, sit down at the terminal, and fix it right then and there. A working build is fully ingrained into their culture, and they've come to depend on it so much every developer needs the *working build* to do *any* of their work.

It always has to be up and running.

Integrate Early and Often

The longer we wait to integrate the harder it is, so we want to integrate all the time.

This is easy to do as long as integration is painless, so make integration happen with a single click of a button and make it happen fast. People ask me how often we should integrate…

Tell your developers to integrate at least once a day.

This is a little trick, actually. What happens is that the last person to integrate usually winds up with this huge burden of failing tests and ends up not going home for dinner. That's the last time she does that.

Instead, integrate *all the time*—every hour or so, or even more frequently—as soon as you have the tiniest bit of functionality to add. Since you're integrating only a little piece, it's not very difficult. It's easy to find and fix a problem since typically it's just one or two little things you have to fix to have something that passes all the tests. And if a test fails it was likely caused by the little piece that was just introduced.

It's really simple and in fact it's usually automated. If I type something in and it's an error, it doesn't compile. It tells me to fix it, so I fix it. Now I compile again, my tests pass, and it automatically promotes the code to the build.

There are even automated concurrent testing tools that try to do another build every time you press a key on the keyboard. You don't even have to click the *build* button. You just write your code, and as your code gets compiled—if what you've typed is compilable—it goes into the build. It's done, and it all happens in the background.

We'll cover more on this later in the book when we get a little deeper into test-driven development (TDD). Not only does your code compile, but all your automated tests are running as well. You'll see the green bar, which tells you, "Yes, all your tests have passed." That's like a shot of espresso to me. It wakes me up. It energizes me.

Take the First Step

The first and most important factor in improving software development is to automate the build. Software products, particularly those released on CD-ROM or other media, have a cost associated with releasing and subsequent maintenance. But regardless of when you decide to release, the software being developed should always be *releasable* from day one.

For me, doing Agile and Scrum have little to do with iterations or stand-up meetings and everything to do with when you integrate. If you build in two-week iterations, having each team integrate their code into their own branch, and then integrate all the team's branches at the end of a year, then I have bad news for you—*you're doing Waterfall!*

If you take software to only 99% completion, that last 1% can hold an unknown amount of risk. Instead, fully integrate features into the system as they are built.

A healthy build is at the heart of a healthy project. Remove all branching and integrate continuously using *feature flags* to turn off features that are being built but not yet ready to be used. Then *mock* out components to remove unnecessary dependencies and add automated unit testing for regression. If you do those things, you're halfway there already—as the Korean proverb, *sijaki banida*, says: "The first step is half the journey."[1]

What I find stops people the most is fear. Once you can get past the fear and see what it really takes to make this process work, it's not only less intimidating but really quite exciting. If the worry is these practices are going to make your life more complicated, well, in the very short term, yeah, maybe a little.

Until those old habits are broken—and until you get to the end of a release cycle when everybody used to have to say good-bye to their loved ones for two weeks while they tried to figure out how to get the thing that didn't work to work...and instead you can be home in time for dinner—it may be harder, but it quickly goes from *harder* to *worth it* to *how did I ever think it was okay to do it any other way?*

It's *The Tortoise and the Hare*, where slow and steady wins the race. Regardless of specific roles, we all have to see the bigger picture. There's always a cognitive load for anything different, but if we want to enjoy the benefits of exponential increases in efficiency, scalability, and maintainability, we have to be willing to do that up-front work—now that we've admitted that there is a problem.

And we have to work together to do it.

Let's Get Practical

Here are some ways to put these ideas into practice.

---

1. New Nations Online. "North Korea Update No: 079." November 2009. http://www.newnations.com/archive/2010/January/nk.html

Seven Strategies for Agile Infrastructure

The first step in achieving agility and technical excellence is to set up an infrastructure to support it. An automated build server is vital, since we can only consider a story as "done" when it's fully integrated into the build. Here are seven strategies for setting up the right infrastructure for Agile development.

Use version control for everything

I have not seen any development project in the past twenty years that wasn't using version control. It is an essential tool for all development—Agile, Waterfall, or whatever. But I've seen clients fail to version non-code files that are critical to their build (config files, scripts, stored procedures, and so on) and wonder why their releases were unstable. The fix is easy: version everything that your build depends on!

One-click build end-to-end

Automate the entire build process so code is saved locally and compiled, automated tests are run, and if all the tests pass, the code is automatically checked in, built on the server, and more tests are run—all within a few seconds.

Integrate continuously

Continuous integration does not mean you have to release software every sprint, *but you could if you wanted to!* Continuous integration is a key to making Agile work. The tools are free, for the most part, and the value from the feedback you get is essential.

Define acceptance criteria for tasks

Every task should have well-defined criteria for acceptance to let you know when you're done. This can be automated with an acceptance testing framework such as SpecFlow, FIT, or Cucumber. This not only helps you know when a task is done, it also helps you avoid overbuilding.

Write testable code

Once a team commits to automated testing, life becomes a lot less painful, not just for QA (who doesn't have to waste time regression testing), but also for developers who get instant feedback as to whether an approach they're trying will work. But there is another benefit of writing automated tests: you begin to write code that's easier to test, which is ultimately higher quality than untestable code.

Keep test coverage where it is needed

As an idealist, I strive for 100% test coverage of the behaviors my code creates, even though I know it isn't always achievable. Because I write my tests before I write my code, I tend to have a high percentage of code coverage. However, for those who do not write their tests first, and have a requirement for a certain percentage of test coverage, it is not uncommon to write tests for the easiest code, like getters and setters, and leave the really hard stuff that needs automated tests without test coverage, which can lead to big problems.

Fix broken builds immediately

A working build is the heartbeat of a project. When the build breaks the entire project comes screeching to a halt. Do not let this happen, ever. Everyone who checks in code must be responsible for making sure it works. If checked-in code breaks the build, it must be either fixed or backed out *immediately*.

A successful automated build is the key to knowing if your project is on track. Integration is often the worst part of a Waterfall project and hides problems and true progress. So instead of putting it off to the end of a project, we do a little bit of it every day throughout a project because, until a feature runs in the context of the rest of the system, it is not really done.

Seven Strategies for Burning Down Risk

Developing software is risky and expensive. Software is formless and hard to understand. Subtle interaction can cause software to affect seemingly unrelated components. A good development process focuses on mitigating risk by finding problems early, before they become showstoppers, and while there's still time to resolve them.

Integrate continuously

Creating a system that can be built from day one and continuously integrating software into that system as it's built is the only way to eliminate risk. Delaying integration until one of the last steps before release is a bad idea because integration is the time when we see how our code behaves with other code in the system. It's often when the nastiest bugs are found. A feature remains unproven and carries an unknown amount of risk until it's integrated into the system. Integrating features into releases that are tested in large batches is like going all-in in Vegas. The odds are against you.

Avoid branching

Once code is integrated into the system the risk drops to near zero, but when components are built in branches and integrated before release the risk is unknown until the branches are integrated. Instead of branching, use feature flags to turn off features in the system while they are being built but not yet ready to be activated.

Invest in automated tests

Removing all human intervention for validating a release candidate so tests are entirely automated is essential for dropping the cost of development. Fast automated tests let you run them any time and provide important feedback. If you find it difficult to do test automation in your system, then consider a redesign to something more testable. A lack of testability often indicates a poor design.

Identify areas of risk

Risk often has to do with unknowns or things out of our direct control. Identify what these things are by asking what could go wrong. Identify external dependencies—the things out of your direct control—and then look for ways to mitigate those risks and decouple dependencies.

Work through unknowns

Once an unknown is identified you can work on it for a short period and then check in to measure progress. Spikes are generally focused around a question or series of questions to be answered. By creating short time boxes with check-ins and measuring progress, we hope to avoid going down ratholes and wasting time. Try to keep separating the known from the unknown so the unknown becomes smaller and smaller.

Build the smallest pieces that show value

Smaller problems are easier to understand, solve, prove, and maintain. But how small should you make it? My rule of thumb is to build the smallest thing that shows value. If 80% of the value comes from 20% of the features, then let's build that 20% first. We might not even need the other 80%.

Validate often

Our customers may not know what they want until they see it. Getting validation early and often can help us build a higher-value product and engages the customer in finding better ways of doing things. When development can become a partnership between the customer or PO and the developers, we can often build better features than we could have with all the up-front planning in the world.

Reducing risk in software is about assuring that you're building the right things and assuring that you're building the things right. You know you're building the right things by getting feedback from our users early and often. You know you're building the things right by following good engineering practices for building changeable code that's continuously integrated into the build. By doing these two things you can significantly improve your likelihood and degree of success.

Retrospective

Integrate Continuously, because a story is not done until it's done-done-done. The goal is to take a story from start to finish as soon as possible and this requires an automated build—the heartbeat of a healthy project.

In this chapter, we discovered...

- Integrating code as it is built reduces risks involved in developing software.

- Integration can be painful so Waterfall puts it off until the end, increasing risk and the cost of making changes.

- Automate release candidate validation so the cost of making last-minute changes is negligible.

- Shorten feedback cycles so developers immediately see the consequences of their actions.

- Knowing the importance of continuous deployability, you'll look for ways of automating tasks and use continuous integration to get immediate feedback on how features interact with the rest of the system as it's built.

By integrating code as it's written, we ensure that the risks associated with developing software drop and that developers gain a rich source of feedback. This decreases the cost of making last-minute changes, shortens feedback cycles, and assures the system is always in a releasable state.

CHAPTER 8

Practice 4: Collaborate

The most valuable resource we have is each other.

When we work together, when we can learn not just from each other but with each other, we can do anything. But collaboration doesn't just happen. We have to set ourselves up for success in collaboration the same way we've to set ourselves up for success in anything else.

No one—I hope! —just jumps behind the wheel of a car for the first time ever at the start of a driver's license test. We get a learner's permit, learn the rules of the road, get comfortable with driving around an empty parking lot...

We *learn* to drive, *then* we go take the test.

There are methodologies, techniques, practices, and principles underlying any skill, and the same is true with collaboration.

Software developers are information workers, and information workers depend on information.

This sits in stark contrast to a lot of the ideas still left over from the Industrial Revolution. We were taught to do things in certain ways, and to have certain expectations about the workplace itself. We were told to want our own offices, or at least our own desks. When I worked at IBM that was what senior developers aspired to: an office of our very own, with a door we could close and beautiful furniture inside and lots of privacy. And if you were *really* good you might even have a window!

But as it turns out, that was a big mistake.

Child psychologists have identified a concept known as *parallel play*.[1] When babies are put together in a common area and given a collection of toys, each baby grabs a toy or two and starts playing, but as hard as parents might try to get the babies to play with each other, they simply won't do it. Each baby bangs around with his or her toys, seemingly oblivious to the presence of the babies around them.

Seemingly oblivious—but they aren't actually oblivious to those other babies. They're keeping one eye on their favorite toy and another on the babies around them. They're observing each other, watching what one baby does with the same toy, looking for cues on how to behave, what looks like fun, and so on. But they don't directly interact with each other.

It's almost as if each baby is sitting in his own office, every once in a while cracking the door open to see what the other babies are up to.

But by the age of three or four, they start to interact with each other, share toys—or, to be honest, *steal* toys from each other—and in general start to try to sort out the complex nuances of human interaction that will continue to challenge them well into middle age.

Assuming everyone who's reading this is at least four years old, when you're working as a team it's not enough to be *on* the team—a member of the team, or somehow "team adjacent"—you really have to be *in* the team—immersed in that culture.

I was a contractor at IBM, where contractors "enjoyed" a sort of second-class existence. We didn't get our own offices. We were all thrown into what they called "the bull pen"—a big room with a whole bunch of desks all smashed up against each other so we were working in each others' faces. Even the name had a negative connotation, reducing us to the level of livestock. I've heard of similar setups referred to as "the pit" or "Siberia."

And they couldn't understand how we could get so much more done than the IBM employees who were pulling in salaries much higher than ours.

A big reason for our greater productivity was that we were able to collaborate. I could look up and see my colleagues, ask a question, answer a question, or discuss a question.

---

1. What to Expect. "What's Parallel Play?" http://www.whattoexpect.com/playroom/playtime-tips/what-is-parallel-play.aspx Accessed November 28, 2014.

Extreme Programming

The ideas at the heart of Extreme Programming come from Kent Beck and his initial work in the field. Kent Beck coined the term in his book *Extreme Programming Explained: Embrace Change [Bec00]*, which described the methodology he developed along with his associates Ward Cunningham and Ron Jeffries while working on the Chrysler Comprehensive Compensation System. This was a massive and very expensive project—and it was failing. In an effort to bring it back on track, Chrysler brought Kent Beck in as a consultant to take a look at where they were and where they were headed, and to suggest ways to fix what everyone there knew was broken.

After talking with the team, who all knew the project was in trouble, Kent was asked by the CIO to take over the project, but instead he stayed on as a consultant. One of the things that Kent brought to the project was a new office layout, which you can see in the following picture. Cube walls were taken away in favor of shared desks and a more communal setting, free of "private" spaces.

This "transformative moment" for that project, and for the concept of the workplace in general, actually evolved over the course of a year or so, during which the team was moved into a completely different space. The developers there went from knowing they were in trouble to working closely together to save the project. And part of how they got there was being open to the idea of putting the work ahead of the office space. It's that openness to new ways of thinking—even if it seems, on the surface, to just be the simple act of rearranging the furniture—that cannot be trivialized or ignored.

Communication and Collaboration

Software development is a social activity, one that involves a lot of communication and interaction—constantly learning, constantly interacting, and dealing with and talking about the abstract—so coordination among individuals is of vital importance. What management has to keep in mind is that it's the people on the front lines who know best, and people who don't immerse themselves in building software don't really understand it.

And though there might be some push-back from people who see this sort of communal space as an invasion of privacy, or personal space, as one more "perk" we're no longer getting...think of it this way: if you're in prison and you get in a fight or otherwise misbehave, they throw you in solitary confinement. Being in a tiny little windowless room all by yourself is a *punishment*. How did that turn into a "perk" in Corporate America?

But again, there are skills to learn and practices to employ in order to get the most out of a collaborative environment. Just making a space open and airy is not nearly enough. It's how we interact within that space—how we interact with *each other*—that reveals not just the reason for the common space but the power in it.

Software development is more than a technical activity. It's also a social activity. Team members must be able to communicate complex abstract ideas and work well together. Communication depends more on common understanding than common workspace. So we have to begin with a shared definition of our goals, a shared definition of what "quality" means, and a shared definition of what "done" means. We must have a common language for doing design—shared design patterns, refactoring, and other common practices—and we also have to help each other and pair together.

It's a common mischaracterization that software developers are bad communicators. We're actually excellent communicators. We may not be good at small talk because we like high bandwidth communication, but as I said, we actually like the work we do, developing software, and we like people who also like to develop software. Software development is one of the most collaborative activities in the world.

Pair Program

One of the most valuable, yet one of the most undervalued and misunderstood of the Extreme Programming practices, is *pair programming*, where two developers work on the same task together on one computer.

Managers tell me they don't want their developers to do pair programming because they can't afford to lose half their "resources"—but pairing is not about taking turns at the computer; it's about bringing two minds to bear on the same task so that task is completed more rapidly and at a much greater level of quality than if one person worked on it alone.

Pair programming is one of the hardest practices of Extreme Programming to get most developers to try, but when done correctly it's one of the most powerful. Too often we think of programmers as solitary people and programming as a solitary activity, but software developers can get a lot more accomplished when they work together than when they work alone.

Have you ever tried to move all of your possessions all by yourself?

You carry every piece of furniture all alone, put it in the truck all by yourself, unload it without assistance, and carry it into the new house all on your own? If you don't have any heavy furniture or appliances that might be possible, though time consuming. But if you have any piece of furniture you can't lift on your own.

Which is faster and yields better results: building a house all by yourself, or having a team of experienced carpenters, plumbers, and electricians come in and work together using the best tools of the trade?

Physical activities like moving furniture or building houses are obvious examples—there's only so much weight one human being, however physically fit, can lift. But the fact is, there are mental limits as well. Conceptual, virtual problems can be just as unwieldy as a king size mattress, and having someone help with the mental "heavy lifting" is just as important to the efficiency of a software developer as it is to a building contractor.

Still, a lot of developers resist pair programming and even make fun of it and belittle the concept, almost always without trying it.

But when you actually do it, I assure you it's a very different kind of experience than you might imagine. And of course, it's important to do it the right way. I have seen situations where people have tried pair programming and thought the concept was flawed, but they were doing it wrong. They're simply trading off, like two babies sitting on the floor next to each other, occasionally putting down and picking up the same toy, playing next to each other but not with each other.

Benefits of Pairing

Pair programming disseminates knowledge across a team far more quickly than any other method I know, and for cross-functional teams it's extremely valuable when all team members have some familiarity with the entire code-base. It prevents overspecialization and creates a shared understanding of the system across the team.

Pair programming is especially useful for activities like naming things, which sounds like a trivial activity but is quite important in software development. Virtually everything in software requires a name and the name should reveal the intention behind the thing. Coming up with good intention-revealing names is a critical part of writing good software.

When figuring out complex implementations, close collaboration helps you validate ideas and think through problems more thoroughly.

Pair programming helps get others up to speed very quickly and helps senior developers mentor less experienced developers.

Developers learn from each other and support each other in following good development practices.

People are less likely to take shortcuts and build bad code when they know someone is looking over their shoulders, so pair programming helps pairs make code that's more maintainable. Pairing is also useful for design sessions, debugging sessions, and cleaning up code to improve maintainability.

Pair programming helps support a shared code aesthetic and collective code ownership.

This notion of collective code ownership is quite important in software development. In traditional Waterfall environments, everybody has his or her own little piece to work on and everybody's style is different, making it hard to read the code in the short term and even harder to maintain it in the longer term.

I'm much less concerned with what that style is than the fact that it's consistent across the team.

Ideally, you should never be able to tell by reading the code who wrote it. I don't think there should be a standards document for coding style. That style guide should be the code itself.

Having that shared set of practices, a shared code style, means you'll have to get new team members up to speed, and there's no better, more efficient way to do that than pair programming.

Have the new team member pair with a senior developer, or at least a more experienced developer, for a week or two. Over that short time this might be considered more "job shadowing" than pair programming, with the senior developer acting in the role of mentor more so than in a true pair programming relationship, which is, ideally, a collaboration of equals. The wait staff at a restaurant does this, and with much less at stake than in a multimillion-dollar enterprise software project.

According to Alistair Cockburn and Laurie Williams in their paper "The Costs and Benefits of Pair Programming," when two programmers work together, it's not two people doing the work of one—a drop in overall team productivity of 50%. In fact, pairing decreases total programmer time by only 15%.[2] But even though it consumes a little extra time, that's easily made up when complex problems are solved more quickly.

There are far fewer defects in code that has been pair programmed than in code somebody wrote alone. Pair programming can result in less code being required to solve the same problem. When those things are put together—less code to sort through and that code is better and more efficient—it's clear that would significantly reduce maintenance costs. And the cost of maintenance is very, very high in software.

Developers get fewer interruptions, in fact *very* few, when they're pairing. People are less likely to interrupt when they see two people working together. When you see two people doing something, working together, how comfortable do you feel walking up and essentially saying, "Both of you stop what you're doing so I can take one of you away to a meeting, or so I can ask one of you about this, and did both of you get the new cover sheets for the TPS reports?" or "Hey, how 'bout those Seahawks?"

But when someone's in his cubicle—type, type, type, type, type—people are much more likely to walk right up: "Can you sign off on this, and can you initial this other thing?" Some of those things may be necessary activities. A whole team may be waiting around for your initials on some document. But the ingrained unease that people have interrupting a group of even two people

---

2. Cockburn, Alistair. Williams, Laurie. "The Costs and Benefits of Pair Programming." Proceedings of the First International Conference on Extreme Programming and Flexible Processes in Software Engineering (XP2000). http://dsc.ufcg.edu.br/~jacques/cursos/map/recursos/XPSardinia.pdf

working together helps to separate what's really an immediate priority and what can sit in an inbox for an hour or two.

And not all distractions come from external sources. We're all much less likely to answer emails, check in on Facebook, or wander off into other distractions if we know that someone else is sitting right next to us, waiting for us to finish that and get back on task. Sometimes anyone can get lost mentally—we have to do a lot of thinking when we develop software—but being able to look over to a person next to you and throw out some ideas, or ask a question, keeps you focused.

At the end of a day of pairing I find I'm absolutely wiped out. I'm totally exhausted, and yet I'm supremely satisfied because I know I learned and I got a lot accomplished. When people are paired together, they police each other in a way, and both of them put in a solid day's work.

And this, managers, is why you want to encourage your developers to pair.

How to Pair

Though there's rarely ever just one way of doing anything, there are ways of doing anything more effectively.

Just putting two people in front of a computer and saying, "Okay, start pair programming. I'll be back to check on you in three hours," is obviously not going to be enough. Of course, developers know how to talk to each other and how to code, but we don't necessarily know how to put those two together in a useful way.

In pair programming, as the name clearly states, there are typically two people working on one machine: the *driver* and the *navigator*. A good resource on pair programming is *Pair Programming Illuminated [WK02]*.

The driver is the person at the keyboard, and the navigator is sitting next to the driver with a clear view of the monitor.

But the navigator isn't just sitting there watching the driver code. The navigator and driver talk to each other. This should be a real conversation, too, not just somebody sitting over your shoulder criticizing and pointing out mistakes. It's just as important to recognize what your partner has just done well than it is to say, "Oops, typo there." Even more important is to ask, "Why did you do that, and not this?" Then listen to the answer. It may just surprise you.

Engage, discuss, interact.

Then switch roles.

The driver hands over the keyboard and mouse and becomes the navigator, and the navigator becomes the driver.

The driver and navigator should switch roles frequently—as often as every five minutes but no less often than thirty minutes. I like to switch roles every twenty minutes, but sometimes even more frequently. And that switch should happen organically, not on some kind of timer, though using a timer to start with or as a backup can be helpful. Two people with a common goal and the most basic interpersonal skills should be able to identify those natural pause points, and the vast majority of the time developers do just that. But if you're the driver and you sense your navigator is getting a little bored, then pass the keyboard back and forth more frequently. Sometimes when you have two trains of thought going and one train is traveling a little faster than the other, get that keyboard in the slower person's hands and I guarantee the slower train will speed right up.

Another technique I find very useful is Ping-Pong Pairing: one person writes the test, then the other person makes the test pass, cleans up the code, writes the next test, and then passes the keyboard back to the first person to make the test pass, clean up the code, and write the next test...and so on. This is useful when getting tests to pass will take five to twenty minutes, but if we get stuck on something we may go back to a timer and switch driver and navigator every twenty minutes.

Who to Pair With

The question of who pairs with whom is a logical concern. There are three different ways to approach pairing, each with its own set of advantages and disadvantages.

First, we can match developers based on their strengths and weaknesses, so the pair can play to each other's strengths, and in so doing help each other to overcome their weaknesses, including personality. When pairing based on personality, take a developer who has a strong personality—the outgoing, opinionated type—and pair her up with a developer with a more passive personality—the introverted, silent type. What we're looking for is the discontinuity, the space where those two very different mind-sets come together. Regardless, pairing two best friends, or the most like-minded individuals on the team, may not always be the best approach. Avoid letting two people simply "preach to the choir."

Second, pair the most experienced developer with the least experienced. This is particularly valuable teams adding new members.

If there are significant time constraints on the team or a little less elbow room for finding unexpected synergies, or on a team that's bringing in new people, I'll typically take an experienced person and a non-experienced person and pair them together. Of course, this is meant to put the senior developer in a mentoring role, but what invariably happens is that the senior developer ends up learning almost as much from the act of mentoring as the student does from being mentored. I've been a teacher most of my life and I can tell you with no hesitation that the best way to learn, to really open up your thinking on even the most familiar subject, is to teach it. Explain it to someone else, and when you hear yourself, I assure you you'll be surprised by what you end up saying.

As Plutarch[3] once said, "The mind is not a vessel to be filled, but a fire to be kindled." Teaching is not about trying to get what's in my head into your head. Teaching is about discovering together. It's all about showing our students the thought process that allows them to discover the answers for themselves. Every question they ask is an opportunity to help them learn, so I usually don't answer questions. Most of the time, I help the person who asked find the answer for himself. I'm trying to help people think through problems because it's the thought process that's most enlightening, and most valuable, and not one specific answer to one specific question.

The third option, which I highly recommend, is *randomly* pairing with different people. Random pairing time and time again brings us together with people we just would never suspect would bring out the best in us, and not despite the fact that you have different approaches to coding but precisely because you have different approaches to coding. It's pretty hard to learn something new from someone who thinks exactly like you.

I've sat down to work with that quiet guy in the corner and found myself three times more productive than I was with the developer I was sure would be my best match. And there's no way to know that unless you get a chance to pair with everyone. Pair for a day, pair for an hour, pair for a week—then switch it up.

Another approach to pair programming I find particularly useful is what Llewellyn Falco calls *strong-style pairing*[4] where you follow the rule:

> For an idea to go from your head into the computer it MUST go through someone else's hands.

---

3. http://en.wikiversity.org/wiki/Plutarch_quote
4. See http://llewellynfalco.blogspot.com/2014/06/llewellyns-strong-style-pairing.html

There's a different part of the brain that's engaged when you're speaking as opposed to when you're typing. Describing something to someone else can often help you get clearer on details you might not have considered. This is a way for both team members to stay engaged while pairing.

A great paper on pair programming is "Promiscuous Pairing and Beginner's Mind: Embrace Inexperience" by Arlo Belshee.[5] In it he talks about going to a flow state and how we can do that and be pairing at the same time:

> The Flow mind state is one of intense focus. The entire problem and solution spaces are loaded into the developer's head. Programmers work orders of magnitude better when in Flow.
>
> Pair Flow is similar to Flow. The solution and problem spaces are shared between the minds of the participants. Again Pair Flow works significantly better than pair programming without flow.

We're talking about pairing here in the context of software developers, but I think everyone on any team can find a great deal of value in pairing.

Buddy Program

For teams that have serious trepidation about the idea of pairing together, and there are a few, I'll suggest another practice I use, which I call *buddy programming*.

Sometimes it is better to work by yourself, but developers still want the benefit of feedback. So in buddy programming you work by yourself, in the typical way, for most of the day. Then maybe the last hour of the day you'll get together with your buddy and do a code review of what you both did that day. This is less extreme than pair programming but it still has significant benefits.

As with pair programming, I suggest randomly swapping buddies on a daily, or at least weekly basis. Or by task, by iteration...all sorts of different ways. In a sense, buddy programming is baby steps toward pair programming. Sometimes you have to get people to just *try* something and buddy programming is a safe way to try pairing.

Software development is incredibly personal, and it's our intelligence at stake. Doing that magic in front of somebody is a little scary for some of us. And it's not at all unreasonable to allow people a chance to acclimate to new practices.

---

5. Belshee, Arlo. "Promiscuous Pairing and Beginner's Mind: Embrace Experience." Pasadena, CA: Silver Platter Software. http://csis.pace.edu/~grossman/dcs/XR4-PromiscuousPairing.pdf

Direct experience is critical, and so much of what we're covering here, you'll just have to eventually try. The experience of trying it is very different than reading about it.

I have noticed on more than a few occasions that after trying pair programming for just a few days the person in the group who was most resistant to pairing becomes its biggest supporter on the team.

Spike, Swarm, and Mob

Beyond pair programming and buddy programming, there are a few other configurations for working together that are worth not just mentioning but trying.

Spiking

Spiking is when two or more developers focus on a single task together, usually working for a predefined length of time to resolve some kind of unknown. Spiking is a very powerful tool in that area. We have this unknown, and we have to figure out what we're going to do for it, so we "take a spike" and we do some research. It's like forming a committee to study a short-term problem, and once that problem is solved, the committee is disbanded.

Swarming

Swarming is when the whole team, or small groups of more than two developers each, work together on the same problem, but they're all working simultaneously. This is an especially good approach for solving "showstopper" problems. If the whole team is blocked on something, have the whole team go to work on it. This can be very, very powerful.

Mobbing

Mobbing[6] is a concept brought to life by Woody Zuill and his team. This is when the whole team normally works together on a single story, like a swarm of ants working together to break down a piece of food.

Though this may seem like a highly inefficient way to work, it turns out to be surprisingly efficient for specific kinds of projects.

The team was taking on a complicated project, so when they gathered in a meeting to look at what they needed to work on, they found they were very

---

6.   Zuill, Woody. Blog: Mob Programming. http://mobprogramming.org/

productive together. At the end of that day they decided to try it again the next day, and they haven't stopped since.

The whole team works like this all the time now. They have their offices set up like a conference room with two projectors. They take turns so only one person is at the keyboard and the rest of the team—five to seven people—are the navigators.

You can go to their website to watch a time-lapse video[7] of a day of mob programming condensed down into five minutes.

Watch the video and you'll see everyone working on the project the whole time and it's exciting to see. It brings the idea of collaboration to a whole new level. Some teams find mobbing particularly useful when getting up to speed on new technologies.

Research Unknowns in Time Boxes

In addition to training software developers, I work with scientific research companies. I have one client that's the world authority on things that happen in the air...weather and stuff like that. I have another client that's a world authority on things that happen *underneath* the earth. They study geological topology and do geological cartography, and so forth. Both have a lot of scientists working for them: pure, real research scientists.

What's really cool is that they not only brought their developers to my classes but they brought their scientists to my classes as well. So here I am teaching senior scientific researchers the same techniques I teach developers and they

---

7.   http://mobprogramming.org/mob-programming-time-lapse-video-a-day-of-mob-programming/

find it incredibly valuable. After all, software developers are researchers. They're really *inventors*, and so the same techniques that prove successful for us worked for these scientists as well. I taught them to do spiking and time boxing and iterations and writing their tests first and all that, and they loved it.

Time boxing is valuable for researching what you don't know, and the goal is to spike on that. It's usually best to have a set of questions, goals, or objectives in mind when starting a spike but basically a spike is:

> For this period of time—it can be an iteration of two weeks, it could be an hour, whatever—I'm going to research *this*.

Say, "This is what I know about this, this is what I don't know," and draw a circle around the domain you don't know, and tweak that circle as you're spiking until you can make that circle invisible—it's completely consumed by what you know. Or if you can't do that, then see if you can encapsulate what you don't know so you can deal with it later when you know more.

Schedule Code Reviews and Retrospectives

Pair programming is essentially code review *as you're writing it*. In fact, that's where the term Extreme Programming came from. Kent Beck called it Extreme Programming because what we want to do is take the things that seem to have worked for us in the past and take them to a logical extreme.

Honestly, I don't feel that Extreme Programming is all that "extreme." In many ways it's the way software should have been built all along. Even some of the most conservative and business-minded people in the industry prefer Extreme Programming.

Still, in the thinking of Extreme Programming, if code reviews are a good thing, why don't we review every line of code as we're writing it? That's where pair programming came from. It's an "extreme" version of a code review.

But even if you're reviewing each others' code as you work together, that doesn't negate the need for actual code reviews. You still want other people on the team to understand all of the code in the system, not just your pair's code. The whole team needs to understand the design and talk about the trade-offs and approaches we've each been taking.

Let the team decide how frequently they'd like to do design reviews and code reviews. Once a feature is built the developers who wrote it can show other members of the team how they wrote it. Personally, I enjoy code reviews and learn a lot from them, but I have seen them degrade into no more than arguments about formatting. Design and code reviews should first and foremost address the *why* of the design and say why that design was chosen. Understanding what design trade-offs were made and how straightforward it would be to extend in various ways are good things to cover in code reviews.

Regular retrospectives at the end of an iteration or at the end of a release can be very helpful. Retrospectives help teams improve as a whole, as long as they find actionable problems from that retrospective. The retrospective process has tremendous value even if the problems it discovers are very small. If you can take action on a problem, do something proactive to fix it, and identify the antipatterns that led to the problem in the first place, you can avoid making the same mistake again.

Retrospectives can be fairly informal. Gather the team for an hour or so and give everybody a chance to talk about what worked and what didn't. Doctors call them "postmortems" and the military prefers "debriefings," but the concept is more or less the same: what did we do, how and why did we do it, how could we have done it better, and so on.

Amplify Learning and Spread Knowledge

In the old paradigm, job security came from being a specialist. Knowing something that made you indispensable kept you safe from a round of layoffs, could be parlayed into a raise, and was a sort of corporate currency. And that being the case, who wouldn't want to hold on to that knowledge and not share it with anyone else?

But today, job security—and beyond that, *career* security—comes from exactly the opposite direction. We put more value on those who are willing to spread knowledge and share it around with the team. Pairing, swarming, mobbing...these are all techniques to help bring people together, to help us get more done more efficiently and at a higher level of quality.

Create cross-functional teams that are able to handle the range of tasks needed to design, implement, and test the software they create. And even though you may be a front-end developer on one project and a back-end developer on the next project, as a professional software developer you bring a range of principles and practices to your work regardless of the platform or language you use.

But there's more to pair programming than better code faster—not that that isn't enough. Pairing is *fun*. And the fact is that the more work feels like play the more likely we are to choose work over play. And I'm far from the first person to say that if we love what we do, we'll never really "work" a day in our lives. I'll let you in on a little secret…

One of my favorite things to do is to go to a conference and blow it off.

Instead of the panels and seminars and presentations I'll find a friend, a colleague, and we'll pair together for the whole morning session. I've learned so much that way—things you never got a chance to learn in a formal conference setting. I've learned about keyboard shortcuts this way that have saved me hours and hours and hours of time. That's always been something that really surprises me as a developer. There are so many conventions that are just not written down anywhere. And when I'm pairing with another developer I see some new keystroke and it's like a bolt from the blue—and I throw back a few bolts of my own. And when we discover we've both found the same shortcut but have attached different names to them, it's like meeting another member of a secret society—while at the same time doing precisely what secret societies would rather we not do: share information.

And the software industry just can't afford to be a secret society anymore, much less a whole collection of secret societies with even more layers of other secret societies within each team…and solitary developers who are little secret societies in and of themselves.

Please keep in mind that a lot of developers, most really, do work with proprietary information. This isn't me saying, "Go tell all your customer's secrets to the world." I'm talking about sharing thought resources within a team, to more efficiently work together to get a project done. Professionals still need to be aware of what's confidential, and respect those limits.

Always Strive to Be Mentoring and Mentored

Being a software developer means constantly learning. New tools and new techniques are introduced almost daily, and keeping up with all that can be a challenge. Scott Bain, who is my mentor and dear friend, says, "Always strive to be mentoring someone and to be mentored by someone."

I could not agree more.

As a teacher I get to mentor thousands of developers and, again, I can attest to the fact that the best way to learn is by teaching. I've learned so much from my students and by translating my knowledge into learnable chunks that others can easily grasp. As a developer I draw on my many colleagues and associates to introduce me to new ideas and teach me new skills.

Time and time again in pair programming I come across a tendency to turn inside and to get isolated—I think we've all been there. But when I work against that little cynical voice inside that says, "Don't do it...this is going to be bad...you know this is going to go bad..." it never has gone bad.

Having had a chance to work with over 8,000 developers I feel as though I've assimilated them and they have assimilated me. I can draw on their knowledge and I know many of my students have drawn on mine. People have told me that when presented with a tricky problem they've asked themselves, "Well, what would David say about this?" and an answer would come into their heads. And I do that with them as well. We're all in this together.

And by working and playing well with each other, we can build code that works and plays well with other code.

Let's Get Practical

Here are some ways to put these ideas into practice.

Seven Strategies for Pair Programming

Of all the Agile development practices I teach, pair programming gets the most resistance from managers and also from developers. Managers often ask me how putting two developers on the same task can possibly be more efficient than having them work independently on different tasks...but it most definitely is. You may not find a huge increase in the lines of code written per day, but you will find developers get more done writing less code, which also drops the cost of maintenance, and you will see a huge decrease in the amount of bugs written, which will dramatically speed up the time to delivery. When done correctly, pair programming can be an effective way to propagate knowledge throughout a team, improve everyone's skill level, and bring more job satisfaction. All these things will reduce the overall cost of building software. Here are seven strategies for effective pairing.

Try it, you'll like it
> The experience of doing pair programming correctly is different than what many people think. Trying it in a supportive environment, where team members can learn how to do it properly, can make all the difference between having a bad experience that will be avoided in the future and having a great experience that team members will continue to practice.

Engage driver and navigator
> Pairing is not about taking turns doing the work. Each member of the pair has specific duties, working together, and in parallel. Both the person

at the keyboard (driver) and the one looking over the driver's shoulder (navigator) are actively engaged while pairing.

Swap roles frequently

Taking turns driving and navigating every 20–60 minutes helps keep collaboration at a maximum. Handing off the keyboard also helps propagate knowledge across the pair and ultimately, by pairing with other team members, propagates knowledge throughout the team.

Put in an honest day

Pairing takes a lot of energy. You are "on" and focused every minute of the day. You are far less likely to take breaks or get interrupted by others when pairing. At the end of a day of pair programming, I come home exhausted but I also feel supremely satisfied. I always gain a lot when I pair program, regardless of whether I'm learning something from someone with more experience than me, I'm teaching something to someone with less experience, or we're figuring things out together.

Try all configurations

There are a series of techniques and protocols for effective pairing. Knowing them can help pairs collaborate more effectively and efficiently. Try random pairing by story, task, hour, all the way down to twenty minutes. Often, people who wouldn't think to pair with each other make the best and most productive pairs. See what works and what doesn't, but give all the options a try. The results may surprise you.

Let teams decide on the details

Pair programming—like any of the Agile practices—cannot be forced on a team by management. Team members have to discover the value for themselves. Not everyone is suited to pairing, nor are all tasks. Some people need more alone time than others, but contrary to popular belief, software development is very much a social activity, requiring a great deal of complex communication. Pairing can help.

Track progress

Metrics speak louder than words. Pairing does *not* cut productivity in half. It can boost productivity if you measure time-to-value. Keep track of velocity, defects, and code quality. They are productivity indicators and will show you the value of pairing in your organization.

When done correctly, pairing can significantly increase the throughput of value created while slashing defects. I know of no other approach to software development that can radiate knowledge and skills throughout a team more rapidly than pairing.

Seven Strategies for Effective Retrospectives

It's important to make time to reflect with the team and gain insights on what can be improved. Regular retrospectives are a good way to get the team in the habit of looking at what they did and how they can improve. Here are seven strategies for effective retrospectives.

Look for small improvements

Organizations tend to be either very resistant to change or try to make too many changes at the same time. Organizational change happens most rapidly and easily through baby steps and making small improvements. If you strive for just a 2% improvement every few weeks you'll have at 50% improvement at the end of a year. Small improvements tend to be easier to adopt, and they compound!

Blame process, not people

When things break down it's typically not intentional, and blaming people often makes matters worse. Instead, look for flaws in the process that allowed this problem to happen in the first place. This takes the pressure off people so those closest to the issue can focus on finding ways of preventing this type of issue from happening again.

Practice the five whys

Often, the presenting problem is not the real issue, it's just a symptom of a different and possibly more far-reaching problem. One technique for finding the root cause of a problem is called the "five whys." When faced with a problem, ask why it happened, or what caused it to happen, and with that answer ask why that happened, and so on until you've asked "why" at least five times. After about the fourth "why" you'll often start to discover some interesting problems you may not have been aware of.

Address root causes

Once the root cause, the real issue, is understood, it can and should be addressed. Addressing the root cause of a problem is often easier than addressing the symptoms, and can really deal with the issue instead of being a Band-Aid solution that can cause the problem to show up again in a different form.

Listen to everyone

Retrospectives should engage everyone on the team. Don't just let the most vocal team members get all the say. Instead, solicit opinions from everyone and give everyone actionable objectives for making small improvements. Constant improvement is everyone's responsibility.

Empower people

> Give people what they need to make improvements. Demonstrate to people that you are serious about continuous improvement and support them in making changes. If people fear making changes it's generally because they feel unsupported. Show them that you encourage and reward this kind of initiative.

Measure progress

> It's not enough to set a goal for improvement. You have to have a measurable outcome that everyone can strive for and then regularly measure progress toward that outcome. This takes an idea out of the conceptual and into the practical, making it real for people. When people can see progress toward a goal, they're more apt to strive for it.

Your process doesn't have to be perfect, but when flaws are detected and ways of improving are found, they must be encouraged and supported. The people on the front line doing the work are most likely to see ways of improving it. When workers are encouraged to "stop the assembly line" to make improvements, the whole process can get better.

Retrospective

Collaborate to build high-fidelity communications and rapidly propagate knowledge across a group. We're in this together!

In this chapter, we discovered...

- Use techniques right away to build high-fidelity communications and rapidly propagate knowledge across your team.

- Utilize a range of collaboration techniques, including pairing, spiking, swarming, and mobbing.

- Collaboration skills help in researching unknowns, amplifying learning, and spreading knowledge.

- Receive and act on feedback from code reviews and retrospectives.

- By always striving to mentor and be mentored, we elevate our skill level as well as our team's.

Our greatest resource is each other, and to maximize collaboration it's useful to know some basic techniques and configurations for working together. In addition to pair programming, there's spiking, swarming, mobbing, and buddy programming. By amplifying learning and spreading knowledge, we can improve our teams as well as the whole industry.

CHAPTER 9

Practice 5: Create CLEAN Code

CLEAN code is a shout-out to Uncle Bob Martin's book *Clean Code: A Handbook of Agile Software Craftsmanship*[1] and to Miško Hevery's "Clean Code Talks."[2] Both are outstanding resources for software developers interested in writing cleaner, more testable software.

In this chapter, we'll explore five code qualities that are at the foundation of good software. They are at the core of software development principles and practices. And, as we will see, they have a very special relationship with testability.

We can infer virtually all good software development skills by understanding just a handful of code qualities. And these qualities show up in many other places than code: they are everywhere from a well-written novel or an enthralling movie to the remote control of your TV. When these qualities are present, things are more understandable, clear, and even intuitive. When they're missing, things look messy and complex. This is because our brains are wired to more easily understand things when these qualities are present.

Unlike qualities in goods and services, which can be, well, *qualitative*, the code qualities we'll discuss are actually *quantifiable* and precise.

Code qualities are little things that can make a big difference. An object should have well-defined characteristics, focused responsibilities, and hidden implementation. It should be in charge of its state; and be defined only once.

---

1. Martin, Robert C. *Clean Code: A Handbook of Agile Software Craftsmanship.* Upper Saddle River, NJ: Prentice Hall, 2008.
2. Hevery, Miško. Google Tech Talks. "Clean Code Talks." 2008. http://misko.hevery.com/2008/12/08/clean-code-talks-inheritance-polymorphism-testing/

We have names for these things. These names are:

C ohesive
L oosely Coupled
E ncapsulated
A ssertive
N onredundant

The first letter of each word spells the word CLEAN.

Good code is CLEAN Code. Let's look at each code quality in detail.

Quality Code Is Cohesive

First and foremost, high-quality code is *cohesive*—each piece is *about one thing*. This is my favorite code quality because cohesive code is easy for most of us to understand and work with. It's also easy to create.

If you look up the word *cohesion* in a dictionary you'll find it's a synonym for adhesion, or how well things are stuck together. But to software developers cohesion means software entities (classes and methods) should have a *single responsibility*.

Al Shalloway says, "No God Objects!"

When I asked Al, "You call it a God Object because it tries to do everything, right?" he said, "No, I call it a God Object because when you go to change it you say, 'Oh, my God!' "

Scott Bain told me, "Keep entities single-minded."

In other words, a class should have a single purpose.

This implies that our programs will be made up of lots and lots of little classes that will have very limited functionality. This is true. I didn't understand the value of cohesion when I first read about it.

When I was introduced to object-oriented programming around 1990, I was shown an object-oriented program and I thought the developers who wrote it were crazy. It was a simple program with nearly fifty classes, and I thought they built it that way so that no one else would ever be able to understand it and they could hold onto their jobs forever.

I thought, *They use forty-eight classes and I could do the job with just three*, as though a program is better if it uses fewer classes. But I don't judge literature that way. I don't think one book is better than another because it has fewer words or one poem is more beautiful than another because it's shorter. Expression should be concise but it must also be *complete*.

Using lots of little classes means that each class could focus on a single responsibility and do its job well. It became clear that each class had a unique and specific purpose. When a change was required, it tended to be only narrowly focused to one or a few classes, making the change easier to isolate and implement.

I found this difficult to understand at first because as a structured programmer my "security blanket" for understanding code was to trace through it. I pretended I was the CPU and would follow the instruction pointer as it moved through the code. It turns out this is not a good way to read object-oriented code.

What I learned is that good object-oriented programs are like ogres, or onions, or parfaits (everybody likes parfaits); they have *layers*. Each layer represents a different level of abstraction. This is the way we naturally think, where concepts are nested within other concepts. This helps us "chunk" concepts so we can deal with things at a high level—unless we want to get more detail, in which case we simply dive into the next layer down.

When used properly, layers of abstraction help us see the big picture and how components relate with each other. They also help us focus in on the details only when needed. Reading a good object-oriented program requires a different skill set than tracing through highly procedural code.

But if a cohesive class is about one thing, that one thing is an idea or concept—something that can be named. We experience and understand the world through language, and writing software is, after all, a linguistic activity. If I can name something then I can represent it with a class. People are hardwired to represent concepts with language so if we can easily name something it's usually well defined and understandable. Conversely, if we have difficulty naming something, it indicates the responsibilities are not yet well defined.

I said a class is cohesive when it's about one thing, but how do we model complex things? Let's say I want to create a person class. People are complex. They have walking behavior and talking behavior, eating behavior and speaking behavior, and so forth. How do I model such a complex thing while still keeping that class cohesive?

The answer is *composition*.

For example, a person class would be *composed* of a class for walking, a talking class, an eating class, and so on. The walking class would be *composed* of a class for balance, a forward step class, and so on.

I use classes to represent layers of concepts, and I nest them just like concepts are nested in our minds.

Of course, if a person in my system only needs a name and an address then there's no need for much else, but if I'm building something a lot more complex, nested abstractions may apply.

A class can represent a tangible thing like a wheelbarrow, or an intangible thing like a checking account. A class can also represent an idea, a process, a relationship, or anything else real or imaginary. Classes define the behavior of *objects*, which get *instantiated* at runtime using the new keyword.

Clearly, objects are not these things. They are representations, not because of their names but because of what they *do*. Names are important because they give us clues for what a class does, but in the digital domain, things are defined not by their label but by their *behavior*.

Quality Code Is Loosely Coupled

This code quality is about keeping the relationship between objects intentional and clear. This is often referred to as "loose coupling."

Code that is loosely coupled *indirectly depends* on the code it uses so it's easier to isolate, verify, reuse, and extend. Loose coupling is usually achieved through the use of an indirect call. Instead of calling a service directly the service is called through an intermediary. Replacing the service later will only impact the intermediary, reducing the impact of change on the rest of the system. Loose coupling lets you put *seams* in your code so you can inject dependencies instead of tightly coupling to them.

Rather than call a service directly you can call through an abstraction such as an *abstract class*, or in languages like Java or C# you can use an *interface* to that service. Later you can replace the service with a mock for testing or an enhanced service in the future with minimal impact on the rest of the system. This is why I prefer to couple to an abstraction rather than a concrete implementation.

People talk about *tight* coupling and *loose* coupling, but I always forget which is the good one and which is the bad one!

Tight coupling sounds bad, but loose coupling doesn't sound good either. If we have a graphical user interface (GUI) program with an EXIT button, I don't want it loosely coupled to the exit action. I don't want it to say, "I don't feel like exiting today." I want coupling where I intend it to be and no coupling where I don't intend it to be. For this reason, I also use the terms Scott Bain uses in his book *Emergent Design: The Evolutionary Nature of Professional Software Development [Bai08]*: *intentional coupling* and *accidental coupling*, so it's clear which is the good one and which is the bad one.

But how did I get bad coupling in the system?

Was it really an accident?

If gremlins didn't put it in my code when I wasn't looking, then how did bad coupling end up in my code?

The answer is that accidental coupling shows up when other code qualities are lacking. For example, if I have an uncohesive method that deals with many different issues, I'll have many unrelated reasons to couple to it.

This is why I avoid writing "Uber-APIs": fragile APIs that try to do too much, are difficult to maintain, and couple code across classes that have no business linking to each other. Code reuse is good because it helps eliminate redundancy but not at the expense of other code qualities. In the name of reuse, developers write "Uber-APIs" too often.

If different callers of an API share some of the same implementation or state for different reasons, don't expose this fact. Instead, hide it by creating multiple APIs that internally use only the part that's needed for each caller. By doing this, you not only eliminate the bits of redundancy, but you increase cohesion, encapsulate the right pieces, put the responsibility in the right places, and probably improve testability.

Notice how good design choices don't usually force you to sacrifice one quality for another. I say "usually" because there are times when performance or other considerations can force you to make code quality trade-offs. But these should only apply when these considerations are real and not supposed. More often than not, the right design choices improve code qualities.

Coupling is a particular problem with redundancy or when there is split functionality. When all or part of the same issue is spread out across a system, all the parts have to stay in sync in order for the issue to be handled correctly. If you break coupling in that situation, you can get incorrect or corrupted results. These are nasty bugs to have to try to track down.

Quality Code Is Encapsulated

Quality code is *encapsulated*—it hides its implementation details from the rest of the world. One of the most valuable benefits of using an object-oriented language over a procedural language is its ability to truly encapsulate entities. By encapsulation, I don't just mean making state and behavior private. Specifically, I want to hide *interface* (what I'm trying to accomplish) from *implementation* (how I accomplish it).

There are many things that can be encapsulated, and the process of writing a good program is the process of hiding as much as possible while still getting the job done. For our purposes, let's redefine encapsulation to mean hiding *what* something does from *how* it does it. The more you can hide how you implement something, the more freedom you have to change the implementation later without affecting other parts of the code. This helps keep code more modular and simpler to work with.

Well-encapsulated software comes about by designing from the *outside-in* rather than the *inside-out*.

Outside-In Programming: Outside-in programming, as I call it, designs features from the consumer's perspective. A service is designed based on the needs of the clients of that service. Name things after *what* the service does and hide *how* the service works. This helps create strong contracts between services that decouple components.

Inside-Out Programming: By contrast, the way most developers write software is to decompose the problem down into small pieces and stitch the pieces together to form a solution. I call this inside-out programming because the problem is decomposed to get right to the solution so developers can start coding. But when developers jump into implementation without first seeing the big picture, they tend to build brittle code whose responsibilities aren't well defined, making it harder to encapsulate.

Ultimately, developers need to see their code both *inside-out* and *outside-in* but it's a question of sequence. If you start with the details and ignore the big picture, it may become difficult to integrate pieces into a larger whole. Start by focusing on the big picture, the *what* and *why* of each component, and you can more readily create a space for it in the code.

So much of software comes down to how you think about the domain you're working in and how you represent it in the software you write. The domain model should be understandable to a domain expert without a computer background. If I'm writing an accounting system, the objects in my domain model will be things like Account, Asset, Balance, Checks, and other terms familiar to accountants.

Therefore, I want my domain model to be as separate from implementation details as possible. This helps provide flexibility, consistency, and understandability. It starts from the experience of using the software versus how the software was built, and continues down into every object in the system.

When we look at the world around us, we notice that everything has its own limited perspective. When we model things in the world we also want to model their limited perspective as well. This is important because what you can hide you can change later without breaking other code that depends on it. This is the way the non-software world works and it allows us to leverage concepts as well as the implementation of concepts in our code.

Encapsulation helps reduce the "ripple effect" that change can have on a system, and it can do much more than that.

If I want to know how much cash everyone in a room has on them, it's not appropriate for me to reach into their pockets and take it. Furthermore, some people may not carry their cash in their pockets; they may keep it in a purse—or in their socks, for that matter. I don't want to be concerned with the details of where and how each person accesses the money he has on him. Instead, I want to ask: "How much money do you have on you?" and have each person figure it out separately and give me the result.

When implementing a system with objects, put the responsibility for each object with the object itself, where it belongs, and this gives each object in the system its purpose. Every entity in the system has its own responsibilities and if those responsibilities change, it can be hidden, to a large degree, from other parts of the system, driving down the cost of making such changes.

There are many other things that can be encapsulated, including relationships, processes, varying behaviors, the number of steps in a process, the order of steps in a process, and so on. You can hide a concept behind an abstraction. You can hide the way you implement an algorithm behind a method signature. You can wrap foreign code in your own code using the Adapter Pattern or Facade Pattern. "Encapsulation is making something which is varying appear to the outside as if it is not varying," as Scott Bain said to me.

And there are many, many ways to encapsulate: you can hide an implementation behind a method call, hide an idea or ways of doing something behind an abstraction or interface...

Every design pattern cataloged by the Gang of Four in their book *Design Patterns: Elements of Reusable Object-Oriented Software [GHJV95]* encapsulates something different. Seeing patterns by what they encapsulate is a very powerful way of understanding and wielding patterns to solve problems.

Patterns say, "What you don't know can't hurt you."

That's not always true in life, where sometimes the things that hurt us the most are things we didn't know about, but in software that's *always* true. If you don't know about something you can't couple to it. Fewer dependencies make code easier to change.

Encapsulate by policy; reveal by need.

In other words, hide as much as you can and only reveal what is required to solve the problem. For example, start by making all of your data *private* and then later, if you find you need to expose more, create *getter/setter* methods to access the data that is *protected*, *package*, or *public*. It is generally much easier to expose something that is hidden than to try to hide something that's already exposed. Only expose what is *required by the problem you are solving* and hide everything else.

When encapsulation becomes a habit, you'll design from the *caller's perspective* and give each little bit of functionality its own method that can be called, making its parameters and what it returns explicit. This makes clear exactly what data it needs and what is expected to be returned. This not only limits system interactions to reduce side effects, it also clearly documents the code so you know exactly what is required and expected of each method.

Perhaps the most basic and fundamental form of encapsulation is hiding the implementation of a behavior behind a method's signature. This is echoed in the advice from *Design Patterns*: "Program to an 'interface,' not an 'implementation.'"

Only expose what is required by the problem and hide everything else. The process of creating great software is, in many ways, the process of encapsulating as much as possible. Anyone can fulfill a specification, but great programmers are also able to encapsulate their code for maximum flexibility.

Quality Code Is Assertive

Quality code is assertive—it manages its own responsibilities. Software entities should be assertive, as opposed to inquisitive. This is a code quality I don't see many people talking about, yet it's highly valuable in helping to determine where to put behavior and give objects the right responsibilities.

For example, should the code to control printing a document be part of the Document class or part of the Printer class? When I ask developers this question their immediate answer is usually to say the Printer class should have the code to control printing the document, but let's think about this for a moment. When we consider who knows about the document to be printed, it becomes clear that only the Document class knows about itself and therefore should be the one in control of printing itself. This doesn't mean that the Document class needs to know any details about the printer; it delegates the task of printing to the Printer class, but it is the Document class that's in charge.

I do a lot of training in California and developed a specific way of describing the quality of assertiveness to my students there. Many people in California are into self-improvement. Therapy is a thriving profession on the West Coast because people want to be self-responsible, self-reliant, and "masters of their own domain."

Think of making our objects assertive as "object therapy." Make objects self-reliant, self-responsible, and in charge of themselves. Don't let other objects do their work for them—unless there's good reason.

As a rule of thumb, an object should be in charge of managing its own state. In other words, if an object has a field or property then it should also have the behavior to manage that field or property. This doesn't mean that an object has to do all the work. In the case of the Document class example, it's not controlling the ink flow on the printer—that's the printer driver's responsibility. The Document class's responsibility is to convey the information about itself so the Printer class can exercise its responsibility to print the document.

This also keeps objects well defined and puts the behavior where it needs to be. When deciding what objects should contain a behavior, look for the object that has the state the behavior depends on. Sometimes a behavior depends on the state of more than one object to do a task, and in that case, if there are no other reasons compelling you one way or the other, pick the one it depends on the most.

Objects shouldn't be inquisitive; they should be *authoritative*—in charge of themselves.

Unassertive code is overly inquisitive; it has to constantly access the state of other objects to do its job. Because it's making a lot of calls to other objects, it's not as efficient as if it were just managing its own state. Overly inquisitive objects must call other objects to access their state in order for them to do their work, which breaks encapsulation and degrades performance. In his book *Refactoring: Improving the Design of Existing Code [FBBO99]*, Martin Fowler refers to this as "feature envy" or "inappropriate intimacy" to describe the code smells related to lack of assertiveness.

When code becomes inquisitive and unassertive, the rules for a process become spread out among multiple objects and split functionality ensues, where multiple objects must remain in sync in order to achieve the correct results. Behaviors end up in the wrong place—in objects that should not have those concerns, weakening the object's cohesion and coupling separate issues together.

This can sometimes happen when a design lacks classes that should be in the model but are forgotten or remain undiscovered. Since some behaviors are recognized as needed, they're put into existing classes rather than creating new classes where the behaviors really belong.

The quality of assertiveness shows us where to put behavior. If we have a method that heavily depends on data from another class, we may want to move that method to the other class.

Inquisitive smells can be subtle. Classes may have many collaborators, so it may be hard to find the right place to put a behavior without careful consideration.

Quality Code Is Nonredundant

Quality software should contain no redundancies—it should not repeat itself. Quality software should contain no redundancies—it should not repeat itself.

You see, redundancy in learning can be good. We learn by repetition. But redundancy in software always costs more to maintain and is therefore a burden.

I have to be careful here. I was teaching a software design class several years ago outside Dallas/Fort Worth, and I didn't know it but I had two senior NASA developers in the room. I said, "Redundancy is always bad." One of them stood up and said, "Wait a minute, redundancy saves lives!"

He was right but he was talking about a particular kind of redundancy—intentional redundancy. If you've ever worked on mission-critical applications, you know what I'm talking about.

I define a mission-critical application as one where if a bug gets into production someone could likely die. Under those circumstances you think about the software you build differently than if you were writing a social media app—at least if you have a conscience and you want to sleep at night. Development becomes about reliability at all costs. These two developers from NASA build mission-critical applications.

For example, there were five computers on the space shuttle, and for mission-critical computations they each did the computation separately and then voted on their answer. If they concurred, there was a high likelihood the computation was correct, but if there were discrepancies they may have needed to recompute.

Those NASA developers are right—having intentional redundancy for mission-critical applications can save lives. But what I'm talking about here is *unintentional* redundancy—and that's *always* a maintenance issue.

People use the acronym DRY (Don't Repeat Yourself) or phrases like "Once and only once," but finding redundancy isn't always so easy.

Most redundancy is obvious and easy to see in code. However, redundancy can also take subtle forms that make it not so easy to spot, which is why I prefer the term *redundancy* instead of the term used in Extreme Programming: *duplication*.

I may recognize that I'm introducing redundancy when I *inherit from the clipboard*—if I copy something to the clipboard, before I paste it, I could ask myself if I really need it in both places or if I could put it in its own place and call it from both places. If I want to call something in more than one place, I can surely name it so I can wrap it in a method and call it.

I would say that 95% of all redundancy is easy to recognize in code and once seen it is easy to get rid of. It's that last 5% that can be hard to find, but often it can be worth the extra effort. I'll hunt for it if I have the time because redundancy in code can hide the true nature of a problem, and without understanding a problem, it's difficult to find a concise solution that solves it. If I can rid my code of every bit of redundancy, I often discover patterns in the problem that I didn't see before. This can collapse complex code into a much simpler solution.

There are many forms of redundancy. I'm not just referring to redundant state or redundant behavior; many other things can be redundant—redundant relationships, redundant tests, redundant concepts, redundant construction, redundant processes where most of the steps are identical but some of the steps are different so you create two algorithms that must be maintained forevermore. There are patterns that can help with these issues.

For me, redundancy in code is trying to do the same thing in multiple places regardless of the way you do it. Nonidentical code can be redundant and identical code can be nonredundant. Redundancy is not necessarily a repetition of form. Redundancy is a repetition of *intent*.

Code Qualities Guide Us

Code qualities are little things that can make a big difference. An object should have well-defined characteristics, focused responsibilities, hidden implementation, be in charge of its state, and be defined only once.

These code qualities help guide developers in building better software:

- When code is *cohesive* it's easier to understand and find bugs in it because each entity is dealing with just one thing.

- When code is *loosely coupled* we find fewer side effects among entities and it's more straightforward to test, reuse, and extend.

- When code is well *encapsulated* it helps us manage complexity and keep the caller out of the implementation details of the callee—the object being called—so it's easier to change later.

- When code is *assertive* it shows us that often the best place to put behavior is with the data it depends on.

- When code is *nonredundant* it means we're dealing with bugs and changes only once and in one location.

Quality code is *Cohesive*, *Loosely coupled*, *Encapsulated*, *Assertive*, and *Nonredundant*, or CLEAN for short.

It's interesting to note that all the principles and good developer practices we discuss in this book can be inferred from these code qualities. Code quality is my yardstick for measuring what is good in software and everything we'll discuss supports good code quality.

Code that lacks these qualities is also difficult to test. If I have to write a lot of tests for a class, I know I have cohesion issues. If I have lots of unrelated dependencies, I know I have coupling issues. If my tests are implementation dependent, I know I have encapsulation issues. If the results of my test are in a different object than the one being tested, I probably have assertiveness issues. If I have to write the same test over and over, I know I have redundancy issues.

Testability then becomes the yardstick for measuring the quality of a design or implementation. In the old days when faced with two approaches that seemed equally valid, I used to have to take the time to code them up both ways to find which was the better one. Now I simply score them based on their code qualities, or based on how easy it is to test each one, and I usually find the better approach much more quickly.

CLEAN code qualities support each other. Since improving one will often improve the others, don't worry about all of them; just pick one or two that make the most sense to you and focus on those.

Kent Beck, in his easy-to-read and deceptively simple book *Test Driven Development: By Example [Bec02]*, says that if you just pay attention to consistently eliminating duplication in code, you'll end up with high-quality code, and he's right. But the same can be said for all the code qualities we've discussed. They're actually aspects of the same thing, facets of the same gem, so to speak: good code.

When one aspect is improved, the others tend to as well. When we improve one code quality and the others improve, it tells us we're on the right track to improving the overall quality of our code.

I like to focus on cohesion. For me, cohesion is easy to spot and fix, and focusing on it helps me name things for what they do, which makes my code easier to understand. I notice that when I make my code more cohesive, the other code qualities improve as well. You may prefer to focus on encapsulation or assertiveness.

Whatever qualities you focus on, if you improve one and you see the others improve, you know you're on the right track.

Increase Quality Today to Increase Velocity Tomorrow

I always tell teams the way to increase velocity tomorrow is to increase code quality today. Focusing on code quality keeps the software we write clear and easy to understand.

Our brains have been conditioned to understand information when it contains these qualities, so code that exhibits these qualities is easier to understand and work with. Quality software helps us extend our software without creating a mess and this allows our projects to scale.

Quality software is also much easier to debug. This helps us deliver faster and makes the code easier to maintain, reducing the total cost of ownership and paying for itself very quickly.

Ward Cunningham[3] coined the term *technical debt* to express what can happen when developers don't factor their learning back into their code as they're building it. Nothing slows development down and throws off estimates more than technical debt. What should take an hour can take a day or more and sometimes adding a feature can require a great deal of code to change. Improving code quality can bring down the cost of change and make estimation more predictable.

Sometimes developers have to go fast, and sometimes that means being sloppy. If you have to cut corners, you also want to clean up after yourself before you make too much of a mess. When you adopt practices that support quality, it won't take much more time to write code that is higher quality in the short term and it will save a lot of time in the long term. Sure, you have to type a few more curly brackets to encapsulate code in separate classes, but since when was typing the bottleneck in software development?

I have a friend who is a professional chef and responsible for putting out more than two hundred plates a night. He says, "I don't have time to make a mess," because he knows working fast is working clean. His workstation is always neat and tidy. His sleeves are clean and dry. The faster he works, the cleaner he works. And so should we.

You probably remember these code qualities from an old book or computer science course you took, terms like cohesion and coupling or encapsulation. I keep discovering that many of these ideas are at the foundation of the best software I've seen. The most successful organizations—the ones whose velocity was so great they could consistently respond to the business and provide the best software to their customers—all had a base of high-quality software to work from. They built a culture that focused on code quality and everything else flowed from there. I think this was one of their keys to success.

And once you know how to write CLEAN code, the best way to be sure you're writing high-quality, testable code is to write the test first, and that is the topic of our next chapter.

Let's Get Practical

Here are some ways to put these ideas into practice.

---

3. http://c2.com/cgi/wiki?WardExplainsDebtMetaphor

Seven Strategies for Increasing Code Quality

People define quality in software in many ways. Some define quality as software that does what the customer wants. Others define quality as software that runs fast. Still others define quality as software that's error-free. We all agree these are good things, but are they all effects of a single cause, and if so, how do we start to write quality code? Here are seven strategies for increasing code quality.

Get crisp on the definition of quality

> Quality in software is different than quality in tangible goods. Just as a baker can't mix random ingredients together, throw them in an oven, and expect to get a cake, understanding the "ingredients" that make up code quality is important. What characteristics should quality code have? Quality code should be clear, easy to understand, and easy to extend.

Share common quality practices

> In addition to sharing a common definition of "quality" to create quality software, we must share common practices. Leveraging Agile processes can help. For example, focusing on building features keeps development centered on giving each method a cohesive purpose.

Let go of perfectionism

> Voltaire said, "Don't let the perfect be the enemy of the good." Most of us know perfection is unobtainable in software and hold no illusions of achieving it. But when we're unclear as to how our code will be used, even great isn't good enough. Having clear acceptance criteria can help us build only what's needed so we can move on without gold-plating features.

Understand trade-offs

> Developing software is about making a series of the best trade-offs for a given situation. Understanding the implications of the trade-offs we make can help us make better decisions that address the needs of the current situation. We may have to pay a price in one area to gain benefit in another area, and knowing this can help us build a better product overall.

Hide "how" with "what"

> Encapsulate implementation details and present an interface that callers can use to ask for *what* they want without worrying about how they get it. This gives us the freedom to change implementation details later without breaking our callers.

Name things well

> The first and most important documentation of any program is the software itself. Name entities and behaviors for what they do, not how they do it. Keep names meaningful and metaphors consistent. This makes software easy to understand and work with. Avoid abbreviations and acronyms—instead spell it out in CamelCase. And don't worry that it's long—most IDEs have autocomplete, so after you type it in the first time you only have to type the first few letters and pick it from a list. Make names descriptive, active, stated in the positive, and reflective of how the system is changed as a result of being called.

Keep code testable

> Software that is not tested carries a great deal of risk, so testing is important. But beyond verifying that our code works, we want to ensure it's testable because testable code correlates to high-quality code.

Software quality is not something that just happens, nor can it be created with heavyweight processes like Six Sigma and Waterfall. Software quality comes from paying attention to the problems we're addressing and how to model them accurately. This helps us get rid of redundancy by centralizing decisions, keep methods and classes focused, and put behavior in the right place. The result is a codebase that is easier to maintain and extend.

Seven Strategies for Writing Maintainable Code

Maintainable code is code that is understandable and easy to work with. It's design is clear, entities are well named, and developers aren't scared to change it. Maintainable code doesn't happen by accident; it requires attention but it can make a big difference for those who have to work in the code. Here are seven strategies for writing maintainable code.

Adopt collective code ownership

> Collective code ownership means that any of the team members can work on any part of the code, even if they didn't write it. The team should adopt the same coding standards so no one can tell by reading the code who wrote it. This makes the coding style consistent and easier to work with. In addition to sharing a common coding format, the team should be working from the same domain model, and have common development practices and a shared vocabulary for describing designs.

Refactor enthusiastically

> Refactoring is a central part of writing code and happens throughout the development process. Developers should refactor code as they're writing

it and once a new behavior is working. Refactoring is not an excuse for writing messy code. Refactoring teaches us to build supportability into code so it's easier to work with later.

Pair constantly

Pair programming is the fastest way to propagate knowledge across a team. Pair with different people every day until you find the people you pair best with, but still pair with different team members occasionally in order to continue learning from each other. Some teams pair on all tasks, but you should at least pair when designing, coding, refactoring, debugging, and testing.

Do code reviews frequently

Code reviews are still valuable even when you pair program on everything because it gives others who you didn't pair with a chance to see your code and give feedback. Code reviews should focus on the reasoning behind decisions and discuss design options and trade-offs.

Study other developers' styles

Reading other people's code and learning how other developers write code is a great way to improve your skill level as a developer. Virtually every developer has his or her own style. Learning how other developers address issues can make you a much better developer yourself.

Study software development

Twenty years ago there were only a few good books on software development that were must-reads for developers. Today there are hundreds. Being a professional developer requires ongoing study. Doctors devote 8–10 hours per week reading up on their field. Developers should do the same.

Read code, write code, and practice coding

In Stephen King's book *On Writing,* he suggests that in order to be a great writer you should read a lot and write a lot. When Henny Youngman was asked how to get to Carnegie Hall he said "practice, practice, practice." The same is true in software development. Read other people's code, write code, and practice.

Clean code is easier to work with. Since on average code is read ten times more than it's written it usually makes sense to put effort into keeping it clean. As you make these practices into habits, you'll find it takes no effort at all but pays back dividends quickly by making code more maintainable.

Retrospective

Create CLEAN Code, or code that is *Cohesive, Loosely coupled, Encapsulated, Assertive*, and *Nonredundant*. CLEAN code is quality code.

In this chapter, we discovered...

- Cohesive code reduces side effects.

- Loosely coupled code is easier to test.

- Encapsulated code is easier to extend.

- Assertive code makes software more modular.

- Nonredundant code reduces maintenance issues.

If we define good code as code that's simple to understand and work with, we can identify specific code qualities that support this. While these code qualities may seem like small things, they add up, and paying attention to them can guide us to build more maintainable software.

CHAPTER 10

Practice 6: Write the Test First

Isn't TDD dead?

Some people are claiming that the practice we'll discuss next, test-driven development (TDD), is dead and gone. It was a nice idea, they say, but hasn't worked out in practice. They speak of "test-induced damage" caused by over-testing where people write too many tests or implementation-dependent tests that end up being a burden rather than an asset.

And they're right.

I've seen "test-induced damage" before—when developers don't know when to stop writing tests.

A key benefit of the tests software developers create by doing test-first development is they support us when we have to change existing code. But when developers write too many tests, or write implementation-dependent tests, those tests can become more difficult to change than the code itself, and rather than supporting changeability those tests become a liability, making code changes harder and more time-consuming.

I've been told by TDD practitioners to write tests *until bored.* They reason that at the point of boredom you probably don't need more tests. The problem with that approach is we all have different thresholds for boredom. "Until bored" doesn't really tell me how many tests to write.

Tests are specifications; they define behavior.

If you think of tests in this way it becomes clear how to write the proper number of tests for any behavior and how to implement those tests to create that behavior. Driving development with tests in this way not only gives you the right number and kind of tests to support safely working with the code later, it keeps implementation focused and makes it clear when you're done and ready to move on to your next task.

Just like any complex activity, there are only a few ways to do it right and millions of ways to get it wrong. Don't blame TDD as a practice if it wasn't correctly applied.

This particular way that I'm advocating for using TDD to drive development gives clear guidance on *how to use TDD correctly* and avoid the pitfalls of test-induced damage. Write just enough tests to specify the behaviors you're building and only write code to make a failing test pass.

The Things We Call Tests

There are several different things called "tests" in software development. Each is very different from the others and they are used for very different purposes. Before diving into TDD, let's look at a few of the different kinds of tests used in software development.

Acceptance Tests = Customer Tests

Customer tests, or *acceptance tests*, help clarify the behavior of stories and give developers a way of having real interaction with their Product Owner or customer representative. Developers can formalize that conversation by writing explicit tests they can run through an automation framework, or just do it informally by jotting down some different examples of a story on their story cards.

Acceptance tests help developers understand where the edge cases are—what the exceptions are to a particular scenario so they know how to handle these other paths of execution. By defining acceptance criteria, acceptance tests help answer the question: "How will I know when I'm done?"

This, by the way, is one of the most important questions any developer might need answered. You may not know exactly how the code you're writing is going to be used and in what situation, and therefore, we all have a tendency to overbuild it. With a limited amount of time, when you overbuild in one area it means you're underbuilding in another area. Knowing what constitutes "done" lets you move on when you need to and gives you that feeling of satisfaction and completion developers always crave but rarely experience. Instead developers tend to wonder, "Gee, did I cover this case? Did I make it robust enough?"

But when you have an acceptance test that turns green and you've hit that acceptance criteria, you can comfortably move on, knowing that if there's more of the feature to build you'll do it in the next iteration, when it's identified. There's so much ambiguity in software and in how it's built, which is hard to deal with for any human being but especially software developers, who like things to be binary: "Did I cover it or not?"

There are tools to automate acceptance tests. It can be as easy as writing English-like tests in a language called Gherkin (implemented in acceptance testing tools), which is based on three criteria—given, when, and then:

Given this setup *when* this trigger occurs *then* we should see this result.

Given is how you set up the test; it specifies the preconditions that must be true in order to run the test. *When* is the trigger, where you invoke the behavior you want to test. *Then* is where you compare the expected result with the real result, and that tells you whether or not the test passed.

Remember, we want to have that "binary" result—pass, fail—and we want that result to be automatic.

My two favorite books on acceptance test-driven development (ATDD) are Ken Pugh's *Lean-Agile Acceptance Test-Driven Development [Pug11]* and Gojko Adzic's *Specification by Example [Ad 11]*.

Unit Tests = Developer Tests

Unit tests are for testing smaller units than a whole story. Developers write unit tests to drive the development of code when doing TDD.

Unit tests also serve as internal documentation, which frees up a lot of time and provides a full suite of regression tests to catch mistakes made in any future changes. Those tests are automated now, and when you run your test suite all the tests you wrote are executed.

We'll focus primarily on unit tests in this chapter, but I want you to know about some of the other tests we use in software development.

Other Tests = Quality Assurance Tests

There are several kinds of "tests" used in software development in addition to acceptance tests and unit tests. Many of these tests are part of the quality assurance process, like *integration tests*, which test the interaction between components during a workflow. Unlike unit tests, which mock out all dependencies, integration tests use the real dependencies to test the interaction of components, making the test more brittle and slower. Complex workflows may require many integration tests, which can significantly slow the build.

I'd prefer to test as much as I can at the unit level, in isolation from its dependencies. This speeds up and simplifies testing.

I know teams that use tools that simulate user input in order to test their features. These tools certainly have their place in the world of testing and are valuable in some situations, but if this is the only way you can test the functionality of your system, you may have some design constraints you might want to rethink. Sometimes you're stuck with an existing system that forces you to make trade-offs, but whenever you can you should strive to write code that is unit testable so it can be easily verified.

There are many other tools and approaches for testing software to assure quality. For our purposes here, we'll classify tests in two categories:

- those that are needed to validate a release candidate
- and everything else.

It's important to automate as much of testing as possible, but it's especially important to automate all testing involved in validating a release candidate. Just as good code has as few dependencies as possible to minimize the things that could go wrong, so too should our software development *process* have as few dependencies as possible. Having a dependence on human intervention to make the build succeed introduces a dependency: something that can go wrong.

Usually, many manual steps are involved in validating a release candidate in a traditional quality assurance process. This raises the cost of a release candidate and forces us to build in bigger batches.

However, with automated tests you can usually remove all human intervention from the build so you're constantly adding to a system that is releasable at any time. Some software requires human intervention. You can't fully test GPS software without taking it out in the field. But you can isolate and simulate components so being out in the field doesn't remain in your critical path for release.

Quality Assurance

The quality assurance (QA) kind of testing can take many forms.

- *Components tests* look at how units work together.
- *Functional tests* take those units and put them together to make a full end-to-end behavior.
- *Scenario tests* are more the way a user would interact with the system.

- *Performance tests* ask, "Can this system handle a very large load? We tested it in isolation but what happens when a million users hit it simultaneously?"

- *Security tests* look for vulnerabilities in the code.

And so on.

The kind of QA testing needed for a project varies by the amount of risk involved. Testing a pacemaker requires a very different approach than testing a social media app.

Quality Engineering (QE) has become a specialized role. Companies like Microsoft, Amazon, and Google are realizing that they need to focus on quality as a form of engineering, so they've removed a lot of people who were just manually running scripts and replaced them with developers who can automate those tests—and it's working.

This is in alignment with everything else we've said about getting to the point where we can take a story from start to finish as quickly as possible because "finish" has to include automated tests to verify that it really works, and do all that as quickly as possible.

TDD Doesn't Replace QA

The software development industry is saying it's okay to have tests for our code, but they're still mostly practicing test-after, which ends up being considerably more work.

Having whole teams seated just to do test-after or QA is like sending auditors in *after* the savings and loan scandal, or opening the black box *after* a plane crash. I see why people do that, at least in an effort to gather data that might prevent a later crash, or to assign responsibility, but the auditor can't return everyone's life savings, and the investigation can't bring crash victims back to life.

Postponing QA to the end of a development cycle just before a release can only give you bad news. Once you find a bug, it's too late, and as time elapses between a bug being written and that bug being found and fixed, the cost grows exponentially.

It helps QA to have automated regression tests from doing test-first development, but you may have to go back later and add more tests to cover additional test cases.

When you start to see test-first development as a way of *specifying* behaviors rather than *verifying* behaviors, you can get a lot clearer on what tests you need. Doing TDD in this way gives you a lean, mean test base to support you in safely cleaning up code, but it doesn't take the place of a QA effort.

Unit Tests Can't Do Everything

There are things that are appropriate for unit testing, and there are things you can't do at the unit level but that you really want to see, like *end-to-end tests*, which tell you whether an application is functioning as desired from start to finish.

Most systems still incorporate some code that was built without using TDD, and as such can be difficult to test: code that interacts with the user interface, code that interacts with the database, code that's multithreaded, or a lot more advanced code.

Still, I have not seen features that are inherently untestable as long as you're willing to change the design.

But sometimes you can't change your design, like if you're interfacing with code that's already written or you're using an existing package that requires doing things a certain way. If you have control over the environment, very often with the change in architecture you can make code that's hard to test much easier to test. When you do that, you also see that it's more affordable, more maintainable, more extendable—all those good things.

However, unit tests are a great start and as we'll see, when we do test-first development—where we write the test before we write the code to make the test passes—developers gain a great deal more than just a suite of automated unit tests; it helps build out a system where a flexible design can emerge.

Write Good Tests

Most developers I've met assume they know what a good test is and how to write one, but in my experience few developers really understand how to write good unit tests. As with most things, these are skills that have to be learned.

Many managers—and developers—have strange notions about what TDD really is. Much of that confusion stems from how they talk about TDD. There are many different ways of doing test-driven development and I'm a proponent of *test-first development*, where developers write a test for a small bit of functionality and then make the test pass by implementing that small bit of functionality. It's the ping-ponging back and forth between taking the perspective of your test (outside-in) and taking the perspective of your code (inside-out) that gives us the feedback we need to make steady progress.

I know people who write all their tests up front and then implement code to make them pass. I don't really see that as TDD. There is some benefit to doing that, but it's not as big a benefit as gaining the frequent feedback that doing test-first development provides.

In what I call "test after development" you write the code and then write the test. There's definite benefit to doing that: you get a suite of automated regression tests that can be run any time a change is made to the system to verify the rest of the system is still working as it's supposed to. But writing those tests after you write the code often reveals that the code you wrote is hard to test and requires significant cleaning up to make testable, which can become a major project. Better to write testable code in the first place, and the simplest way to write testable code is to write it test-first.

One of the other significant benefits of writing a test first is that you're only going to write code covered by tests and so will always have 100% test coverage. There's not a line of code that's not intrinsically about making a failing test pass, so you'll always have all the code you write covered by tests when doing test-first development the way I recommend doing it.

Writing code to make a failing test pass assures that you're building testable code since it's very hard to write code to fulfill a test that's untestable. One of the biggest challenges we have as developers is that we tend to write code that's not inherently testable. Then, when we go to try to test it later, we find ourselves having to redesign and rewrite a lot of stuff. Doing test-first development prevents developers from getting into that situation.

It's Not a Test

When I write a unit test before I write the code necessary to make the test pass, what is it I'm testing? There's nothing there yet, so what I'm writing clearly can't be a test because I'm testing nothing.

So what is it if it's not a test? Think of it more as a *hypothesis*.

When I write the test first, what I'm doing is *hypothesizing* that I understand the requirements. I'm hypothesizing how to invoke a service and what I expect back. I'm hypothesizing my criteria for completion.

Once I write the code that makes the test pass, it becomes a real test because now it's exercising some behavior; there's something for the test to verify. And it continues to provide value throughout the life of the software, validating that nothing has changed that could affect it and verifying that the code still works as expected.

So therefore, this thing we call "tests" actually plays a dual role. On one hand it's a hypothesis—or a specification for behavior—and on the other hand, it's a regression test that's put in place and is always there, serving us by verifying that the code works as expected.

In a way, tests are *sensors*, like the check engine light in your car. They will always be there, ready to tell you if something's gone wrong and if some new line of code has been added that moves it from green to red.

Units of Behavior

TDD has a major effect on how we think about solving problems, but TDD can be done wrong. It's easy to understand how anyone, even very experienced software developers, can get confused when so many of our terms are misleading. When we talk about "unit tests," many developers assume that a "unit" is a piece of code.

But it's not.

A test is not a test when it's written, and a unit is not a unit of code either. When I say "unit" in "unit test" it does not refer to entities like methods, classes, modules, functions, and so on, like many developers assume.

A unit is a *unit of behavior*—an independent, verifiable behavior. It must create an *observable difference* in the system and not be tightly coupled to other behaviors in the system.

Understanding this properly is critical.

The term "unit" was adopted to put forward the notion that a behavior is independent from the rest of the units of behavior in the system. This doesn't mean that every class should have a test class or every method should have a test method. It means that *every observable behavior* should have a test associated with it.

Code should always produce observable behavior.

Then when it comes time to clean up the design, new tests typically don't have to be added as long as the behavior isn't changing. Even if you do have to add more classes or methods, because the behavior is the same, the test shouldn't break. There should be no need for new tests.

This may sound simple, but it's the most common thing developers tend to get lost on when starting to adopt test-driven development. I've heard developers worry that every time they create a new class or method they write a new test and their code gets bigger and bigger, more tests are added, and it soon becomes unscalable.

But that's not how it works.

What a "unit" represents is a *behavior*, and if the *behavior* doesn't change, then the *tests* don't need to change either.

The purpose of writing the test first is to help build out functionality effectively and to support you so you can *easily* clean up your code later, if needed. You don't want your tests to create a burden when you clean up your code. That defeats much of the value of having an automated suite of regression tests in the first place. Always write the minimum number of tests to specify behavior.

TDD Gives Rapid Feedback

The cheapest way to develop software is to prevent bugs from happening in the first place, but the second cheapest way is to find them *immediately* so they're fixed by the same person or team that wrote them rather than fixed later by a different team entirely, as the ship date looms ever closer.

Russian physiologist and father of the behaviorist school of psychology Ivan Pavlov showed that for a stimulus-response transaction to take hold in the psyche, the response must immediately follow the stimulus. "If you hit this bar we'll feed you *eventually*" doesn't work for dogs, and—comparing *myself* to a dog—the same is true for software developers.

If I make a mistake and am told about it three months later, it's not going to click and I'm likely to make the same mistake again in the future. By then I'm deep into another project, and would have to stop that work in order to be brought back up to speed and shown a bug I couldn't possibly remember writing.

And that's why things haven't changed, because developers don't have that rapid stimulus/response. Test-driven development will provide that.

TDD Supports Refactoring

Refactoring has been practiced to some degree since the dawn of computing, but it was really Martin Fowler who turned refactoring into a software development discipline when he published *Refactoring: Improving the Design of Existing Code [FBBO99]*, in which he defines refactoring as "the process of changing a software system in such a way that it does not alter the external behavior of the code yet improves its internal structure." This is a book every developer should read and understand as it also contains a wealth of information on good programming practices.

Refactoring code gives developers another chance to make their software easier to work with. Sometimes when developers are deep into implementing a feature, they tend to be a bit sloppy with their naming. Sometimes developers don't really know what something should be named while they're in the middle of implementing a behavior. For these reasons it may become necessary to go back and review code later, looking for opportunities to improve names and make the code more maintainable.

In Agile software development, where you don't get all the requirements up front and figure things out as you allow your designs to emerge, it's easy to make a few wrong turns now and again. It's still far more efficient to build software iteratively than to try to figure it all out up front. When you do take a wrong turn that limits your ability to extend a design in a certain way that may now be needed, you can refactor your code to accommodate the change without degrading the existing design.

But refactoring can also be dangerous because most code is so intertwined that changing one part can cause bugs to emerge in other areas.

Code that's supported with tests is safer to refactor. That's because if you make a mistake, it'll likely cause one of your tests to fail, so you'll know about it immediately and can fix it right away.

Write Testable Code

I taught a TDD class for a very large client—one of the largest Internet properties in the world—and right before the class started, Monday morning at about 8:45, one of the senior managers came in and said, "I'm told you're teaching a TDD class here."

I said yes, and he replied, "We don't do TDD here. We don't want to do TDD here. Why are you teaching our people TDD? That's wrong."

I told myself, *Okay, calm down. Take a breath.* Then I said, "Honestly, I don't care whether your developers do test-first development or not. What I care about is that they write *testable code* and TDD is the fastest way to show them how to get there." And he was pleased with that answer. That made sense to him.

There's a strong correlation between testability and code quality. TDD does not design for you, but it gives you a framework to draw from and it supports the way we naturally think when we're successfully designing. Separating out different ways of thinking into the various stages of the development cycle of TDD makes problems a lot easier to deal with.

I'm an old guy. I've been a software developer for over thirty years. I can tell you that when I was younger I had a phenomenal memory. I could remember details—unbelievable details—all the time. I could write code out of my head. I could hold that thousand-line procedure in my head and just code it up.

But as I get older, those facilities are fading. The good news is, wisdom replaces focus, attention, retention, and concentration. TDD is a way of helping support us in the way we naturally think, helping us concentrate and produce a better result. It simplifies the process and makes it easier to work through tougher problems.

Even though there's a lot of technique involved to make it happen, you'll find yourself faced with one of two situations:

"Oh, I can write tests for that—I understand that."

Or: "This is impossible—I can't do that."

How come?

When I get to that situation, where it doesn't work, it's telling me I've got some design issues and it's time to rethink.

So suddenly then these antipatterns—these bad things that have come up as a result—are not really bad things. They're clues to give me ideas on how to get back on track.

I've done some video editing, and found that when I have a bad cut I don't see it until about five seconds later, and I'm already into a completely different scene and now I have to rewind to get back to that bad cut. But I don't just move on and hope it'll all work out in the end. I listen to that voice.

And in TDD there's always something I can do to stay productive. I can clean up code or write another test for new behavior; I can break down a complex problem into lots of smaller problems. Doing TDD is like having a difficulty dial, and when I get stuck I can always dial it down to "pathetically simple" and stay there a little while until I build up confidence and feel ready to turn the dial up to raise the difficulty. But all the while *I'm* in control.

In order for me to write a blog post or teach a class I have to be well rested and heavily caffeinated. But I can write code test-first half asleep on a transcontinental flight. I can write code test-first in bed at night half watching a movie with my wife. That's how powerful the process is, and for those of us who have relied on our brain power to help us build complex code, it's a welcome relief. But it doesn't just appeal to my sense of laziness; I actually produce a better result and that's why I advocate it.

TDD Can Fail

As valuable as TDD is, I've also seen it utterly fail in some organizations. A client once told me, in no uncertain terms, that TDD doesn't work. He said they'd had to abandon it. When I asked him why, he said it would take a day to clean up their code and a week to clean up their tests.

They were under crunch time, so they had the choice to either continue with TDD and cause the project to fail—and watch the whole company then go out of business—or stop doing TDD. If anyone is faced with that choice, abandoning TDD is most certainly the right thing to do.

Don't try to implement TDD when you're ready to release. Don't put the burden of a new learning curve on your developers when they can't handle it.

But this client was doing something wrong. They'd bought into code quality, they'd bought into CLEAN code, they'd bought into good development principles, and so on, but they failed to see tests as code, so they had enormous redundancy in their tests. They were seeing tests as things tacked on rather than things that are integral to the whole.

They put their QA hat on and said, "More tests are better tests," and therefore they wound up writing too many tests and their tests were testing against an implementation—the way they do things—instead of testing against an interface—what they want done. As a result, it made it hard to clean up their tests when the time came to clean up their code. Remember, unit tests are about supporting you in cleaning up code, so we have to write tests with supportability in mind.

The same client said to me, "It takes hours to run our tests so we don't run them very often. Why are they so slow?"

Then he added, "Well, we have to get a connection to the database, and then we have to use the database to do some stuff..."

And I said, "You're not Oracle. You're using the Oracle database, but you're not Oracle. They're down the street. Why are you testing Oracle's code?"

"Our code interacts with the database so we need to open the database so we can interact with it."

That's not how we write unit tests.

Unit tests are only meant to test *your* unit of behavior.

If you interface with the rest of the world, you need to mock out the rest of the world so that you're only testing *your* code. I showed that client a whole variety of techniques on how to make untestable code testable using mocking, shunting, dependency injection, and endo-testing, among other techniques.

All these techniques can help you only test the unit of code you want to test. When you only test the code you need to test, you wind up with tests that run really fast.

Introduce TDD to a Team

I've been asked if TDD is something that individual software developers—or really *teams* of developers—can introduce into companies essentially on their own, without making some kind of formal switch-over or involving management in what is ultimately a technical paradigm shift.

As it turns out, that's how TDD has been taking root in at least some of the companies that practice it. In some cases management says, "Look guys, do whatever you feel is going to help you build quality software and make your deadlines." Other organizations say, "What? You want to take twice as much time—write twice as much code now? You're crazy!"

So it very much depends on management's preconceptions of what TDD is and isn't. And we're dealing with developers' preconceptions, too. Those are very different preconceptions. Both groups may have different reasons for *not* wanting to do TDD, but when everyone sees the benefits of doing TDD for themselves they start getting excited.

There really isn't one single way to learn how to do TDD correctly. It's not a matter of copy and paste. It starts with good common sense—just a few key rules you must follow to get benefit from the practice.

Become Test Infected

Some developers have told me they feel uncomfortable having to write the test first. This is the biggest challenge for many developers when getting started with TDD because we're trained to focus on going straight to writing the implementation. As soon as you put a keyboard in most developers' hands, they start writing production code. It took me a long time to break that habit and write the test first. But the developer is the one who straddles the world of the *what* and the *how*.

Developers should start with the *what* because that's what the interface is. That's what the test is. The test is all about the *what*. Starting with the *what* is always a good idea because it helps to keep knowledge about implementation from leaking out into the rest of the system and it helps keep code more focused and encapsulated.

First, specify the *what*—what the method you're calling is going to look like: its name, input parameters, and return value. Then you can focus on the how: how it will perform its work. So it's really just stepping back and thinking, *Before I actually start coding, what do I want to create?* and then having a context for that. This is the natural way we should all be approaching problem solving most of the time, from the outside in, and not from the inside—the implementation—out.

When you break the habit of going straight to writing production code—and it's just a habit—you'll naturally think *test-first*. There's a term for this, coined by Erich Gamma,[1] one of the early proponents of test-driven development. He calls it being *test infected*.

You're "test infected" when you find so much value in doing TDD that it's all you want to do. I'm test infected. You couldn't pay me enough money to write code that isn't developed test-first.

Let's Get Practical

Here are some ways to put these ideas into practice.

Seven Strategies for Great Acceptance Tests

Acceptance tests can be applied at any level, from story to task. They can be formalized with a testing framework like Cucumber or SpecFlow, or they can be informally jotted down on the other side of a story card. Acceptance tests tell the team when they're done building a feature, and they help everyone to share a common understanding for what's to be built. Here are seven strategies for great acceptance tests.

Get clear on the benefits of what you're building
> Writing acceptance tests forces you to get clear on exactly what you're building and how it will manifest in the system. Just having this conversation between the Product Owner and the developers is valuable and gets people thinking about how to improve what they're building.

---

1. Gamma, Erich. "Test Infected." http://junit.sourceforge.net/doc/testinfected/testing.htm

Know who it's for and why they want it

In addition to knowing *what* the user wants, developers want to know *who* it's for and *why* they want it. This can help developers find better ways of accomplishing a task so that it's also more maintainable. Personify the user and give him a backstory. Getting clear on who the feature is for and what its purpose is can help developers make that feature more valuable.

Automate acceptance criteria

Defining automated acceptance tests can be a valuable experience for both customers and developers. The conversations that come from working through examples and defining acceptance criteria are helpful for getting everyone on the same page with a shared understanding of what is to be built.

Specify edge cases, exceptions, and alternate paths

Acceptance tests can also specify alternate paths through code. Defining these edge cases up front can help developers address the most important issues first. It also helps developers focus on what could go wrong and build robust ways of handling those problems.

Use examples to flesh out details and flush out inconsistencies

Working through an example of using a feature is a great way to start to understand the implementation issues around that feature. Examples let you think about and discuss something concretely. Start with concrete examples. Once you've worked through a few, you can start to generalize and abstract the code to handle it.

Split behaviors on acceptance criteria

Every acceptance test should have a single acceptance criterion that will either pass or fail. Different behaviors should have different acceptance criteria. This helps drive the creation of features so they're both independent of other features and focused on a single criterion for acceptance.

Make each test unique

Every acceptance test should be unique and independent of all other acceptance tests in the system. Unique acceptance tests help assure that code is nonredundant and focused around a singular acceptance criterion.

Acceptance tests tell developers what needs to be built, and most importantly, when they'll be done. Knowing when a feature is done stops developers from overbuilding and gives them the confidence to move on to the next task without having to second-guess themselves.

Seven Strategies for Great Unit Tests

Unit tests can be either an asset or a liability depending on how valuable those unit tests are when you're refactoring. If your tests depend on implementation, they'll need to be refactored when your code is refactored. That will cost time instead of save time. Here are seven strategies for great unit tests that support refactoring.

Take the caller's perspective

Always start the design of a service from the caller's perspective. Think in terms of what the caller needs and what it has to pass in. Forge method signatures and be willing to refactor them as your design emerges.

Use tests to specify behavior

Writing tests to efficiently drive the development of features helps your designs emerge and leaves you with a good suite of regression tests. Those tests then become *living documentation* for the system. With the click of a button they can be verified as still being up-to-date.

Only write tests that create new distinctions

Make tests *unique*. Every unit test should drive development forward and create some new observable behavior on the system. If you take this approach, all your tests will be unique.

Only write production code to make a failing test pass

If you want to write some code, first write a test that fails. Then write the production code that will make the test pass. This discipline assures all code written is covered by tests.

Build out behaviors with tests

There are several approaches to building out behaviors with tests. You can start with the *happy path* and then peel off exceptions, or you can start with error cases and drive to the happy path. The approach you take depends on the situation at hand.

Refactor code

As requirements unfold and understanding deepens, it's important to refactor code and keep it maintainable. Keeping code clean and supportable is an important key to iterative development.

Refactor tests

If you test behaviors and not implementations, when you refactor code you won't have to add or change any tests. Your tests will support you when you refactor your code. But tests are code too and can end up suffering from poor code qualities unless you take the time to improve the code to make it supportable and easier to work with.

A good set of unit tests provides regression and supports developers in safely refactoring code. Using tests to specify behavior clearly shows how code is to be used so it becomes the definitive form of *internal* documentation. When software is built test-first in this way, it supports the creation of higher-quality software that costs less to maintain.

Retrospective

Write the Test First, and then write only the code needed to make the test pass. This keeps the software you build focused and testable. Tests should support you in refactoring safely and test code should be kept as CLEAN as production code.

In this chapter, we discovered...

- The *why* behind test-first development, not just the how.

- Test-first development can easily be done wrong if you write too many tests or write implementation-dependent tests that can impede refactoring code.

- Our tests should support refactoring code, and to do this write only the tests needed to specify the behavior you're creating.

- Doing test-first development helps quality assurance, but it doesn't replace QA.

- Test-first development involves building features by writing a failing test, then writing just enough code to make that failing test pass. Then refactor as needed and repeat by writing another failing test.

When done correctly, test-first development helps developers create testable code that's more maintainable, but TDD can become more of a burden than an asset when done poorly.

CHAPTER 11

Practice 7: Specify Behaviors with Tests

Tests provide immediate feedback so you can see if anything you do adversely affects any other part of the system, and if it does you can automatically roll back those changes and let life move merrily along. Having independent verification of code through unit tests immediately flushes out any logic errors. A whole class of elusive bugs that kept many of us up late at night, bleary eyed, staring at our debuggers, are caught by our unit tests and aren't introduced into code so they don't have to be found later and removed.

Developers get instant feedback about what works and what doesn't, and this changes the whole dynamic of software development. With instant feedback, you can figure things out really quickly and experiment aggressively, knowing your tests will help catch mistakes. Once you establish the simple infrastructure for instant feedback, all the developers on your team can leverage that and use it as a learning tool for building better systems. Of course, learning about good coding practices can save a lot of time, but I feel confident that a lot of developers will discover many good coding practices on their own with the feedback from their tests.

I once got a great deal on a used car but it had a subtle electrical problem. I took it to three different mechanics and they couldn't find the source of the problem. The headlights kept going out and the blinkers didn't work either. When they replaced the headlights, the blinkers started to work but only for a short time. Finally, the fourth mechanic discovered the problem—actually it wasn't *a* problem; it was *two* problems.

The circuit for the blinker was shorted in two places, and that's why the previous three mechanics failed to discover the true source of the problem. Compound problems like this, which are caused by multiple issues interacting, can be nearly impossible to find in software. When they happen—and they do happen—it can take hours or even days to track down and resolve.

More than half a developer's time is spent reworking decisions that were previously made, according to Capers Jones in his book *Patterns of Software System Failure and Success [Jon95]*. All of these things eat up valuable time and resources, and these are the issues that test-driven development directly addresses.

So when managers or developers say to me that they don't have time to write their tests before writing implementation, I'm not surprised. They don't have time to do test-driven development because they're not doing test-driven development. But we all—developers and managers alike—have to get off the treadmill at some point. Our industry doesn't have all the answers, and TDD doesn't solve all software problems, but it is a step in the right direction.

TDD also helps us all better understand the code we write because it frames building code in the context of a concrete example, which is how we best understand things. Humans think and visualize in the concrete, yet very often language describes things in the abstract. We have to make that translation.

Tests are concrete requirements because they exercise the code with specific parameters. Concretizing requirements is incredibly valuable for helping to discover good implementations. When you build software in this way, it helps eliminate a whole other source of potential bugs.

Red Bar/Green Bar/Refactor

There are three distinct phases to test-first development. We call them *red bar*, *green bar*, and *refactor*, because those are the visual cues you get from your unit testing framework. When all your tests pass, you get the green bar. When you have a test that's failing, you get the red bar.

When you first write the test there's no code to test yet. It can't fail yet—it can't even compile. If you're using a modern integrated development environment (IDE), you'll see feedback that says, "I don't know what you're referring to with this production code. You want to add one and one. I've never heard of a method called add(). What is that?"

The next thing you do is you "stub out" the production code so that you can compile the test. So you write the method called add() but you stub it out. You've taken two numbers as input parameters but you just returned zero because you're not worried about the implementation yet.

This is a very simple example, and you don't need to figure out a lot to add two numbers. But imagine it was a double-declining amortization algorithm or something else very complex. First, you want to decide how you're going to call it. What does it need? What do you expect to get back? But for now you're just going to return a dummy value. That's called "stubbing out a method."

Once you stub out that method, you can compile and run the test. Of course it fails, and it tells you it's failing by displaying the red bar. Observing the red bar at this point is a test of the test. It tells you the test *can* fail, and that's important to prove because a test that can't fail is worse than no test at all.

Move on to implementing your code by writing the simplest code needed to make the test pass. Once you do that, you should see the green bar—your test passes. The next step is to clean up the code for quality, if necessary, so the code is easier to read and work with in the future. Also clean up your test. Then go back to step one and create something else—another little bit of intention or behavior.

What you're saying when you write tests is, "Hey code, can you do this?" And of course the code can't do it, so it fails. It says no and you reply, "Okay, let me show you how." Then you implement it and say, "Hey code, can you do this now?" And you go back and forth like that.

It's sort of a dialogue with your code, which is very nice. Do this in the small, over and over, this cycle of red bar/green bar/refactor, red bar/green bar/refactor, over and over and over. Build a whole system that way.

From the outside this may appear a bit tedious, but it's not. Not at all. It's a rhythm, like the drumbeat in a song.

An Example of Specifying Behaviors Test-First

Let's walk through an example in detail. This example illustrates how to create the right kind and number of tests for a specific behavior to drive the development of that behavior.

If you're not a programmer and you don't read source code, don't worry. You should be able to understand the gist of what the code is doing if I've named things well. Even if you don't understand exactly how this code works, you'll certainly get a sense of many things developers must consider when building software.

Let's say I want to create a Person class that has a name and an age. I am programming in *Java* using the *Eclipse*[1] development environment.

---

1. Eclipse IDE for Java Developers, Version 4.2 (Juno) and JUnit 4.

Write the Test

I start by writing a test for the *happy path*:

```
1  package person;
2
3  import static org.junit.Assert.*;
4  import org.junit.Test;
5
6  public class PersonTest {
7      String personName = "Bob";
8      int personAge = 21;
9
10     @Test
11     public void testCreatePersonWithNameAndAge() {
12         Person p = new Person(personName, personAge);
13         assertEquals(personName, p.getName());
14         assertEquals(personAge, p.getAge());
15     }
16 }
```

After the first line declares the name of the test's package, the next two lines import the packages that define the unit testing framework, junit. The sixth line declares the class, PersonTest, which will contain our test.

The next two statements on lines 7 and 8 define *variables* to hold the name Bob and the age 21 that will be used in the test. Rather than typing "Bob" in several places in the test (which I could accidentally misspell) or using the number 21 (which may not be clear in context that it represents someone's age), I define variables to hold these values and give them meaningful names. Now, if I misspell personName, the compiler will tell me, and when I reference personAge it's clear that variable holds a person's age. This technique of using variables with intention-revealing names instead of hardcoded values in my tests is called *instrumentation*, and it's one of the most valuable techniques for making tests serve as specifications.

Line 10 uses the @Test annotation to indicate that the method declaration on the next line is a test method. I've given the test a verbose name to make clear what this method tests. Line 12 is the setup for this test, where it creates a new Person class. Notice the red circle with an X inside to the left of the line number and that the word Person has a red squiggly underline, indicating the compiler doesn't recognize what a Person class is because it hasn't yet been defined.

The last two lines assert that once I create the Person his name field is set to the value of personName ("Bob") and his age is set to the value of personAge (21). This is done with two versions of the test method assertEquals(). The first takes two strings or sequences of characters. The first string contains the expected result, "Bob," and the second string will come from the name field in Person.

assertEquals() will compare the two strings and verify the sequence of characters are the same in both. If the strings don't contain the same sequence of characters, the unit testing framework puts up the red bar.

The second assertEquals() compares numbers. The first parameter contains our expected result, 21. The second parameter will come from the age field of Person and if it matches our expected result, 21, the test passes. If age doesn't match the expected result, the unit testing framework puts up the red bar.

Stub Out the Code

I can't compile this code yet because the test references symbols that don't exist, the Person class and the methods getName() and getAge(), so I'll let Eclipse "stub them out" for me.

In Eclipse, if I move my mouse over the first instance of the word Person on line 12, a little window will pop up with an error that says "Person cannot be resolved to a type." This means that I want the system to instantiate a Person but the system doesn't know what a Person is because it hasn't been defined yet. The pop-up also contains a list of Quick Fixes, the first one being "Create class 'Person'." If I select that option, Eclipse will create a stubbed Person class for me that looks like this:

```
public class Person {
}
```

The Person class is empty; it doesn't do anything yet, but it now exists and the error in my test on the first occurrence of Person is gone. But there's another error on the same line after the equals sign that says: "The constructor Person(String, int) is undefined." This means that I'm trying to create a Person with a name and age but the Person class doesn't have the ability to receive these fields because it doesn't have a special matching method called a *constructor*. Again, I'll let Eclipse stub this out for me by selecting from the pop-up "Create constructor 'Person(string, int)'." This adds the following constructor to the Person class:

```
public Person(String string, int i) {
        // TODO Auto-generated constructor stub
}
```

I'll replace string with name and i with age so the meaning of these fields is clear, and I'll delete the TODO comment so the Person class now reads

```
public class Person {
        public Person(String name, int age) {
        }
}
```

This fixes that error, but it also reveals two more errors in the test: getName() and getAge() do not yet exist so I'll have to stub them out as well.

Notice that even though I just want to test that I can create a valid Person instance, I also have to define *getters*—code that "gets" and returns information from fields—for name and age because that's what the test will use to retrieve the information from Person so it can be verified. So I'll autogenerate a stub for getName() that looks like this:

```
public Object getName() {
        // TODO Auto-generated method stub
        return null;
```

Then I'll autogenerate a stub for getAge() that looks like this:

```
public double getAge() {
        // TODO Auto-generated method stub
        return 0;
}
```

I'll clean up the stubs so getName() returns String instead of Object and getAge() returns int instead of double. Now there are no errors in my test and my stubbed Person class looks like this:

```
public class Person {
        public Person(String name, int age) {
        }

        public String getName() {
                return null;
        }

        public int getAge() {
                return 0;
        }
}
```

I'm ready to compile. All the references in the test can be resolved so I'll run my test and when I do I get...the red bar! My test fails because I'm not yet keeping track of the name and age field so what is returned doesn't match what the test expects.

But remember, in TDD our initial goal is to get to the red bar and *prove our test can fail*. I've proven that but I've also done a lot more—I've defined a class for Person that will have a name and age. I just haven't implemented it yet.

Implement the Behavior

I'll define fields for name and age, set those values in the constructor, and return them in the getters. This is what the finished code looks like:

```java
public class Person {
        private String name;
        private int age;

        public Person(String name, int age) {
                this.name = name;
                this.age = age;
        }

        public String getName() {
                return name;
        }

        public int getAge() {
                return age;
        }
}
```

Now when I run the test, I get the green bar telling me the Person class now works as expected. At this point, I can create a person object instance with a name and an age.

Introducing Constraints

But what happens if I try to set age to a negative number or a very large number? Maybe I should introduce some constraints on age.

I'll start by defining some constants for Person, test-first of course.

```java
17    @Test
18    public void testConstants() {
19        assertEquals(Person.MINIMUM_AGE, 1);
20        assertEquals(Person.MAXIMUM_AGE, 200);
21    }
22 }
```

I get the red squiggly line under MINIMUM_AGE and MAXIMUM_AGE because they haven't been defined yet. I'll let Eclipse autogenerate them in the Person class and then I'll clean them up so they read

```java
public static final int MINIMUM_AGE = 1;
public static final int MAXIMUM_AGE = 200;
```

This defines the symbols I'll use to set the lowest and highest ages I'll accept to 1 and 200. I've never heard of anyone living to 200, and by the time somebody does I'll be long gone so I won't need to update the program.

And what I just did right there is to create what might actually become an example of legacy code. It's like writing banking software (or any software) that assumes the first two digits of every year will be 19. What I'm depending on here is that, when we do get to a point where people are routinely living past the age of 200, anyone who might need to revise my code accordingly will easily find the constant marked MAXIMUM_AGE, and be able to change that to equal 300 or 500 or 5,000, because I have used simple language and *intention-revealing names*—which we'll cover in more detail in the next chapter.

Write the Test and Stub Out the Code

Next, I'll write a test to verify that the age passed in is not too small. Since the data type I'm using to hold the age is an int, which in Java is 32 bits, it can hold numbers from -2,147,483,648 to 2,147,483,647, so I have to guard against negative numbers. I'll write a test to verify that when I pass in an age that is one less than MINIMUM_AGE it will *throw an exception* to signal an error. I'll add the following test method to the PersonTest class.

```
23   @Test(expected = AgeBelowMinimumException.class)
24   public void testConstructorThrowsExceptionWhenAgeBelowMinimum() {
25       Person p = new Person(personName, Person.MINIMUM_AGE - 1);
26   }
```

This is a special annotation that tells JUnit that when setAge() is called with a value of 0 (MINIMUM_AGE - 1) then it should expect a Person isn't instantiated. Instead an AgeBelowMinimumException is *thrown*, which is underlined because it doesn't exist yet. I'll let Eclipse generate the stub for me:

```
public class AgeBelowMinimumException extends RuntimeException {
}
```

Now everything is defined and I can run my tests and I get...

Red bar!

Implement the Behavior

I have a test but I haven't implemented the new behavior in my code yet, so I'll do that by updating Person's constructor:

```
public Person(String name, int age) {
    if (age < MINIMUM_AGE){
        throw new AgeBelowMinimumException();
    } else {
        this.age = age;
    }
    this.name = name;
}
```

This says that when an instance of Person is created and the age passed in is less than MINIMUM_AGE then throw an exception instead of creating a new instance of Person. When a parameter makes no sense, I should probably throw an exception and exit instead of creating an invalid instance of Person that could end up doing who knows what to the system.

Notice that this test tests things in reverse, so to speak.

If I try to create a Person with an age less than MINIMUM_AGE, I want the system to *throw an exception.* If it doesn't that's bad, so my test verifies that the system *throws an exception* when age is less than MINIMUM_AGE and if it doesn't *throw an exception* JUnit will put up the red bar.

Finally, I'll write a test that expects an exception when an instance of Person is created with an age greater than MAXIMUM_AGE:

```
28    @Test(expected = AgeAboveMaximumException.class)
29    public void testConstructorThrowsExceptionWhenAgeAboveMaximum() {
30        Person p = new Person(personName, Person.MAXIMUM_AGE + 1);
31    }
```

And I'll let Eclipse stub out the exception:

```
public class AgeAboveMaximumException extends RuntimeException {
}
```

In practice, I'd probably use a single exception, AgeOutOfRangeException, instead of AgeBelowMinimumException and AgeAboveMaximumException, but I wanted to demonstrate that a range has two boundaries and I could do something different for each boundary condition.

Once again I can compile. When I run the test I get the red bar again telling me I have to handle this new exception in my code. So I'll handle it by adding to the *constructor* of Person:

```
if (age > MAXIMUM_AGE) {
        throw new AgeAboveMaximumException();
}
```

What I Created

In this little example, I created four classes: PersonTest, which I used to drive the creation of the Person class as well as the two exception classes, AgeBelowMinimumException and AgeAboveMaximumException.

The Java source code for this Eclipse project is available for download at the Pragmatic Programmers web page for this book.[2]

---

2.   http://pragprog.com/book/dblegacy.

Here's the PersonTest class:

PersonExample/tst/person/PersonTest.java

```java
package person;

import static org.junit.Assert.*;
import org.junit.Test;

public class PersonTest {
        String personName = "Bob";
        int personAge = 21;

        @Test
        public void testCreatePersonWithNameAndAge() {
                Person p = new Person(personName, personAge);
                assertEquals(personName, p.getName());
                assertEquals(personAge, p.getAge());
        }

        @Test
        public void testConstants() {
                assertEquals(Person.MINIMUM_AGE, 1);
                assertEquals(Person.MAXIMUM_AGE, 200);
        }

        @Test(expected = AgeBelowMinimumException.class)
        public void testConstructorThrowsExceptionWhenAgeBelowMinimum() {
                Person p = new Person(personName, Person.MINIMUM_AGE - 1);
        }

        @Test(expected = AgeAboveMaximumException.class)
        public void testConstructorThrowsExceptionWhenAgeAboveMaximum() {
                Person p = new Person(personName, Person.MAXIMUM_AGE + 1);
        }
}
```

Here's the Person class:

PersonExample/src/person/Person.java

```java
package person;

public class Person {
        public static final int MINIMUM_AGE = 1;
        public static final int MAXIMUM_AGE = 200;
        private String name;
        private int age;

        public Person(String name, int age) {
                if (age < MINIMUM_AGE) {
                        throw new AgeBelowMinimumException();
                }
```

```
            if (age > MAXIMUM_AGE) {
                    throw new AgeAboveMaximumException();
            }
            this.age = age;
            this.name = name;
    }

    public String getName() {
            return name;
    }

    public int getAge() {
            return age;
    }
}
```

And here are the two exception classes:

PersonExample/src/person/AgeBelowMinimumException.java
```
package person;

public class AgeBelowMinimumException extends RuntimeException  {
}
```

PersonExample/src/person/AgeAboveMaximumException.java
```
package person;

public class AgeAboveMaximumException extends RuntimeException {
}
```

Notice that my test contains three assertions: an assertion for the happy path when age is MINIMUM_AGE, which is the first valid age. I have another assertion where age is one less than MINIMUM_AGE, and a third assertion where age is one greater than MAXIMUM_AGE.

You may wonder why I don't suggest having a fourth assertion to test for MAXIMUM_AGE. Well, that test would be redundant to the MINIMUM_AGE test since they would both pass and fail together for the same reason. We want our tests to be *unique*, so I omit that fourth assertion.

Some people feel that having the fourth assertion for completeness is a good thing. If you're in that camp, I won't argue with you. On the contrary, I'll praise you for having any tests at all!

Because I think of tests as specifications, I like to have test coverage for all my code, even trivial code. It would be part of the specification and so it should be part of the test suite. I even have tests for my constants. For example, notice I have the following test in my code:

```
@Test
    public void testConstants() {
            assertEquals(Person.MINIMUM_AGE, 1);
            assertEquals(Person.MAXIMUM_AGE, 200);
    }
```

Now, if someone decides MINIMUM_AGE should be 18 and they change the code, one of the above assertions will fail. Anything that could cause a change in behavior should be covered by a test.

Tests Are Specifications

I think of unit tests as specifications. This is especially useful when I'm trying to figure out what tests to write.

I talked about how to write a test for a linear range from MINIMUM_AGE to MAXI-MUM_AGE—a number between 1 and 200—and determined that I needed three assertions in order to do that:

- one for MINIMUM_AGE – 1 or 0, which returns an exception because if I want a value from 1 to 200 and we passed in zero, that's bad.

- one for the first valid value in the range, MINIMUM_AGE or 1, which returns with no error.

- one for the next invalid value, MAXIMUM_AGE + 1 or 201, which again returns an exception.

Notice that those three assertions—0, 1, and 201—are unique. They wouldn't fail for the same reason. Tests should always fail for different reasons, and each test should fail for only one reason. Build the rules into the code itself.

And that's another huge benefit of having a suite of unit tests as opposed to a requirements document. It's difficult—even impossible—to tell if a requirements document is out of date. But with a click of a button I can run all my unit tests and verify that all my code coverage is up to date. They're *living specifications.*

For any feature or any behavior in the system, there's an optimum *number* of tests to write and an optimal *kind* of test to write that would verify that behavior. Each one of those tests is unique, and they should be named accordingly.

Be Complete

There is an assumption that a suite of tests tells the whole story and is a complete specification. If you don't specify a test for a behavior, that behavior is assumed to be false. Anything that's not part of a test suite is assumed not to exist. So you have to have a *complete* set of tests to cover all the behavior in your system. If you're really practicing test-first development, you'll have that complete set of tests. Always write a test to create behavior.

And because you're creating testable code as you're writing it, you'll see a dramatic positive increase in the overall quality of the finished product. There's a tight correlation between testability and code quality, but please don't put on your QA hat.

It's very enticing for a developer or a manager to say, "Hey, we're going to kill two birds with one stone. We're going to do TDD and that's going to do QA at the same time." But when you do that, you're not really doing TDD. You'll write too many tests. You'll write tests that are not about specifying behavior, and you'll start to skew the test specification for the code, making it harder to read, understand, and later revise.

QA is about making sure you have enough coverage to be able to handle certain cases that developers shouldn't be thinking about at this stage of the game. Put your editorial mind aside and just focus on *creating behavior*, then go back and clean it up as needed. It's easier—just like it's easier when you're writing a book or an article to write first and then go back and edit. Every writer knows this. You're not supposed to edit yourself as you're writing—that's a recipe for writer's block. The same is true for coding. First create the behavior, and then go back and make it supportable.

But this notion can be a difficult sell to management. They tell us to do TDD instead of QA. And yes, TDD can help make code more testable and provide more test coverage, but that additional step of focusing on what could go wrong, on nonfunctional requirements, and on other things that the QA process traditionally works out, is still there.

Instead, look at those possible problems well before a final QA pass—soon enough that you can still do something about any problems you may find. But you can't do it at the same time. It's okay to have a quality engineer working with the developer, but those two things can't happen in the same brain at the same time. Write your tests in TDD to focus on specifying behavior and put that QA mind-set aside for the time being. Then, after the code is working, go back and write tests with a QA mind-set to try to break the code and see what could go wrong. Adding many QA tests can slow down the build, so it's more efficient to add them after the code is mostly working.

Make Each Test Unique

The criteria for a good test are that the test fails for a *known reason*—not any other reason—and that it's the *only test in the system* that fails for that reason. In other words, *tests should be unique*.

When you have unique tests and you don't have redundant tests, then you get clean feedback when something fails. Typically one test will break, rather than a whole suite of them, and you won't have to spend weeks trying to clean up those tests.

This is a primary way teams fail when they adopt TDD. They think: *Two tests are good, three tests are great, so ten tests must be fantastic. Let's just write a whole bunch of tests.*

But then you end up with test redundancy in the system. When you go to refactor your code, it means you may have to refactor a lot of tests, which slows you down considerably. It means that when something fails, you're going to have multiple tests fail for the same reason. That makes your tests noisy—we've got to figure out what the real problem is.

Test-first development is a *design methodology*. It helps developers build high-quality code by forcing them to write testable code and by concretizing requirements.

If you're going to write a test for something, you need to have some way to verify it in the first place. So write things in manageable chunks—the smaller, the better. Further, write code that's *focused* and *about one thing*. If you have multiple issues in a class, you start to have multiple reasons that the test could fail. As a result, there's an exponential increase in the number of tests you have to write for the number of issues you have in a class.

Cover Code with Tests

Many companies have standards for the percentage of code with unit test coverage they should have. To me, the only number that makes sense is 100%.

Knowing that we're not always going to be able to achieve that, as developers, we still want to strive for it, even when we have dependencies on other services that may make parts of our code untestable.

Code coverage tools show you where your code is covered by unit tests. The discussion of what is the best percentage of code coverage to shoot for can set us up to game the system. I've seen companies have test coverage targets of 60%, 80%, or whatever, and developers use it as an excuse for not writing tests. They leave the hard-to-test code untested and cover trivial code since it's easier to test. Conversely, I know developers who cover complex code but refuse to write tests for trivial code, such as getters and setters. They reason that because it's unlikely to introduce bugs in trivial code there's no need to write tests for it.

I strive for 100% test coverage because I use my tests as specifications for building code. I'd define even trivial behavior such as getters and setters in my specification, so I put it in my tests as well. Since I don't write code unless it's to make a failing test pass, I always get 100% test coverage.

If you have multiple paths through code, indicating the code is more complex, you want to have test coverage for that code. Each code path can produce a different result, so you need unit tests for each one.

As the number of code paths increases, the number of unit tests needed to cover those paths grows exponentially, so TDD rewards you for writing simpler code.

Bugs Are Missing Tests

Every bug exists because of a missing test in a system. The way to fix bugs using TDD is first write a failing test that represents the bug and then fix the bug and watch the failing test turn green. This not only fixes the bug but it ensures it will never come back because you have a test in place that will fail if anyone makes changes to the system that produce that bug.

Bugs in software can be grouped into several different classifications. We have syntax errors or typos, and we have more serious problems like logic errors or design flaws. Test-driven development addresses *all* of these issues.

Tests provide a level of feedback the compiler can't. Traditionally, the only feedback developers got before running a program was the syntax checker in the compiler, which checked that your source code made syntactic sense but didn't check that it made logical sense. Compilers can only check syntax and a few basic kinds of errors. They can assure that code is well formed, but that doesn't assure that it's logically correct or that it does the right thing.

Unit tests bridge that gap between syntax errors and conceptual errors. They catch mistakes no other tool can. They catch mistakes you might have missed but your customer would find. I would much rather have one of my tests fail than get a call from an upset client. I don't write perfect code—no one does—but I prefer that those blunders stay between me and my unit tests.

Test Workflows with Mocks

Unit tests can be useful for specifying parameters, results, how algorithms should behave, and many other things, but they can't test that a sequence of calls are in the right order, or other similar scenarios. For that you need another kind of testing called *workflow testing*.

Workflow testing uses something called *mocks*. Mocks are stand-ins for real objects. They're only used in the context of the test, and they verify how the code you're testing interacts with an external dependency. Anything external that's needed in the code you're testing has to be mocked out, and a variety of techniques and tools are available to do that.

Condition the mock to say that when it's called with a certain set of values it should return a specific value. After you run the test that talks to the mock, you interrogate the mock. Ask the mock, "Were you called correctly? Were you called with the right parameters?" That helps you understand how your code interacts with the external world without it interacting with the external world.

Create a Safety Net

Practicing TDD provides the cadence for building software, and it also gives developers a safety net for building code. You could discount the idea of a safety net, but it's just as important for software developers as it is for an acrobat. Who would go up on the trapeze five times a day knowing that one small slip would be her last? Having that safety net is psychological assurance. It bolsters the confidence needed to try stuff and gives you the freedom to experiment that leads to true innovation.

The greatest of the many benefits of doing test-first development is the end result: software developers are writing more testable code, which costs less to maintain.

Developers who are practicing test-after will sometimes discover in the process of writing tests later that they have to change their code to make it more testable. Doing that first, because you're writing the test first, is much more efficient. You never have to rewrite code for testability when you're doing test-first.

So even though it is against conventional wisdom, which says you should create the test after there is something to test, it makes a lot more sense to start by writing the test first. Similarly, most developers have been taught to start with the design, but it turns out that you'll know much more about the right design late in the project. So I'm a proponent of another practice that goes against conventional wisdom: implementing the design *last*. This is the topic of our next chapter.

Let's Get Practical

Here are some ways to put these ideas into practice.

Seven Strategies for Using Tests as Specifications

Writing unit tests to specify behaviors keeps development focused on building only what's needed. It also helps you limit the tests you write to only those that specify the behavior you're creating. Not only do these tests document how to use the behaviors you create, they also show the sequence in which you built a feature, which gives insight as to how the software was designed. Here are seven strategies for using tests as specifications.

Instrument your tests

Instead of using hardcoded values as parameters, assign those values to variables that are named for what they represent (for example, maxUsers instead of 20). This makes generalizations explicit so the test can read like a specification.

Use helper methods with intention-revealing names

Wrap setup behavior and other chunks of functionality into their own helper methods. This lets you create several different setup options while removing redundancy in individual tests. This also provides the opportunity to wrap the helper method in a meaningful name so it's easier to read in the test.

Show what's important

Name things for what's important. Call out generalizations and key concepts in names. Say what the test exercises and state it in the positive. Instead of passing hardcoded values, pass variables named for what the value represents (for example, anyInt instead of 4).

Test behaviors, not implementations

Tests should exercise and be named after behaviors and not implementations. testConstructor is a bad name; testRetrievingValuesAfterConstruction is better. Use long names to express exactly what the test is supposed to assert. Focusing on behaviors helps keep code testable and development focused.

Use mocks to test workflows

Asserts can test values and behaviors, but they can't test workflows or how one object interacts with other objects. When you want to test your code in isolation from its dependencies, *mock objects* can stand in for external dependencies.

Avoid overspecifying

It's easy to overspecify behavior with tests. Sometimes you write more tests than needed to understand an algorithm. Once the abstractions are found and the algorithm is written, it's important to go back and delete the redundant tests, making sure every test in the system creates a new distinction.

Use accurate examples

Tests concretize abstract requirements by asserting real behaviors. Use examples that reflect how the system will be used so behaviors are exercised the way they're used in the system. Working through accurate examples will often reveal inconsistencies and other design issues before coding starts so they can be dealt with early.

When you allow behaviors to emerge using test-first development, you end up with *living specifications* expressed in your test suite. You can run your tests at any time and prove that the specification is up-to-date when you see the green bar. Unit tests that specify behaviors are valuable assets that support refactoring and document how a system is used.

Seven Strategies for Fixing Bugs

Bugs are the bane of the software industry. They can be difficult to find and costly to fix. How we deal with bugs has a big impact on our software development process. Strive for zero bugs or at least avoid accumulating them in a backlog of bugs so they're dealt with as soon as possible. We can use bugs to show us ways of improving our process so that similar bugs aren't created again. Here are seven strategies for fixing bugs.

Don't write them in the first place

You know the old joke: The patient raises his arm and says to his doctor, "Hey, Doc, it hurts when I do this," and the doctor replies, "Well, then, don't do that." We want to avoid writing bugs in the first place and can do so by focusing on creating high-quality code and using our tools to help us prevent mistakes.

Catch them as soon as possible

If we're going to write bugs, we should have a process for finding them as quickly as possible. When time elapses between when a bug is written and when it's fixed, the code containing the bug becomes less familiar to the developer who wrote it and takes longer to fix. But with a set of automated regression tests, developers can get instant feedback on whether or not their code has most kinds of bugs. Reduce to zero the cycle time from when a bug is written to when it's repaired, and the cost of fixing the bug is the lowest it will ever be.

Make bugs findable by design

No matter how good your regression tests are, some bugs will get away from us, and when they do, it would be good if they were easier to find. Your ability to find bugs in code is directly related to the code's qualities. For example, software that is highly cohesive and well encapsulated is less likely to have side effects that can cause bugs. Software that is cohesive and well encapsulated is also easier to read and understand, so it's also easier to find bugs in it.

Ask the right questions

Since developers spend most of their time and effort in debugging trying to find the bug in the first place, figuring out how to quickly locate bugs is important. I had a professor in college who used to say that it didn't matter if your experiment succeeded or failed—what mattered was that you learn something. This is good advice for debugging too. When I find myself hunting down a bug, I try to construct scenarios that give me good information on where the bug could be—or at least where the bug isn't—and I'll try to narrow down sections of code until I find it.

See bugs as missing tests

Once I find a bug and before I fix it, I write a failing test for it so that when I fix the bug the test passes. The bug came about because of some false assumption. By figuring out what that false assumption was and embodying it in a unit test, we get regression test coverage for that issue and will never have to deal with that bug again.

Use defects to fix process

When I find a bug I ask why the bug happened in the first place. Sometimes this leads me back to a problem in my software development process, and fixing the process can potentially rid me of many future bugs. Look for ways to let our tools help us do the right things.

Learn from mistakes

If bugs represent false assumptions or flaws in our development process, it's not enough to simply fix the bug. Instead, fix the environment that allowed the bug to happen in the first place. Use bugs as lessons on vulnerabilities in your design and process so you can look for ways to fix them. Use mistakes as learning opportunities and gain the valuable message each of our problems hold.

Bugs are a huge expense to software development, costing billions of dollars per year. Bugs aren't just problems in code—they're also problems in the software development process. By seeing them as such, we can use them to find ways of improving our process, thereby eliminating similar bugs in the future.

Retrospective

Specify Behaviors with Tests to create *living specifications.* We walked through an example of building some basic functionality test-first and saw how to use tests to specify behavior. When developers see the benefit of doing test-first development, they can become *test infected* and want to do all their development test-first.

In this chapter, we discovered...

- How to use your test suite to not only verify behavior but also to specify it.

- By *instrumenting* tests, you can clearly state their purpose and they become a form of *living specifications.*

- Tests provide a "safety net," allowing you to refactor code and instantly know if you've made a mistake.

- By writing tests to specify behaviors, you'll always know the right kind and number of tests to write to build out any behavior.

When done correctly, test-driven development helps developers create testable code that's more maintainable, but TDD can fail when done poorly. By seeing tests as executable specifications for code, you'll know exactly what tests to write for any given behavior. We walked through an example of doing test-first development so you can grasp the basic concept even if you're not a programmer.

CHAPTER 12

Practice 8: Implement the Design Last

While I'm not advocating putting off *all* design until the end, some design activities in software are actually more effectively and efficiently done *toward* the end of the development cycle. The kind of design I'm talking about here doesn't happen on whiteboards; it happens in code when the code is already working and fully supported by tests. This is the ideal time to design supportability into software.

Tests support safely cleaning up code, so it often makes sense to wait until tests are in place and code is working before shaping the design of the code. I find more opportunities toward the end of a project to discover design patterns and better understand what the system is supposed to do than at the beginning of a project.

This usually occurs in the opposite sequence. Traditional development focuses on getting code to work. And then they remove as many bugs as possible at the end of the development cycle. But with this practice we turn that on its head and learn to better support our efforts to write more maintainable code.

Let's write the test first. Let's do the design last.

Impediments to Changeability

Supportable code is flexible and easy to modify because it's readable and understandable, not just by the developer who wrote the code but by other professional software developers as well.

We've seen previously that one aspect of "good code" is that it's easy to change. When I ask developers what makes code easy to change, they usually say things like it's well documented, it uses intention-revealing names, it follows a consistent metaphor, and so on. These and other things can definitely help make code easier to understand and easier to change.

Are there guidelines developers can follow that show them how to make code easier to change? I believe the answer is a resounding *Yes!* We've already discussed several principles and practices that help make code easier to change. But let's ask the converse question, because sometimes knowing what to avoid is just as important as knowing what to strive for.

What makes code difficult to change? Are there things developers do that make their code hard to change later?

I believe that some commonly accepted developer practices are actually impediments to creating changeable code. Changeability impediments can become roadblocks for easily working with code. Many of these impediments are little things, and individually, they may not be a problem. But when created regularly, as a practice, such impediments can seriously slow down development.

Let's start by looking at some common developer practices that can be impediments to change. This can get a little technical, so nondevelopers, please bear with me.

Here's my short list:

Lack of Encapsulation

The more one piece of code "knows" about another, the more dependencies it has, whether it's explicit or implicit. This can cause subtle and unexpected problems where one small change can break code that's seemingly unrelated. As soon as one piece of code "knows" or depends on the way another piece of code is implemented, it can become difficult to change without causing the other parts of a system to break.

Overuse of Inheritance

Inheritance is an important and valuable part of object-oriented languages, but it can be easily overused and misused, linking together unrelated issues, producing steep inheritance hierarchies, and causing maintenance problems.

Concrete Implementations

When key abstractions are missed, so are commonalities between two or more behaviors. This tends to introduce redundancy and needless complexity that make code harder to work with. Concrete implementations are more difficult to change or add new variations to in the future.

Inlining Code

It was considered an efficient practice on constrained systems to copy and paste code inline, as needed, rather than wrapping the code in its own method and calling it. But this can make code harder to read while it also introduces redundancies. Today, most compilers can optimize indirect method calls away, and extracting code into their own methods gives us the opportunity to improve readability by providing meaningful names for them rather than preceding the block of code with a comment.

Dependencies

The way you handle dependencies is also important. If you do not separate them correctly, you can end up coupling multiple issues together that don't need to be coupled. This makes it difficult to break those issues apart later.

Using Objects You Create or Creating Objects You Use

This was a difficult one for me to understand at first, but it turns out that this is one of the most important things *not* to do for writing extendable code—code that's able to be extended with minimal effort.To instantiate an object, you need to know a great deal about it, and this knowledge breaks type encapsulation—users of the code must be aware of sub types—and forces callers to be more dependent on a specific implementation. When users of a service also instantiate that service, they become coupled to it in a way that makes it difficult to test, extend, or reuse. This will be discussed in more detail later in this chapter.

These are just a few impediments to easily changeable code. They can be small things that when done occasionally can be no big deal. But when done repeatedly throughout millions of lines of code, they can add up to big problems.

I have a friend who is a hardware engineer. He designs chips. He says, "Software is too forgiving," and he is not paying our industry a compliment. When he designs a circuit, he knows that one little mistake can invalidate his entire design and saddle his company with hundreds of thousands of dollars in re-fabrication costs. As a result, he's extremely careful—even obsessive—in his practices, checking and rechecking his designs before passing them along to manufacturing. He thinks that most of us software developers are undisciplined, shoot-from-the-hip slobs who focus on the wrong things and create little messes in code everywhere we go.

I can't argue with him.

The problem is developers *can* get away with being a little sloppy—but only to a point—and most developers weren't taught to be highly disciplined when writing software. The kinds of programs they wrote in school over a semester were relatively trivial and small compared to the kind of enterprise systems they find themselves writing professionally.

You can get away with being sloppy on small projects but at some point, when a project gets big enough, the results of our cumulative sins inevitably catch up with us.

Sustainable Development

In order for software development to be sustainable—that is, in order for us to rapidly build features now and easily extend them in the future—we must pay attention to maintainability.

Here are five of the items on my short list for writing sustainable code:

Delete Dead Code

Dead code—code that's never executed because it's commented out or no longer being called—serves absolutely no purpose except to distract developers.

Delete it.

If for some reason you actually do need it, it's in the version control system so you can roll back, get that code, and add it back to the working system as needed.

Keep Names Up-to-Date

Rename methods and classes to have good, intention-revealing names. As you go through the process of building software and figuring things out, the code's functionality can change a little bit. When you change code, change its name to reflect what it currently does.

Centralize Decisions

Centralize decisions so they're made only once and help remove redundancy in code. If it turns out a decision needs to be changed, there's only one place that's affected. This makes changing code safer and simpler.

Abstractions

Create and use abstractions for all external dependencies, and create missing entities in the model because, again, your model should reflect the nature of what you're modeling. This also makes code easier to test, extend, and repurpose.

Organize Classes

Anyone can miss entities in the domain being modeled, and when you do it can be hard to understand what's going on. So make sure the model is complete in terms of how you're using it, and organize classes so they have the right behavior and manage the right attributes.

Coding vs. Cleaning

Writing software requires a number of different mental activities. Developers have to keep track of many things in their heads. A lot of details are involved and a great deal of discipline is required.

It's hard!

There's a lot of stuff developers have to be aware of and think about in a level of detail that isn't normally required in the everyday world. At the same time, we have to abstract, we have to implement, we have to design—and we have to do all these things every day.

Separating out these different mental activities into different tracks can help developers get more mental clarity, but that's hardly the only benefit. The designs you come up with when you do this kind of development are far better, far more resilient, and far more reflective of the nature of the problem, so they're easier to understand and cost less to maintain.

I find it helpful to distinguish between coding versus cleaning and treat them as separate tasks. When I'm coding I'm looking for solutions to a specific task at hand. When I'm cleaning I take working code and make it supportable. I separate these activities because I find it easier to do them as separate tasks. Coding is easier when I focus on just getting a behavior to work and my tests to pass. Cleaning is easier when I have working code that's supported with tests and I can focus on making the code easier to understand and work with.

Pay attention to good coding practices. As you continue to touch your code and improve it in little ways, you'll get on an upward spiral as opposed to the typical downward spiral that involves accruing technical debt.

Pay off that technical debt both in the small—during the refactoring step of test-first development—and in the large—with periodic refactoring efforts to incorporate the team's learning into the code.

There are times that technical debt simply accumulates as you go. You may need to change your design to accommodate new features or because you've found a better approach. These things can't really be eliminated in the TDD refactoring step. In these situations—every couple of months, typically—do some paying down in the large. Pay back bigger chunks of your technical debt by doing some larger refactoring. But even then unit tests support you in doing that.

Software Is Read More than It's Written

Though most people would be surprised to hear it, code is something to be read, like a book or a newspaper article. On average software is read ten times more than it's written.

For efficiency's sake, and for the sake of extendibility, software should be much easier to read. Write your code for the reader (someone else) as opposed to the writer (yourself). Software development is not a "write once" activity. Software development is actually a "write many" profession where code is continually enhanced, cleaned up, and improved.

In order to keep up with the changing needs of your users, make your code flexible, changeable, and easy to work with. You now know to use intention-revealing names instead of comments to convey the meaning of your code. You may want to use comments to describe *why* you're doing something but not to describe *what* you're doing. The code itself should say *what* it's doing.

There are exceptions to this, of course, like a range of APIs that don't quite work as documented. Some of the Windows APIs are flawed in terms of what they're supposed to do and what they say they do. So what I'll do is I'll have a *what* comment that says: "You're supposed to call this this way but I found it didn't work for me so I call it this way instead and it does work."

In this case I'm embedding knowledge into the system, and that's good. But if a comment was written because the developer didn't feel a reader would understand what's going on just by looking at the code, it's far better to rewrite the code to be more intention revealing than to keep the comment.

Program by Intention

If I have a public API, a method, or some service I'm providing that I'm exposing to the outside world, I won't put any implementation in that method. I will simply delegate to other methods.

I do that because it makes the code easier to read. If you delegate some code, and then do some of the implementation, you're switching perspectives, dealing with things on the conceptual level at times and at the implementation level at other times. When you do that, you may find there's a little task switch that flips in your head. It's not much but when you do it over and over and over again, it becomes very taxing.

Remove that repetitive effort by simply delegating all bits of functionality to separate methods in all your public APIs. That way code can be read like a script or a menu because it's at the same *precision* or level of abstraction. *It does this step, it does that step, it does the next step...I understand.*

We call this technique *programming by intention* and it gives code a *cohesion of perspectives*, meaning that all the code is at the same level of abstraction so it's easier to read and understand.

If there's a bug in one of the steps, you know exactly where to go to find the problem. You don't have to look through this huge amount of code because you've abstracted the ideas—each little piece of the idea—in the correct way.

Think of object-oriented code in layers. This is how we naturally think. If we think about the high-level things we need to do today, we're not thinking about all the little details. Then, when we think about how we're going to do that step, we unfold the top layer and start looking at the details. Understand and look at code the same way, with those levels of abstraction. This goes back to the *what* versus the *how*. If I write a to-do list for today, I write down *what* I need to do, not—in any detail at least—*how* I'm going to do it.

When you look at the *how*, when you jump into that level inside the *what*, you find a bunch more *whats* that have to happen to implement that *how*. That's how to think about the *whats*, and it delegates the *how* to others and so on until you work down the chain.

It sounds like a shell game from the outside, and at first I thought it was. I thought OO was a big scam. But actually it turned out that at each level of abstraction I understood my own code at a deeper level. That understanding needs to be reflected in the code.

Code is like thinking, though I suspect perhaps sometimes developers resist that notion. We don't want to worry about having to organize our code in that way. But that turns out to be helpful—just like it's helpful to think clearly.

If I have the item "pay car payment at bank" on my to-do list, that's the *what*. It's what I'm planning to do. I don't also have to write down "Get your keys. Put your shoes on. Get into the car. Turn the car on..." The list of *how* to actually get to the bank and pay this one car payment gets to be pretty complex after only a few steps, and I actually do have to do all of those things in order to make it happen.

But do I have to write it all down?

Part of my implementation of *how* is "drive to the bank," but how do I implement that? "Write the check" is another, but how do I implement that? I can unfold this task down and down, but what is the lowest level I can unfold it to?

It turns out that the very lowest level in programming we can unfold to are the three logic gates: *and*, *or*, and *not*. Everything boils down to that, though along the way we have sorted groups or clusters of these ideas into meaningful chunks called *abstractions*.

It's a disciplined, useful, and powerful way of thinking.

Reduce Cyclomatic Complexity

Cyclomatic complexity was first described by Thomas J. McCabe in his December 1976 paper "A Complexity Measure."[1] It represents the number of paths through code.

Code with just one conditional or if statement has a cyclomatic complexity of two—there are two possible paths through the code and therefore two possible behaviors the code can produce. If there are no if statements, no conditional logic in code, then the code has a cyclomatic complexity of one. There's only one possible behavior the code can produce. But this grows exponentially. Two if statements have a cyclomatic complexity of four, three have a cyclomatic complexity of eight, and so on. Drive cyclomatic complexity down to as low as you can because, generally speaking, the number of unit tests needed for a method is at least equal to its cyclomatic complexity.

You can't always achieve a cyclomatic complexity of one, because that's code with *no* conditional statements. It's code that doesn't branch. It doesn't take anything into consideration. In fact, the very definition of a computer is a programmable system that wouldn't be possible without conditional statements. But your methods should have *as few conditional statements as possible*.

Conditional logic is expensive. If we look at the cost to maintain code based on the keywords of the language, we find that the thirty or so keywords of any programming language don't have equal costs associated with them. The vastly more expensive keywords are the ones that change control flow: *if, switch, unary processing, loops, exceptions*…all of these conditional statements

---

1.   McCabe, Thomas J. "A Complexity Measure." *IEEE Transactions of Software Engineering* Volume SE-2, no. 4 (1976) http://www.literateprogramming.com/mccabe.pdf

change the flow of control. They make it more difficult and more taxing for the brain because suddenly there's a bifurcation—we have two code paths instead of one, and that splits our attention.

For example, if you have an if statement in your code you must think about and test the true condition and the false condition. This means holding those two conditions in your head, and that can be difficult. I was just looking at some code from a client that had a series of six conditions—a cyclomatic complexity of *sixty-four*. I can't hold anywhere near that many conditions in my head. Most people can't, and that's why the higher the cyclomatic complexity, the higher the probability that it will have bugs.

If you build each entity with a low cyclomatic complexity, you need far fewer tests to cover your code. I prefer to use techniques like polymorphism in my code, which moves the conditional statements into the creation phase of objects rather than the usage phase. Separating these two phases is one of the most important keys for making code less coupled, simpler to work with, and more maintainable.

Separate Use from Creation

In object-oriented programming, there's the creation of the object—we call it *instantiation*—and then there's the *usage* of the object. It makes a lot of sense to separate out those two phases so that one group of objects are only dealing with creating objects and another group of objects are only dealing with using objects. The objects that create objects are called *factories*. Factories simply encapsulate the new keyword. The new keyword is the way we create runnable objects from their class definitions. new has a requirement, which is that it has to know what is newing up.

Suppose I said to you, "I would like you to do something for me."

And you reply, "Fine, what?"

Then I say, "Something. Now do it."

You're probably going to laugh at me.

Don't do that in code. In code you want to be able to *create* something. When you new up an object, it requires that you pass in the type of object you're newing. It's an absolute requirement. Just like if I ask you to do something for me, you have to be told what it is I want you to do or you can't do it. It's not new's fault if it doesn't know what to do without being told.

But one of the techniques used a lot in OO is called *polymorphism*. It's a big word but a simple concept: We want to be able to *do* a task but not have to worry about the *details* of how the task is accomplished.

For instance, say I want to decompress a file with the corresponding decompressor that was used to compress it. If it was zipped, I want to *unzip* it. If it was packed I want to *unpack* it. But maybe I don't care about that distinction. I just know that I have a file and it was compressed in some way and I want to decompress it in any way that'll get the job done.

Now, that's almost as hard for a computer as me saying to you, "Do something for me," and not telling you what. The computer needs to know *exactly* what decompression routine to follow. So I can have another part of my system figure that out. In this case, the object that would figure out which decompressor to use would have access to the object that was compressed because that object knows how it was compressed. It shouldn't be the responsibility of the client code of the other program to figure out how it was compressed. The client code should be able to say "decompress yourself" and have the right decompressor applied as if by magic...but it's not really magic.

That's what polymorphism does. It allows you to build blocks of code independent of each other so they can grow independently from each other. For example, when someone comes up with a new compressor that was never envisioned before, the existing code can automatically take advantage of it because it's not responsible for selecting the compressor to use. It's just responsible for delegating to the compressor it's given. As long as it can handle the job it's supposed to, everybody's happy and the code works. That technique is great for making your code independent from other code in the system and allowing you to extend a system in a safe and effective manner.

But in order to do that correctly you need to create objects separately, in a different entity than the entity that's using the object. By isolating object creation we also isolate the knowledge about which concrete objects are being used and hide it from other parts of the system.

Not only does this decouple business rules from their actions, but it also decouples the dependencies between the caller and the services they use. You can then mock those services and isolate your code from the services they use so they can be tested in isolation.

Separating creation of objects from their usage lets you break dependencies to improve testability. It decouples code so it's easier to modify and maintain, and it simplifies code because factories only create objects but never use them so they're easy to test—just pass in your business rules and see what objects the factory returns. And this approach also simplifies our usage code because it has fewer conditional statements and doesn't have to be concerned with instantiating objects.

Of course, if I need to use a feature of the language or framework I'm using then I'll just new up the object inline. But for my own classes that I might want to extend in the future, or for external dependencies that I'll definitely want to mock out for testing, I'll make sure another entity instantiates and passes in a service object that another object uses.

Emergent Design

Iterative development lends itself well to emergent design where we start with a single, testable behavior and continue to enhance it until our design emerges. Building software incrementally through test-first development while paying attention to design principles and practices as well as technical debt helps us build and create better designs than trying to do it all up front.

As you pay attention to the challenges you're having as you're building software, those challenges are actually whispering in your ear: "Hey, there is a better way to do something. Hey, there is a better option." So suddenly you can take the things that are the worst—the bugs, the pain, the nagging customer not getting what he wants, all the horrible things on our debit side, things you don't want—and turn them into assets.

They hold the clues to how to do things so much better. If you use the information you're getting in that way, they're really blessings in disguise. It's very often easier to change something you have in front of you than to try to pull it out of a vacuum. As new requirements come in, figure out how to handle those requirements and build them. Sometimes we call this *just-in-time* design. It prevents overbuilding because you don't have to anticipate; you're only building what you need. It gives you options to allow requirements to evolve as you go. Pay attention to the forces of the problem. It helps you to understand the problem deeper and naturally create better designs.

But in order for emergent design to work, we have to pay attention to quality and testability as well as apply good principles and practices. If you just write crappy code, as you go back into that code again in the next iteration you'll find it harder and harder to work from. Maybe it's not going to happen in a few weeks, but I know lots of teams that in their four- to five-year time frame build completely unmaintainable systems; then they're left with, "Well, how do we deal with this? Let's start over."

No one wants to get into that place.

Let's Get Practical

Here are some ways to put these ideas into practice.

Seven Strategies for Doing Emergent Design

Emergent design, sometimes called just-in-time design, is an advanced technique for incrementally building software. When done correctly, it can be a highly efficient way of building quality software. But it is not a beginner technique and requires a deep understanding in many areas. Here are seven strategies to help you master emergent design:

Understand object-oriented design

Just using an object-oriented language doesn't make software object oriented. Most of the software written between the curly braces of a class statement is procedural. Good object-oriented code is made up of well-encapsulated entities that accurately model the problem it's solving.

Understand design patterns

Design patterns are valuable for managing complexity and isolating varying behavior so that new variations can be added without impacting the rest of the system. Patterns are more relevant when practicing emergent design than when designing up front. You'll find many more opportunities to apply patterns as you're building software.

Understand test-driven development

Beyond the safety net of having a suite of regression tests to support any changes to a system, when done correctly test-driven development supports good design principles and practices.

Understand refactoring

Refactoring is the process of changing one design to another without changing external behavior. It provides the perfect opportunity to redesign in the small or in the large with working code. I do most of my design during refactoring once I've already worked out what needs to be done. This allows me to focus on doing it well and so the right design can emerge.

Focus on code quality

Code quality underlies all good software. Without making code CLEAN—cohesive, loosely coupled, encapsulated, assertive, and nonredundant—it quickly degrades into legacy code that people are afraid to touch. Paying attention to code quality will reveal better ways of building more maintainable software that gives you design resilience and makes code easier to change.

Be merciless

It's easy to get attached to a design, even when you don't have all the facts. Knowing the limits of a design and being willing to change it as needed is one of the most important skills for doing emergent design.

Practice good development habits

The Agile practices of Scrum and Extreme Programming are valuable tools for doing design, but tools do not create designs. To create good designs, first understand the principles behind the practices and make good development practices into habits. That way, you'll derive benefit from using them all the time.

Emergent design is about knowing your options as you build software and how to avoid painting yourself into a corner. When you understand and are able to use good development practices, you'll have the ability to easily change designs with the confidence that you can handle any changes in the future. This makes developing software less stressful and more fun.

Seven Strategies for Cleaning Up Code

Okay, you got the time and management approval to clean up some code. What do you do with it? Refactoring legacy code can be like unraveling a knotted rope, and it can be hard to figure out where to start. Here are seven strategies for cleaning up code.

Let code speak for itself

Write code clearly using intention-revealing names so it's obvious what the code does. Make the code self-expressive and avoid excessive comments that describe what the code is doing. When I see a lot of comments explaining code, I wonder if the developer who wrote it was nervous I might not understand the code just by reading it.

Add seams to add tests

One of the most valuable things to do with legacy code is to add tests to support further reworking of the code. But often, legacy code is so inter-twined it's difficult to isolate what needs to be tested. In his book *Working Effectively with Legacy Code [Fea04]*, Michael Feathers shares a series of techniques for adding seams to make legacy code more testable. These techniques make software more independent and simpler to test.

Make methods more cohesive

Perhaps the two most important and useful refactorings are Extract Method and Extract Class. Methods are often made to do too much. Other methods and sometimes entire classes can be lurking in long methods. Break up long methods by extracting new methods from little bits of functionality that you can name. Uncle Bob Martin says that ideally methods should be no longer than four lines of code. While that may sound a bit extreme, it's a good policy to break out code into smaller methods, if you can write a method name that describes what you're doing.

Make classes more cohesive

Another typical problem with legacy code is that classes try to do too much. This makes them difficult to name. Large classes become coupling points for multiple issues, making them more tightly coupled than they need to be. Hiding classes within classes gives those classes too many responsibilities and makes them hard to change later. Breaking out multiple classes makes them easier to work with and improves the understandability of the design.

Centralize decisions

As classes and methods become more cohesive, it's possible for business rules to become spread out across a system, making it difficult to read and modify. Try to centralize the rules for any given process. Extract business rules into factories if at all possible. When decisions are centralized, it removes redundancies, making code more understandable and easier to maintain.

Introduce polymorphism

Introduce polymorphism when you have a varying behavior you want to hide. For example, I may have more than one way of doing a task, like sorting a document or compressing a file. If I don't want my callers to be concerned with which variation they're using, then I may want to introduce polymorphism. This lets me add new variations later that existing clients can use without having to change those clients.

Encapsulate construction

An important part of making polymorphism work is based on clients using derived types through a base type. Clients call sort() without knowing which type of sort they're using. Since you want to hide from clients the type of sort they're using, the client can't instantiate the object. Give the object the responsibility of instantiating itself by giving it a static method that invokes new on itself, or by delegating that responsibility to a factory.

Refactoring code is a necessary part of development. It drops the cost of accommodating new features. They say hindsight is 20/20, and refactoring code can take advantage of that fact to clean up your design and make code more maintainable.

Retrospective

Implement the Design Last and program by intention to reduce complexity and support changeability.

In this chapter, we discovered...

- You really can't assure quality; you can only create it. So, instead of focusing on verifying quality, focus on building it in.

- Code that is readable and understandable is inherently flexible, which makes it easy (and therefore cost effective) to modify.

- Programming by intention results in a cohesion of perspective: all code is at the same level of abstraction so it's easier to read and understand.

- Improve testability and break dependencies by separating the creation of objects from their usage.

- Emergent design is not for beginners, and it requires strict attention to quality and testability.

Paying attention to maintainability and changing design to reflect what we've learned along the way can pull us out of the death spiral of legacy code and into code that continues to improve as it evolves, becoming easier to work with and less costly to maintain.

CHAPTER 13

Practice 9: Refactor Legacy Code

Refactoring is restructuring or repackaging the internal structure of code without changing its external behavior.

Imagine you're where I was a few years ago, saying to your manager that you want the whole team to spend two weeks, a full iteration, refactoring code. My manager said to me, "Good. What new features are you going to give me?"

And I had to say, "Wait a minute. I'm talking about *refactoring*. Refactoring is changing the internal structure but not changing the behavior. I'm giving you *no* new features."

He looked at me and asked, "Why do you want to do this?"

What should I say?

Software developers are faced with this situation too often. Sometimes we don't quite know what to say, because we don't speak management's language. We speak developers' language.

I shouldn't tell my manager I want to refactor code because it's cool, because it feels good, because I want to learn Clojure or some other technology…Those are all unacceptable answers to management. I have to specify the reasons for refactoring in a way that makes sense to the business—and it does.

Developers know this, but we need to use the right vocabulary to express it—the vocabulary of business, which comes down to *value* and *risk*.

How can we create more value while at the same time reduce risk?

Software by its very nature is high risk and likely to change. Refactoring drops the cost of four things:

- comprehending the code later,
- adding unit tests,
- accommodating new features,
- and doing further refactoring.

Clearly, you want to refactor code when you need to work with it some more to add features or fix bugs—and it makes sense in that case. If you never need to touch code again, maybe you don't need to refactor.

Refactoring can be a very good way to learn a new system. Embed learning into code by wrapping or renaming a method that isn't intention revealing with a more intention-revealing name. You can call out missing entities when you refactor and basically atone for any poor code written in the past.

We all want to see progress and meet deadlines, and as a result we sometimes make compromises. Refactoring code cleans up some of the mess we may have made in an effort to get something out the door.

Investment or Debt?

I first told the following story on my blog in April 2009:[1]

> Some businesses think software is a write-once activity. It is true that once written software does not change, but the world around us does and static software quickly becomes out of date.
>
> Code rot is real. Even if a system was well written at one time we often cannot anticipate how a system will need to be changed in the future. And that's the good news! If software does not need to be changed then it probably isn't being used. We'd like the software we build to be used and for software to continue to provide value it must be easy to change.
>
> You can build a house out of cardboard and on a nice summer day it will hold up well but in the first rainstorm it'll collapse. Builders have a whole set of standards and practices they follow religiously to make their buildings robust. We as software developers must do the same thing.
>
> I have a client on the East Coast who is one of the leading financial companies on the planet. They are particularly challenged by their huge amount of legacy code. Most of it was built by contractors or their top developers who were pulled onto the next project as soon as the first version was completed. Junior developers now maintain those systems, some who do not understand the original design so

---

1. Bernstein, David Scott. *To Be Agile* (blog). "Is Your Legacy Code Rotting?" http://tobeag-ile.com/2009/04/27/is-your-legacy-code-rotting

they hack away at it to make changes. Eventually they ended up with, well, a mess.

At a meeting with several of their senior managers and developers I said, "So let me get this straight. You became a leader in financial management by going out and finding top fund managers to manage your funds, have them research and acquire the best investments, and then you freeze the portfolio and pull the managers off onto other projects."

They said I got the first part right but the fund managers stay with the funds and continually adjust their portfolio because the market is constantly changing.

"Oh," I said, "so you go out and hire top software developers, have them design and build a system and then you pull them off when they're finished to work on a different project."

"So are you saying that our software is a critical asset, and like any asset it needs to be maintained?" one of the managers asked.

Bingo.

Would you buy a $90,000 Mercedes and then insist on never taking it to the shop because you paid so much for it? No. No matter how expensive and well made the car, it still needs some maintenance. No one builds a house thinking no matter how long it may stand they'll never replace the carpeting, buy a new kitchen appliance, or throw on a coat of paint. On the other hand, why replace the transmission on that Mercedes three days after pulling it out of the lot just because you're pretty sure you're eventually going to have to fix it? But if the day after you pull it out of the lot it won't go into reverse, how long do you just drive it around trying not to have to back up before you get that transmission looked at?

Some things are good to put off until later. Some things are not good to put off until later. Knowing the difference between the two is absolutely critical.

For technical debt, for the things that accumulate, almost always—and there are definitely exceptions to this—but most of the time, paying off technical debt as soon as possible is the right choice. When technical debt is lying around in the system, and developers are working on that system, they're bound to have collisions. They're running into that technical debt and paying the price over and over again. They can't get the car into reverse so they start to modify their behavior—their driving habits and routes to and from places—in order to never have to put the car in reverse. That one problem is starting to cause more and more problems. The sooner you deal with technical debt, the cheaper it is—just like credit card debt.

Become a "Deadbeat"

Technical debt is very much like financial debt; the interest can consume you.

I've worked with the financial and credit card industries, and there's a term they don't like to advertise but that they use for people like me. I'm a person who always pays his bills in full, as soon as I get the bill. I never let any balance accrue. Credit card companies call customers like me "deadbeats." They hate us because they don't make any money on us. They love the guy who builds up a balance and keeps making the minimum payment. I know someone who owed a major credit card company $17,000. If he paid only the minimum payment due each month it would have taken him 93 years and $184,000 to pay that back.

Like financial debt, ignoring the problem doesn't make it go away. I want you to become a technical "deadbeat."

Sometimes, we do have to let technical debts lie there for a bit, either because it's not the right time to fix it because we don't know what to do, or simply because we have no time at that moment. We end up having to live in that world more often than we'd like. But that's the difference between making the minimum payments on a credit card for a few months to get through a rough patch and then paying it all down plus a few dollars in interest, and just pretending all's well until sometime early in the twenty-second century.

We're not trying to create perfect code. I can't stress this enough. No one can achieve perfection, and software developers don't *want* to achieve it. We have to always be aware that there are trade-offs. Do I ship with problems in code sometimes? Yes. I have to. If I didn't, I would go out of business.

When Code Needs to Change

Even the worst-written legacy code can continue to provide value if we simply leave it alone—as long as it doesn't need to change.

This kind of judgment call should be made on a case-by-case basis. Mission-critical software requires different standards than video games. The good news about software is that, unlike physical machines, bits don't wear out. But what about the legacy code that *does* need to be changed or extended?

When software is actually used, people find better ways to use it and that leads to change requests. If you want to support your users in finding more value in the software you've created for them, support them as their needs change by finding ways to safely improve your code.

Now that we know some of the characteristics of good code, use the discipline of refactoring to safely and incrementally change your code to be more maintainable and extendable. Take poorly designed legacy code and apply safe refactoring that gives you the ability to inject mocks and make software testable so you can retrofit unit tests into the code. This safety net will allow you to perform more complex refactoring to safely accommodate new features.

Cleaning up legacy code in this way—making incremental changes, adding tests, and *then* adding new features—allows you to work with legacy code without the fear of introducing new bugs. When you have the right unit test coverage, you can safely drive new development and refactoring from the green bar. This is a much safer and cheaper way to drive changes to software.

As an industry, we have a lot of code—legacy code—that isn't working as well as we need it to work, and that's all but impossible to maintain, let alone extend. But what can we do about it? What *should* we do?

For the most part, nothing.

As an industry, we need to see legacy code not as *time bombs,* but as *land mines.* If code is working, and it doesn't need to be changed or upgraded, then leave it alone. That goes for the vast majority of all the legacy code in the world. Like they say: "If it ain't broke, don't fix it."

As soon as we start mucking around in legacy code we're bound to cause problems. If code is working the way you want it to, keep using it. This is true for most of the existing software in the world. Generally speaking, the code you want to refactor is the code that needs to be changed.

If your code has bugs or you want to add or modify features, it makes sense to go in and make changes to existing code. Changing code is risky and expensive, so be prudent about doing it. But when it does make sense to go out and change code, do so using a methodology that allows it to be done safely. It turns out that the techniques for doing this are the same techniques we've been talking about for writing good-quality new code.

You can refactor existing code just like you refactor new code.

Retrofit Tests into Existing Code

Although this approach can sometimes be a lot more challenging than writing code test-first—because it can require changing existing code so that it's written to be more testable—the overall effect is to improve the maintainability and drop the cost of change to existing code.

Change requests are good. It means that someone cares and wants to see some of our code improved.

When this happens you want to be able to respond and provide new features for existing software so your existing customers can get more benefit from using it. Of course, there's a lot of code out there that no one cares about anymore. That code can quietly rot away, but the bits that are used—the ones customers depend on and that are likely to change—that's the code you want to target for refactoring.

Refactor Bad Code to Learn Good Habits

Refactoring is a discipline that not all developers are currently aware of, but refactoring can also be a craft that can help build good development habits and demonstrate how to build more maintainable code. These are the skills that will always be in high demand for software developers.

Refactoring legacy code sounds boring, but it's actually quite exciting and challenging. It gets far easier with a little practice. When you get good at refactoring, something very interesting happens: you stop writing bad code and following poor development practices and begin *pre-factoring* (see *Prefactoring [Pug05]*), which means writing cleaner code to start with. Refactoring code is one of the fastest ways I know to learn what *not* to do when writing software and what *to* do instead.

Postpone the Inevitable

Our goal as software developers is to create value by building valuable software. This means the software we develop has to create value now and continue to produce value into the future.

In order for software to continue to produce value into the future, the cost of ownership must drop so it's cost-effective to improve and extend software. Make the supportability and maintainability of software a priority, and you'll reduce the cost of ownership for software.

But at some point, software must die. I'm surprised at how long some of the software I've written has survived. I wrote code when I was a kid that I wasn't proud of then but that has lived on in some form to this day.

Software tends to either die on the vine or outlive all of our expectations, and you can never accurately predict when a piece of code is written whether it will be one kind or the other. But we all want our software to be of value as long as it remains alive. The return on investment should be as high as we can make it, while at the same time reduce the cost of ownership.

Refactoring Techniques

As you clean up code and it becomes more testable, it also becomes simpler to extend and drives down the cost of future changes. Here are some techniques I use to refactor code.

Generally, refactoring legacy code starts out at the feature level, so there is some observable behavior that you can write a pinning test against.

Pinning Tests

A *pinning test* is a very coarse test. It may test a single behavior that takes hundreds or thousands of lines of code to produce. Ultimately you want more tests that are smaller tests than this, but start by writing a pinning test for overall behavior so that at least you have some support in place. Then as you make changes to the code, you rerun the pinning test to verify that the end-to-end behavior is still correct.

Since pinning tests are very coarse grain, they have to be run frequently in order to know if the last thing you did affects the code under test. This provides enough of a safety net to perform some of the safer refactorings to allow the addition of seams for injecting dependencies. It effectively decouples objects from the services they use, allowing you to mock out those services so code can be tested in isolation. This makes smaller units of behavior testable and adds finer-grain unit tests to support more complex refactoring.

And that's the way it works, little by little, making small, incremental improvements. Legacy code got the way it is because over time developers have made small changes to the code that degraded its quality. The way to counteract that is by making small changes to the code that *improve* the quality, and then little by little, legacy code will become less of a burden.

Dependency Injection

We talked earlier about the value of separating object creation from object usage. This is a critical step in making code more testable, but it's also important to making code independently deployable. When the construction of an object graph is separated from its usage, you can inject dependencies as needed without creating tight coupling in a system. This is a fundamental technique in object-oriented programs.

Frameworks that use this technique, like Pivotal Software's open source Spring and Red Hat's Hibernate, are called *dependency injection frameworks*.

The idea is simple: instead of creating the objects we use ourselves, we let the framework create them for us and inject them into our code.[2,3]

Injecting dependencies as opposed to creating them decouples objects from the services they use. This makes software more testable as well as more extendable. Instead of injecting the real dependency, inject a mock dependency to more easily test your code. Dependency injection also helps make code more maintainable. It helps centralize business decisions and simplify object usage. Generally, one of the first places I go to look in order to understand a new system is object instantiation. I look to the factories, dependency injection frameworks, or wherever object instantiation is happening. This will tell me a lot about a system and how to improve it.

System Strangling

When I need to replace a component over time without bringing the system down, I often use *system strangling*, which was first described in 2004 by Martin Fowler.[4] In this technique I basically wrap an old service with my own new one and let it grow slowly around the old one until eventually the old system is *strangled*.

Create a new interface for a new service that's meant to replace an old service. Then ask new clients to use the new interface, even though it simply points to the old service. This at least stops the bleeding and allows new clients to use a new interface that will eventually call cleaner code.

Now you can refactor the existing system at your leisure until the old interface is no more than a thin shell that calls into the newly refactored code. Choose to support legacy clients, or ask them to refactor, in order to use the new interface and retire the legacy system entirely. System strangling is a valuable technique for refactoring legacy code while it's still in production.

Branch by Abstraction

The last technique I'll mention here is another one from Martin Fowler he calls *branch by abstraction*.[5] Despite its name, this is a technique for version control designed to help *eliminate* branching. The idea is to extract an interface

---

2. Spring. http://spring.io
3. Hibernate. http://hibernate.org
4. Fowler, Martin. *Martin Fowler* (blog). "Strangler Application." June 2004. http://www.martinfowler.com/bliki/StranglerApplication.html
5. Fowler, Martin. *Martin Fowler* (blog). "Branch by Abstraction." January 2014. http://martinfowler.com/bliki/BranchByAbstraction.html

for the code you want to change and write a new implementation, but keep the old implementation active while you build it, using feature flags to hide the feature that's under development from the user while you're building it.

When you're ready, you can flip the switch on the feature and replace the old implementation with the new one. This is a simple and pretty obvious approach, but it eliminates the need for version branching in software—a real big problem in a lot of software development shops. And as we've seen, as soon as we start feature branching we postpone integration and are basically doing Waterfall development.

Sometimes systems are so tightly coupled that you can't break dependencies in one area of the code without breaking dependencies many other places. In these situations there's a book by Ola Ellnestam and Daniel Brolund called *The Mikado Method [BE12]* to help extract intertwined dependencies.

Refactor to Accommodate Change

Certainly, there are a lot of other techniques for working with legacy code. The basic idea, however, is simply this: clean it up, make it more maintainable and easier to understand, and then retrofit in tests to make it safer to change. Then, and only then, with the safety of unit tests, refactor the code in more significant ways.

I call refactoring a discipline but it still has a long way to go. We need to develop it as a discipline that shows standard ways of transforming code. I would much rather have a methodology that shows me how to safely and repeatedly change code that I could share with other developers than to just have an intuitive feel that I couldn't express to others on how to go about fixing code, even if that's more efficient.

The goal of refactoring software is to make the things the customer wants to change easy to change. This is not done by trying to read the customer's mind or predict the future, but by following supportability standards and practices that can accommodate changes to code when needed. This includes having a suite of unit tests, modeling the domain accurately, calling out abstractions, writing CLEAN code, and following other good technical practices. When you do these things, it takes the sting out of change so you're more able to go in and make changes to code and give your customers more of what they want.

Refactor to the Open-Closed

These are five words that changed my life. It's a way to help get out of this rut of legacy code. Refactoring is changing the design without changing the external behavior. *The Open-Closed Principle* says software entities should be "open for extension but closed for modification." In other words, strive to make adding any new feature a matter of adding new code and minimally changing existing code. Avoid changing existing code because that's when new bugs are likely to be introduced.

Refactoring to the Open-Closed is a way to add features to software safely and cost-effectively. Always make every change in a two-step process. First, refactor the code you want to extend so that it can accommodate the new feature. That doesn't mean adding the new feature yet, but creating a space for it in the software by adding abstractions for it or defining an interface for it...something like that. When unit tests are in place and you refactor code to accommodate a new feature, you're doing it safely, in the green, and if you make a mistake your tests tell you immediately. This is a safe and cost-effective way of making changes to code.

Once the code has been refactored to accommodate the new feature, the first step, the refactoring step, is done. Then go to the next step, which is the enhancement step. First, write a failing test that specifies the new behavior you want to implement. Next add the new behavior and turn the one failing test green, doing it in an open, additive way. You're only adding code because we already changed the code in the previous refactoring step. You're adding code without having to make a lot of changes in the code, and because of that it's safe. Finally, refactor your newly added code to make sure it's understandable and maintainable.

If you try to do all of these steps together at the same time, which is what most developers do, it's easy to get confused and do the wrong thing—and pay a big price for that. But doing these steps separately and with the support of unit test coverage makes changing software much simpler and less risky.

I always make every change to code in a two-step process. I do this when I build features using TDD. When I need to go back and add a feature to an existing system I use the same techniques. Many of the techniques that we touched on in all the practices applied to working with legacy code as well as writing new code. Once we understand what good code looks like, it's easier to get a sense of what we should strive for when refactoring legacy code.

Refactor to Support Changeability

Changeability in code does not happen by accident. It has to be intentionally created in new code, or carefully introduced in refactoring legacy code, by following good developer principles and practices.

This is true in any profession. A doctor doesn't just magically heal her patient. And though sometimes patients heal on their own, software never writes or rewrites itself. You have to make the computer do what you want it to do.

Supporting changeability in code means finding the right abstractions and making sure code is well encapsulated. Ultimately, changeability comes from understanding what you're modeling and imbuing your model with that understanding—with those distinctions—so it's accurate and consistent.

These practices don't do design for you. TDD helps with design, but we can't just turn our brains off and let TDD come up with code. TDD is a tool to help you identify the sequence of efficiently building changeable code, and sequencing is absolutely critical.

One thing science may have over art is that there's very often a sequence to science, a process, or a procedure. It's like cooking from a recipe. We can all start with the same recipe, tweak it in different ways, and come up with all sorts of interesting variations on the same dish. But we're still sharing certain basic practices—this is how you sauté something, chopping vegetables before cooking them tends to work better, you don't want to serve raw chicken, and so on.

Sequence is critically important in software development. While every problem is different and often requires a different approach to find a solution, general guidelines exist for sequencing approaches to solving software problems, some of which are not totally intuitive, like writing the test first or implementing the design last.

Do It Right the Second Time

TDD uses concrete examples to define behavior. Driving development from concrete examples is easier than thinking abstractly. It helps build more stable interfaces, and when we have two or three examples it's far easier to generalize in the code than if we have a single example. I have a favorite saying:

Do it right the *second* time.

Developers sometimes look at me like I'm crazy when I say this. We've always been told to do it right the *first* time.

But when you do it right the first time—or *think* you've done it right the first time—you're setting yourself up for a lot of extra work. It's very hard to generalize with one example. Write concretely the first time if you only have one example, but when you get the second or third example, it's much easier to generalize. Now you can see what's the same about the examples and what's different. You can generalize, and then you can find the right abstractions.

Triangulation is a familiar practice from celestial navigation. Having multiple points on the horizon or multiple stars to get a fix on results in a much more accurate measurement than just a single point. The same thing is true in coding.

If you have a very complex algorithm, some behavior that you're not quite sure how to create in all its glory, create a couple of examples. Typically with two, or at the most three, examples you'll be able to infer what the algorithm really should be. This is far easier than trying to guess at it with just one example.

With two examples I can start to generalize each step and that tells me the right abstractions to use. So if I only have a single example of something then I'll generally code it up concretely using test-first, of course. That gives me the right unit tests to drive the development of the behavior I want. It also gives me a safety net to refactor in the green when I get a second example.

Software is *soft*, and by leveraging this fact we can build better, more flexible code more easily. That's the name of the game.

But having to get it right the first time adds a lot of pressure. And that's true across the board. Knowing you can always go back, you can always edit, you can always clean things up—you can always *refactor*—gives you an enormous amount of freedom.

Study refactoring to best know how to go from one design to another. Most of the time that's trivial, and when you understand that you can transform one design into another, it means you don't have to find the right design up front. You can try anything and then later, when you know what the *right* design should be, you can refactor to improve your design.

It can seem like a weird strategy when we're used to certainty. It recognizes that we're living in an ever-changing world of unknowns. But by getting comfortable with an approach like this, much better code can be built much faster and you won't need all the requirements in to get started. It's quite freeing, which is why I've found it resonates with developers.

Let's Get Practical

Here are some ways to put these ideas into practice.

Seven Strategies for Helping You Justify Refactoring

Refactoring gives developers another chance to improve their designs and often gives management a cheaper and less risky way to ready an existing system for adding new features. Here are seven strategies to help you justify refactoring code.

To learn an existing system

Refactoring code is a great way to learn the code and to embed what's learned into the code. For example, replacing or wrapping a poorly named method with a better named method gives us the opportunity to improve the code's readability. At the same time, you're learning how a system works and embedding that knowledge into the source code, in this case by providing a better name.

To make small improvements

Safe refactorings are the subset of refactorings that are relatively straightforward to perform. Many are automated by development tools to do things like easily rename, extract, and move methods and classes within a project. I constantly use these refactorings as I'm writing code so that it continues to reflect my evolving understanding of the parts I'm building.

To retrofit tests in legacy code

All refactoring reduces the cost of four things: understanding the code later, adding tests, accommodating new features, and more refactoring. As you refactor code, you'll find opportunities to improve the design and add more unit tests. As you add better tests, you gain more confidence to perform more involved refactorings, which reveals even more opportunities to write better tests, and so on.

Clean up as you go

Refactoring should be something you do all the time. Coding is often a process of discovering what works. You may not know the right approach as you're figuring things out, so as you learn more you get the opportunity to improve your code, update names, and so forth. This is vital for keeping your code easy to work with. If you do TDD, you know one of the key steps in the TDD process is to refactor code once you get an implementation working. Doing so improves supportability, reduces the cost of maintenance, and increases extensibility.

Redesign an implementation once you know more

Even with continuous refactoring, it's still possible to accumulate technical debt during development. When you get new information that changes your existing design, or you need to implement a new feature that your current design can't handle, it may be time to refactor in the large. This can include a major redesign and reimplementation of code to make it simpler to add new features later.

Clean up before moving on

Once you get something working, before moving on to the next task refactor the existing code to make it more supportable. Now that you know what each method is really doing, ensure they're named well and clearly express their intent. Make sure the code is easy to read and well laid out. Break out small methods from larger ones, and extract classes when necessary.

Refactor to learn what not to do

The majority of software in production today has accumulated much technical debt and is in bad need of refactoring. This may seem like a daunting task, and it can be, but refactoring code can be pretty fun. I find I learn a lot when I refactor code, and after a long session of cleaning up other people's mistakes (or my own) I tend not to commit the same acts of irresponsibility when I write new code. The more I refactor, the better developer I become.

Refactoring is all about reducing risk and waste. High-performing development teams can appear to spend up to half their time refactoring code, but they're also improving their designs and building in supportability, which can quickly repay the effort. Since code is read ten times more often than it's written, refactoring to clean code can pay for itself very quickly.

Seven Strategies for When to Refactor

Given that there's more code that could be refactored than our industry can handle, we have to decide what code should be refactored and what code doesn't need it. If production software works fine and doesn't need to be extended, there's no need to refactor the code. Refactoring code is risky and expensive, so we want to make sure the ends justify the means. Here are seven strategies for when to refactor code.

When critical code is not well maintained

Most software is in a state that makes it unsafe to refactor. If code is in production and working, touching it—even in seemingly minor ways—can break it in unexpected ways. For this reason, it's often wise not to touch legacy code. But there are times when critical code is not well understood and it becomes enough of a liability to warrant a cleanup effort. In these cases, retrofitting tests to support more complex refactoring can be useful.

When the only person who understands the code is becoming unavailable
The software you write should be easy for anyone on your team to work with, but sometimes existing code has "experts" who are the only people who can work with it. This is not a good place for a company to be. If code needs to be maintained or updated, the larger cost of cleaning code up later can be avoided by having the key person spend time cleaning up the code before moving on.

When new information reveals a better design
Requirements, and our understanding of them, are constantly changing. When the opportunity for a better design presents itself, and the benefits outweigh the costs, then refactoring code can be a good option. This is an ongoing process that helps keep software clean and up-to-date. Improving design through a series of refactorings can be a safe and effective way to keep software maintainable.

When fixing bugs
Some bugs are typos, whereas other bugs represent flaws in the design. Often, a bug in code is the symptom of a flaw in the development process. At the very least a bug represents a missing test in the system that should have been there. It might be missing because it was difficult to write, in which case we can refactor the code to make the test easier to write and then write the test. Then, when we fix the bug, the test passes and all is right with the world again.

When adding new features
The cheapest, safest way to add features to a system that cannot already accommodate them is to first refactor the code so it can accommodate the new feature, and then once the code is refactored, add the new feature. We never want to get into a situation where we're making several kinds of changes to code at the same time. Refactoring code to accommodate new features often involves adding abstractions and interfaces that make it easier to enhance a system with new features in the future. After refactoring, adding the feature to the code should be straightforward.

When you need to document legacy code
Some code is hard to understand and can be helped by some simple refactoring and cleanup before documenting. The purpose of creating documentation is to increase supportability, and this is also a major reason for refactoring.

When it's cheaper than a rewrite

It's almost never wise to abandon a legacy system in production for a total rewrite. Rewritten applications often end up with as much technical debt as the original. If you don't do things fundamentally different when you do a rewrite, you'll likely end up with the same problems you had before. Refactoring is a safe, systemized way of cleaning up code a bit at a time while the system remains in production.

Refactoring is expensive and there's a lot of code that needs it. In order to make the best choices with your limited resources, you have to be selective with what you refactor. When you need to touch code—to fix bugs or add features, for example—it's usually a good opportunity to refactor. By taking these refactoring opportunities, you keep code more maintainable and easier to work with.

Retrospective

Refactor Legacy Code as needed when code needs to change. Use refactoring techniques to help form a discipline around changing code. As a profession we need to move from assuring quality to creating quality by refactoring code to improve maintainability and drop the cost of ownership for the software we write.

In this chapter, we discovered…

- Learn effective ways of cleaning up code to pay off technical debt.

- Separating accommodating a new feature from adding the feature vastly simplifies the task and reduces the risk of introducing bugs.

- Clean up code more effectively and understand why it's important to improve the design of software as it's being built.

- When you get good at refactoring code, you start to write cleaner code naturally.

Refactoring, and the skills necessary to do it well, are important for cleaning up legacy code. Refactoring is a first step before changing or updating existing legacy code, as well as for cleaning up new code so it doesn't end up as legacy code. It's also a highly efficient way to learn an existing codebase.

CHAPTER 14

Learning from Our Legacy

So we've talked about writing new code and what good, maintainable code looks like. Solid principles and practices from object-oriented programming and Extreme Programming will begin to help developers write code that's far less expensive to maintain and extend. As more maintainable practices for software development are adopted, the cost of software maintenance will drop, and that will allow users to get more value from their software over its lifetime. This points to a bright future, but what about *right now*?

What about all of the existing legacy code out there? What about software that wasn't built with maintainable development practices?

Despite the fact that I'm responding to a serious, current problem, this book has mostly focused on writing new code because I want us all to understand what good code looks like—what kinds of things we should all be looking for to make software maintainable. We can't refactor legacy code to something better without knowing what that something better is.

We also looked at how we got here: sitting on top of a mountain of legacy code that developers are essentially scared to touch.

And unfortunately, the legacy code crisis is likely to get worse before it gets better. As we've seen in Chapter 2, *Out of CHAOS*, on page 19, ineffective software development processes cost businesses at least tens of billions of dollars every year in the United States alone. People have lost their *lives* because of poor-quality software, and unfortunately that's not likely to change anytime soon.

Of course, there's no easy way to go back and retrofit all existing software to conform to the practices we've discussed, or any other set of practices. That ship has long since sailed. But these nine practices can help us move forward as a profession, writing much better software from here on.

So then what if everybody starts writing code using these nine practices right now so that every new software package is more maintainable? At what point does all that old legacy code work its way through the system and disappear?

The software industry is a big ship and it takes a long time to turn a big ship. The way most companies build software isn't likely to change in the near future. Scrum was supposed to support doing Extreme Programming. At least that's what Ken Schwaber and Mike Beedle say on the cover of their book *Agile Software Development with Scrum. [SB01]* But Agile and Scrum have been turned into a management practice and much less emphasis has been placed on the technical practices.

While companies may be adopting some Agile technical practices, *mastering* these practices to produce great software represents a goal that has so far eluded most companies that attempt to adopt Agile.

Software development is hard to do, and developers have to get a lot of things right before they can produce viable software. It can be a struggle.

Object-oriented programming has been popular since the 1990s, but few take advantage of the capabilities of object-oriented programming to increase supportability. I've reviewed millions of lines of code for my clients, most of which was written in good object-oriented languages like Java or C#, but the vast majority of this code—and I'm talking about code that's used to run the enterprise systems that drive major industries across the globe—is highly procedural, redundant, and of poor quality, and so it's difficult to maintain.

Practices can be introduced, but those practices can take a while to reach the mainstream, and both developers and managers must understand the underlying *principles* in order to use the practices correctly.

Agile and Extreme Programming were started *by* software developers *for* software developers. In my professional experience, the technical practices are at least as important as the Agile management practices, yet in many organizations little attention is placed on them. You can get some benefit by doing the Agile management practices without the Agile technical practices, but the real value of Agile happens with the application of the technical practices of Extreme Programming.

I've had a lot of success teaching traditional Waterfall development teams some of the Extreme Programming practices like test-first development and emergent design. They've have had great success with those practices, even though their development was happening within a Waterfall framework. If the synchronization points of an organization seem to be working well in their development process, even if it's a Waterfall process, I usually don't have to introduce many of the Agile management practices.

One of the challenges of bringing Agile to existing organizations is that many organizations are set up hierarchically, with gates and processes that closely resemble Waterfall. Bringing their IT departments into an Agile world can be challenging, but I find that virtually every team I work with needs to build more maintainable software more rapidly. The nine practices we've discussed in this book are great for that.

I've taught Agile design and test-first development to developers at Microsoft for many years, and many of them operate within a pseudo-Waterfall process. It doesn't matter how they get requirements. When requirements come in, their developers—some of them at least—build it test-first. This gives them the benefit of being able to make their software highly changeable and responsive to new requirements introduced later in the development cycle.

The technical practices of Extreme Programming like test-first development, refactoring, pairing, design skills, and continuous integration are key to successful software development regardless of the methodology you use. They provide a context to understand and accurately model domains.

Better, Faster, Cheaper

We started with a look at statistics and studies that pointed out the disturbingly high defect rate in our industry and the exorbitant cost of maintaining software. Now we've had a chance to closely examine some new ideas, fresh approaches, and practices that can help drag us out of those doldrums. But Extreme Programming, Lean, and Scrum have been in the mix for a little while now, and many teams have at least been trying to take a new approach to leave the Waterfall world behind.

So how are they doing?

Quantitative Software Management (QSM) Associates, via the Cutter Consortium, looked at the effects of adopting Agile practices and found that large teams trying to meet fast schedules on Waterfall projects showed higher defects, sometimes four times higher than average. High-maturity XP and Scrum teams were the best performers. These project teams showed defects that were 30%–50% lower than average.[1]

---

1. Mah, Michael. "How Agile Projects Measure Up, and What This Means to You," Cutter Consortium, 2008. http://www.cutter.com/offers/measureup.html

In *Realizing Quality Improvement Through Test Driven Development: Results and Experiences of Four Industrial Teams*,[2] Nachiappan Nagappan, E. Michael Maximilien, Thirumalesh Bhat, and Laurie Williams stated that all of the teams they studied who practiced TDD demonstrated a significant drop in defect density: "40% for the IBM team; 60–90% for the Microsoft teams." They concluded that TDD can "significantly reduce the defect density of developed software without significant productivity reduction of the development team."

At Microsoft, Thirumalesh Bhat and Nachiappan Nagappan looked at TDD practices in the Windows and MSN divisions in their paper *Evaluating the Efficacy of Test-Driven Development: Industrial Case Studies*.[3] They observed a significant increase in quality of the code (greater than two times) for projects developed using TDD compared to similar projects that didn't use TDD developed in the same organization.

Boby George and Laurie Williams of North Carolina State University studied two groups of software developers, both working on a "small Java program," and found that the TDD developers produced higher-quality code, which "passed 18% more functional black box test cases." Even though the TDD team spent 16% more time in development, the TDD developers' test cases achieved a mean of "98% method, 92% statement and 97% branch coverage." And when they spoke to the developers themselves, they found that 92% of developers believed that "TDD yields higher quality code."[4]

People will tell you that doing TDD is good for reducing defects, but at a price. You'll write twice as much test code as production code so people assume it will slow you down, but there's a false assumption here. It assumes that the limiting factor in software development is typing.

But that isn't true. Ask any developer; look at any project. Developers spend most of their time in places that *aren't* coding: reading specifications, writing documentation, sitting in meetings, and the biggest time sink—debugging.

2. Nagappan, Nachiappan, Maximilien, E. Michael, Bhat, Thirumalesh, and Williams, Laurie. *Realizing Quality Improvement Through Test-driven Development: Results and Experiences of Four Industrial Teams*. Springer Science & Business Media, 2008. http://link.springer.com/article/10.1007%2Fs10664-008-9062-z

3. Bhat, Thirumalesh, and Nagappan, Nachiappan. "Evaluating the Efficacy of Test-Driven Development: Industrial Case Studies." http://dl.acm.org/citation.cfm?id=1159787

4. George, Boby, and Williams, Laurie. "An Initial Investigation of Test Driven Development in Industry." Department of Computer Science, North Carolina State University. http://staff.unak.is/andy/MScTestingMaintenance/Homeworks/STMHeima7TestDrivenDevelopment.pdf

But doing test-first development removes the need for most of these activities and replaces it with what developers love to do more than anything else: writing code. Tests *are* code but not just any code. Tests are *vital* code because they drive the specification of the functionality being created.

Improving productivity doesn't have to be at the expense of reducing quality. In fact, they often go hand-in-hand. In *Exploring Extreme Programming in Context: An Industrial Case Study*[5] Lucas Layman, Laurie Williams, and Lynn Cunningham found "a 50% increase in productivity, a 65% improvement in pre-release quality, and a 35% improvement in post-release quality" when they compared two releases of the same product. One release was completed just prior to the team's adoption of the XP methodology, and the other was completed after approximately two years of XP use.

The QSM/Cutter Consortium study looked closely at Follet's XP practices and found "a dramatic schedule reduction of almost five months compared to industry norms, with twice the level of quality (half the defects)." Not only that, but Follet managed to save US $1.3 million. Multiplying those savings across six releases is a total cost savings of $7.8 million.

Empirical data on the effect of TDD on code quality is sorely lacking in the literature. In one paper I found called "Quantitatively Evaluating Test-Driven Development by Applying Object-Oriented Quality Metrics to Open Source Projects,"[6] Ron Hilton looked at code quality metrics for a range of open source projects that used TDD and non-TDD approaches. He found that in projects that used test-driven development, the level of cohesion increased by 21.33%, the level of coupling improved by 10.05%, and the level of complexity was reduced by 30.98%.

With so much potential to improve, one would think that most companies would adopt XP practices, but the word hasn't gotten out yet. In the *2013 State of Scrum Report* 40% of companies surveyed use Scrum, 15% use Kanban, 11% use Lean, and only 7% use Extreme Programming. There is a learning curve involved and it takes effort to master these practices, but the potential payoff is real and can be significant.

---

5. Layman, Lucas, Williams, Laurie, and Cunningham, Lynn. "Exploring Extreme Programming in Context: An Industrial Case Study." http://dl.acm.org/citation.cfm?id=1025140

6. Hilton, Ron. "Quantitatively Evaluating Test-Driven Development by Applying Object-Oriented Quality Metrics to Open Source Projects." http://www.nomachetejuggling.com/2009/12/13/quantitatively-evaluating-test-driven-development/

Don't Spend Money You Don't Have To

There are many little mistakes that we make simply because we're human. But when we make a little mistake in the hyper-literal world of the computer, it can turn into a big mistake. Computers don't know what you *meant* to do. They aren't interpreting or translating, or taking code as suggestions or guidelines—they're blindly following very specific instructions. So when you build in the specific instruction to make sure this is working, and test it constantly as you go, you can—surprisingly often—just backspace and fix any bug instantly and then move on. A few seconds have gone by.

But on many software development teams, Agile or otherwise, that don't practice TDD and instead rely on a separate QA process that might take two weeks before developers get feedback on their code, that same simple bug could be a showstopper. It could take the better part of a day for developers to re-familiarize themselves with code they wrote a few weeks ago in order to fix a bug. If it's true that *time is money*—and when we're paying developers, QA engineers, and other people, then, yeah, time *is* money—fixing a bug in a few seconds is cheaper than fixing the same bug over the course of a day or two of concerted effort.

When we focus on *creating* quality through good developer practices rather than solely focusing on *assuring* quality in a separate QA process, we can turn that dynamic around. We can focus on supportability. And that's the only way to decrease the cost of ownership for the software we write. CLEAN, testable code costs less to maintain and extend. That's the bottom line.

If the things we've gone over in this book help remove the overhead of requirements—which take a third to a half of development time—and have addressed horrible integration issues and the whole debugging phase—in which we spend another third of our time—then we're not adding the time it takes to write tests. We're *gaining back more than half of our time and effort.*

That being the case, would you be willing to take half of that gain and reinvest it back into creating quality by cleaning code through refactoring? If you're willing to do that, you're still ahead of the game over traditional development and will end up with a far less expensive product to maintain.

I'm not saying you should entirely eliminate QA. Depending on the project, you may need a big QA effort or none at all. But regardless, you should always focus on creating quality through good developer practices and strive for automating all testing needed to validate a release candidate. Doing these things will significantly reduce the cost of creating and maintaining code.

Walk the Straight and Narrow

There's a straight and narrow path of understanding in software development where everything makes sense. Strive to walk that straight and narrow path because as soon as things stop making sense, you know you've gone off track.

And we don't have the freedom to get even a little bit off track. That one little bit can destroy the whole thing, and destroy it way down the road.

One of the biggest oversights software developers make is failing to identify entities in designs. When entities are missing in the model and you don't know where to put behavior, the model starts to skew. The design then becomes different than your understanding, which is different from the thing you're trying to model, and that's where you get all these bugs, all the poor code...all sorts of problems. That's why I always want to drive back to understanding, in order to be *active* rather than *reactive*. This sense of scrambling around trying to plug holes "putting out fires," which we all hear in the corporate workplace all the time, has always been frustrating for me.

Software development can't be a reactive process. It has to be a thoughtful process, but that doesn't mean it has to be slow. In fact, writing the test first is really not going to slow you down. I know because I've seen it happen so many times. Do this process well, understand it, and go through the learning curve—and there's always a learning curve.

I know developers who are much more productive doing test-first development than they were before. They begin to realize it's not about more typing. What slows us down in software development is debugging. It's writing, reading, and interpreting requirements, and all the stuff that goes into a software development process that isn't writing software. Properly doing TDD helps address these challenges and replaces non-coding activities with writing unit tests. As we've said before, tests are code, so doing TDD means that developers are coding—and therefore providing value—more of the time.

Here's the challenge:

It's hard to learn how to do these practices properly. Good books on the subject aren't plentiful. There is a learning curve. I've seen teams struggle twelve months or more on their own trying to learn these practices or fail to do them effectively because they don't understand the distinctions we've discussed here in this book.

Understanding not just *what* these practices are but *why* they are important gets teams on a fast track for mastering them. Once teams get on a fast track, if they work with another developer who's experienced using these practices effectively and is able to help get them up to speed quickly, then typically it's only a few months before they're even more productive doing test-first development.

But then the real challenges begin when they start to look back on the mass of code they wrote before adopting TDD. Digging themselves out of a hole that may have taken years to get into will typically take years. But the good news is that as they start digging themselves out and paying down on technical debt, they begin to experience becoming *really* productive.

Improve the Software Profession

We need to understand what's important and what's unimportant in software development. We need to focus on sharing principles and practices that are learnable and understandable in order to build the discipline of software development—to make it a true profession.

This is true in every other form of engineering. Skilled tradespeople like electricians or plumbers follow time-honored standards and practices, and the people who created these standards and practices were not solely looking for the fastest and most efficient way of achieving results. They were looking for other factors as well, not the least of which is public safety. They have to properly tap into a municipal water supply and sewer system or the power grid, and those standards are clearly communicated and actionable.

Electricians won't charge you as much to install a single light fixture as they would to rewire a whole house. We all know that some physical things are difficult to change and other things are easy.

But in the less tangible virtual world of software, most nondevelopers have a hard time grasping this and find it difficult to identify the things that are easy to change and those that are difficult.

The software development community sort of closed down in the 1990s. New techniques for building better software came to be considered a competitive edge, but this really isn't a healthy approach. Companies should focus on keeping their proprietary software proprietary but not their methodologies. We should share methodologies across our industry. That's the only way our industry can improve quickly. It works for other industries and it can work for software development as well. Fortunately, I see some of the biggest companies freely sharing methodologies.

The world is looking to us in the software industry to step up and the individuals within the industry—within the *profession* of software development—have to step up and support one another. We have to regulate ourselves. If we fail to do this, the government might try to step in and regulate us—and that would be even more disastrous.

It's unethical for doctors at one hospital to keep information that could save lives from doctors in another hospital. The same thing is true for software developers. Some of the stuff we do actually does save lives, and that's what we most need to share. If we raise the level of professionalism across our industry, it'll come back to us in positive ways. We can share methodologies, patterns, principles, and practices. We don't have to share trade secrets or proprietary details.

Software always has and always will live in the world of the unknown and in a constant state of technological, practical, and theoretical evolution. Software development is a young industry, but though we're growing up quickly, we still have a long way to go.

There are no easy answers here, but let's leverage our unique skills to address these problems. Let's open a debate and share standards. Let's keep an open mind and value the things that are important to us.

Ultimately, building a healthy industry, just like building a healthy civilization, requires each and every one of us to participate. Institutions are only as effective as their members, and already we're beginning to see a new kind of institution emerge that supports software development in ways we couldn't ever dream of before. Open Source and Creative Commons licensing as well as tools like GitHub[7] provide free access to tools and libraries. We *have* the infrastructure to transform our industry. It's just a matter of having the desire to use it. And it is happening.

How do developers share skills and techniques? How do we learn from one another most efficiently and effectively? Developers need more venues for sharing ideas and learning from one another. We need more relevant curricula in schools, and we need other places for professionals to go outside of schools to learn. We must place higher value on development skills and make software development a profession that attracts and retains the brightest people by paying them what they're worth.

We—and by "we" I mean everyone involved in the software industry—have made significant progress in the last few decades. We've built more maintain-

---

7.   GitHub, https://github.com

able code not just through Extreme Programming but through a lot of things that are far less extreme, such as design patterns, the software craftsmanship movement, the clean code movement, and many others. So what are we learning?

The fact that all of this information is compatible is very encouraging. Design wisdom reinforces itself, and its consistency is a good sign. All the principles and practices that we talked about in this book are highly compatible, and they all support the notion of building more testable software that's cheaper to maintain and extend. This shows that we're starting to figure things out and beginning to understand how to build software more cost effectively.

Software is finally coming into its own and we are learning its unique lessons. We're learning effective ways of building software, automating the rote and redundant tasks, and improving on overall efficiency so we can focus on the creative aspects of our work. The future is getting brighter, but we're not out of the woods yet.

In the future, we might be tempted to blame software for upcoming disasters, but this is like blaming the rivets on the *Titanic* or the tiles on the space shuttle. Breakage happens and usually it happens at its weakest points, but that doesn't tell the whole story. TDD, pairing, and other technical practices can help, but again, there is no one-size-fits-all approach for software development. In many situations object-oriented programming and test-driven development *shouldn't* be used.

These are, after all, just tools. Tools do not define a profession. They're simply a means to an end.

A lot of problems in the world are procedural. Lots of things are hierarchical, but many things aren't. We need a way to model the things that aren't hierarchical or procedural, and several paradigms exist for doing this in software development. We've been primarily focused on just the object-oriented paradigm in this book, but there are many paradigms in software development, and with the advent of massively parallel computing, there are even more. But paradigms are, again, just tools. Agile is just a tool. So I really want to drop terms like Agile and Scrum and just say:

We are software developers, developing software the best we can with the tools that we have currently available.

Beyond Agile

When something comes along that's better than Agile, I'll be the first to jump on it. Even though I'm an "Agilist," it doesn't mean I've abandoned all my old practices. I still draw on a lot of the skills I developed in my youth.

It'll take some years before most of what I'm talking about in this book becomes mainstream. But the value of test-first development is so great that most software development *will* be done that way. It may not look exactly like TDD looks to us now, and it may not use the same tools or be within the same language, but some form of separate verification of code as it's written will be incorporated into the software development process, perhaps even into our programming languages and IDEs.

The benefits of doing it are so great it'll simply make sense to do it this way. Building software the way most developers do today will be looked upon in the future the way we look upon people who write code in machine language. Sure, you could do it, but why would you ever want to? Toggling binary switches to enter op codes is a laborious and tedious process. That's what compilers are for, and catching mistakes that we humans inevitably make is what unit tests are for. But the bottom line is that only people can create software.

Far from being a menial job, software development requires a great deal of skill and creativity to do successfully. If we want to improve the software we create, we have to raise our standards and increase the rewards for those who can achieve those standards. If we do this, people will show up who will rise to the occasion. We can make of it whatever we wish, and this is truer for software development than for anything else. Software is a product of pure thought. It goes right from our head, through our fingers, and into the computer.

And it runs everything.

No matter what business you're in—whether it's banking, insurance, trucking, or finance—you're in the software business. Software runs your business like it runs all businesses, and the software that businesses develop often turns out to be the "secret sauce" for their competitive edge.

Software is at the heart of everything. It's our society's *deus ex machina*. It either enables or inhibits us. So we all have a vested interest in seeing it improve and become more valuable. Yet the software we build today radically underutilizes our resources. We've been so constrained in our recent past that we don't often pay attention to creating detailed, accurate models. We build models that are space efficient or that run fast, and because we haven't been trained in how to understand and model domains accurately, the software that we tend to build works for what we intended it for but it's difficult to repurpose, even though, as it turns out, we do a lot of repurposing in the lifetime of software.

When we try to take shortcuts and not build accurate models, our understanding tends to go astray. We miss the big picture, and when we forget the why, things start to become rote.

Embody Understanding

There is no formula for writing good software and I don't think there ever will be—just like there's no formula for writing a good book or writing a song or a screenplay or painting a painting. There are only guidelines you can follow, techniques you can apply, rules you can learn (and then break), and practices you can use.

All of these are just tools, and as with anything, the results you get depend on the skills you apply and how you *wield* the tools. And the more powerful the tool, the easier it is to misapply. You can cut more wood with a chainsaw than you can with a handsaw. You can also hurt yourself much more easily. This is one physical metaphor that holds true in the virtual domain. The more powerful the tool, the easier it is to misapply, and so we have to be very careful with the tools we use and make sure we're applying them well.

We're on the verge of enormous breakthroughs in the physical sciences. Existing quantum computers provide trillions of processors and new technologies on the horizon promise to dwarf even these breakthroughs. Physical sciences are expanding in unparalleled proportions, but it seems that in the virtual sciences—in software development—we've been stuck. We still build software in largely the same way we did for the last half century. Assemblers, compilers, and even object-oriented programming languages haven't fundamentally shifted the way we design and build software.

Test-driven development represents another small shift in the way we build software, and many more shifts will likely occur. We're going to *need* many more shifts if we're going to take advantage of some of these new physical computers. If software is to keep up with hardware, we have to be willing to grow exponentially, and that means, among other things, orders of magnitude fewer errors and greater reliability than we currently have.

The most exciting frontiers in software are yet to come. The software we write today will be considered rudimentary by tomorrow's standards. To solve really difficult problems like being able to model the weather or provide some level of intelligent systems is far beyond the reach of current software technology.

When I was in my early twenties and just starting out in this industry, we used to believe that thinking computers were just a few short years away. Today, we recognize that we're *not* in the golden age of software. We're more like in the Stone Age of software. But we're growing up rapidly and going through a mini-Renaissance. It may take another fifty years to realize the vision of artificial intelligence—or five hundred years.

The next step in our industry is to consolidate and build the foundation. Before we can reach for the stars, we have to firmly plant ourselves on the ground. Software has to become significantly more reliable than it is today, and in order for that to happen, we have to put more value on reliability. To program these new computers that are coming up and to solve difficult problems, we have to conceive of and deliver software very differently than we do today. We can't rush to it. On the contrary, we have to step back and reach effective means of *understanding*. That's what good software does.

It embodies understanding.

The Courage to Grow

We tend to do the same things over and over, even when the results are not what we want. We do this not because we're insane, but because the unknown is so scary. We fear the unknown with good cause. Chaos is hard to deal with, so we tend to stick with what we know, even if it's not ideal.

But it's only in the unknown that something new can be discovered—something no one else has found. Going there takes courage. It may seem strange to consider courage to be one of the greatest qualities of great thinkers, but it is. Courage comes in many forms. As Leo Rosten, author of the book *Passions and Prejudices [Ros78]*, once said, "Those who do not know fear are not really brave, for courage is the capacity to confront what can be imagined." The greater our imagination, the greater our courage must be.

Courage is not only about being willing to face our fears. We need courage to face the possibility of success as well as failure. Anything that threatens the status quo can be scary on a subconscious level. To overcome fear we can't just reason with ourselves; we have to *feel* safe. Words of encouragement can help, but when addressing subconscious fears it's far better to speak the language of the subconscious—with imagery and metaphor.

By recalling a time when we were in a similar situation and survived, the mind can put fear in its place. And in the worst-case scenario, when I'm really scared and can't shake it, I just take my fears with me and do what I was going to do anyway. Fear is a defense mechanism. By respecting the message it brings us, we can help defuse its paralysis.

I want us to have the courage to take the right approach, and so much depends on our understanding of why it is important. Honestly, I could teach an experienced software developer those nine practices in a few hours. We could write it all out in ten pages. But just knowing *what* to do is not enough. We have to know *when* to do it, *how* to do it, but most important, *why* to do it.

We have to understand the nature of software. Once we do—once those things become obvious to us—it'll be as common sense as anything else in our world and a whole lot less scary.

Management cannot impose courage on a software development team. That has to come from the team—from the developers individually recognizing that these practices are going to help them build better software without being a burden. Most of the teams I know of that are successfully doing these practices have organically decided to do them themselves, and said, "Hey, Management, we want to do this"—not the other way around.

Once we truly understand the principles behind these practices, they aren't much of a burden and don't slow us down very much at all. The great developers who I know write highly maintainable, CLEAN code, and they write it faster than anyone I've ever met.

We want to write our software in such a way that we'll be proud of it, just like we can be proud of the fruits of any creative endeavor. I want to shake out this notion that quick is cheaper. When we don't pay attention to good practices, it may look faster in the short term but we'll have that house of cards come toppling down on us faster than we ever thought. And we just have to look at the first part of this book in order to see the enormous record of failures behind us. Our industry is failing far more than it's succeeding, and it doesn't have to be that way. Our customers are getting more sophisticated, and they're not going to put up with being alpha testers and having to pay money for the "privilege" of testing our software.

All I'm saying is let's step back and think about what we're really doing. Building software is a complex activity, but the more we take some time to think about what we're doing, how we're doing it, and why we're doing it, the more we'll be able to focus on doing a better job. And it starts with having the courage to accept imperfection and try new practices.

It's my sincere hope that everything we talked about in this book will help you build better software. But I also hope for the day that these ideas will be superseded by something better. That is the nature of change, and that's what we're trying to do now. It supersedes what we have currently with something a little bit better. And it really is just the next step.

I've seen how many of the world's largest organizations build software. I've worked with several Fortune 500 companies and dozens of other companies. I know how they build software at IBM, Microsoft, and Yahoo! because I've worked with thousands of the developers in these and many other companies, training them in the practices we've been discussing in this book. I've witnessed these practices work in the field.

But all too often I see organizations dead-set on reinventing the wheel. There are very few standards that are universally practiced in software development. Developers know a common programming language but often don't share a common approach to design, or a common aesthetic, or even common goals for how they build features. We all define "good software" differently.

It seems as though everyone has figured out a different piece of the puzzle. I try to share with others the successful techniques I learn from clients. That's one of the great things about being a consultant: I get to learn from my clients

What I've learned is there are many approaches to solving problems. People think and solve problems differently, and the ranges of approaches people have are astounding. Which one is right?

All of them!

Each approach has merits, and when we study them we can glean tools and techniques we can apply to other problems.

In software, there is no "they" who tell us the right things to do. We're all still figuring it out. Knowing we're working in a new way can be very exciting, but it can also be frustrating to have to constantly blaze new trails. Not everyone is cut out to be a developer or an explorer. Thank goodness for Magellan and Lewis and Clark…and for Kent Beck and Ward Cunningham.

Some people understand how to build software. Not only do they do it at a fraction of the cost but they also have a high success rate. These examples are teaching us there's a better way to build software. What we're learning turns our traditional model of quality on its head. It flies in the face of conventional wisdom, yet at the same time it's giving us a glimpse of a deeper understanding of ourselves and the world around us.

The Industrial Revolution gave us large-scale manufacturing that led us to consistency and conformity. Now we're entering the Information Revolution and it's demanding an entirely different approach. This revolution is all around us, asking us to think in ways fundamentally different from how we thought in the past and emphasizing values that are almost diametrically opposed to the materialistic approach of the last century. Instead of consistency and conformity, it's leading us to individuality and innovation.

Bibliography

[Ad 11]   Gojko Adžić. *Specification by Example*. Manning Publications Co., Green-wich, CT, 2011.

[Bai08]   Scott Bain. *Emergent Design: The Evolutionary Nature of Professional Soft-ware Development*. Addison-Wesley, Reading, MA, 2008.

[BE12]   Daniel Brolund and Ola Ellnestam. *Behead Your Legacy Beast: Refactor and Restructure Relentlessly with the Mikado Method*. Daniel Brolund, Ola Ellnestam, http://www.agical.com, 2012.

[Bec00]   Kent Beck. *Extreme Programming Explained: Embrace Change*. Addison-Wesley Longman, Reading, MA, 2000.

[Bec02]   Kent Beck. *Test Driven Development: By Example*. Addison-Wesley, Reading, MA, 2002.

[Bro95]   Frederick P. Brooks Jr. *The Mythical Man-Month: Essays on Software Engineering*. Addison-Wesley, Reading, MA, Anniversary, 1995.

[Coh04]   Mike Cohn. *User Stories Applied: For Agile Software Development*. Addison-Wesley Professional, Boston, MA, 2004.

[FBBO99]   Martin Fowler, Kent Beck, John Brant, William Opdyke, and Don Roberts. *Refactoring: Improving the Design of Existing Code*. Addison-Wesley, Reading, MA, 1999.

[Fea04]   Michael Feathers. *Working Effectively with Legacy Code*. Prentice Hall, Englewood Cliffs, NJ, 2004.

[GHJV95]   Erich Gamma, Richard Helm, Ralph Johnson, and John Vlissides. *Design Patterns: Elements of Reusable Object-Oriented Software*. Addison-Wesley, Reading, MA, 1995.

[Gla08]   Malcolm Gladwell. *Outliers: The Story of Success*. Little, Brown and Company, New York, NY, USA, 2008.

[Jon95]   Capers Jones. *Patterns of Software System Failure and Success*. Intl Thomson Computer Pr (Sd), London, UK, 1995.

[Mey97]   Bertrand Meyer. *Object-Oriented Software Construction*. Prentice Hall, Englewood Cliffs, NJ, Second edition, 1997.

[Pug05]   Ken Pugh. *Prefactoring*. O'Reilly & Associates, Inc., Sebastopol, CA, 2005.

[Pug11]   Ken Pugh. *Lean-Agile Acceptance Test-Driven Development: Better Software Through Collaboration*. Addison-Wesley, Reading, MA, 2011.

[Ros78]   Leo Rosten. *Passions and Prejudices*. McGraw-Hill, Emeryville, CA, 1978.

[SB01]   Ken Schwaber and Mike Beedle. *Agile Software Development with Scrum*. Prentice Hall, Englewood Cliffs, NJ, 2001.

[SW07]   James Shore and Shane Warden. *The Art of Agile Development*. O'Reilly & Associates, Inc., Sebastopol, CA, 2007.

[WK02]   Laurie Williams and Robert Kessler. *Pair Programming Illuminated*. Addison-Wesley, Reading, MA, 2002.

Index

Pragmatic Programming

We'll show you how to be more pragmatic and effective, for new code and old.

Your Code as a Crime Scene

Jack the Ripper and legacy codebases have more in common than you'd think. Inspired by forensic psychology methods, this book teaches you strategies to predict the future of your codebase, assess refactoring direction, and understand how your team influences the design. With its unique blend of forensic psychology and code analysis, this book arms you with the strategies you need, no matter what programming language you use.

Adam Tornhill
(218 pages) ISBN: 9781680500387. $36
https://pragprog.com/book/atcrime

The Nature of Software Development

You need to get value from your software project. You need it "free, now, and perfect." We can't get you there, but we can help you get to "cheaper, sooner, and better." This book leads you from the desire for value down to the specific activities that help good Agile projects deliver better software sooner, and at a lower cost. Using simple sketches and a few words, the author invites you to follow his path of learning and understanding from a half century of software development and from his engagement with Agile methods from their very beginning.

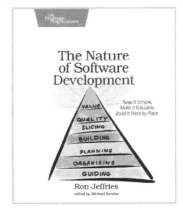

Ron Jeffries
(178 pages) ISBN: 9781941222379. $24
https://pragprog.com/book/rjnsd

Be Agile

Don't just "do" agile; you want to *be* agile. We'll show you how.

Agile in a Flash

The best agile book isn't a book: *Agile in a Flash* is a unique deck of index cards that fit neatly in your pocket. You can tape them to the wall. Spread them out on your project table. Get stains on them over lunch. These cards are meant to be used, not just read.

Jeff Langr and Tim Ottinger
(110 pages) ISBN: 9781934356715. $15
https://pragprog.com/book/olag

The Agile Samurai

Here are three simple truths about software development:

1. You can't gather all the requirements up front.
2. The requirements you do gather will change.
3. There is always more to do than time and money will allow.

Those are the facts of life. But you can deal with those facts (and more) by becoming a fierce software-delivery professional, capable of dispatching the most dire of software projects and the toughest delivery schedules with ease and grace.

This title is also available as an audio book.

Jonathan Rasmusson
(264 pages) ISBN: 9781934356586. $34.95
https://pragprog.com/book/jtrap

The Joy of Mazes and Math

Rediscover the joy and fascinating weirdness of mazes and pure mathematics.

Mazes for Programmers

A book on mazes? Seriously?

Yes!

Not because you spend your day creating mazes, or because you particularly like solving mazes.

But because it's fun. Remember when programming used to be fun? This book takes you back to those days when you were starting to program, and you wanted to make your code do things, draw things, and solve puzzles. It's fun because it lets you explore and grow your code, and reminds you how it feels to just think.

Sometimes it feels like you live your life in a maze of twisty little passages, all alike. Now you can code your way out.

Jamis Buck
(286 pages) ISBN: 9781680500554 $38
https://pragprog.com/book/jbmaze

Good Math

Mathematics is beautiful—and it can be fun and exciting as well as practical. *Good Math* is your guide to some of the most intriguing topics from two thousand years of mathematics: from Egyptian fractions to Turing machines; from the real meaning of numbers to proof trees, group symmetry, and mechanical computation. If you've ever wondered what lay beyond the proofs you struggled to complete in high school geometry, or what limits the capabilities of the computer on your desk, this is the book for you.

Mark C. Chu-Carroll
(282 pages) ISBN: 9781937785338. $34
https://pragprog.com/book/mcmath

Put the "Fun" in Functional

Elixir puts the "fun" back into functional programming, on top of the robust, battle-tested, industrial-strength environment of Erlang.

Programming Elixir

You want to explore functional programming, but are put off by the academic feel (tell me about monads just one more time). You know you need concurrent applications, but also know these are almost impossible to get right. Meet Elixir, a functional, concurrent language built on the rock-solid Erlang VM. Elixir's pragmatic syntax and built-in support for metaprogramming will make you productive and keep you interested for the long haul. This book is *the* introduction to Elixir for experienced programmers.

Maybe you need something that's closer to Ruby, but with a battle-proven environment that's unrivaled for massive scalability, concurrency, distribution, and fault tolerance. Maybe the time is right for the Next Big Thing. Maybe it's *Elixir*.

Dave Thomas
(340 pages) ISBN: 9781937785581. $36
https://pragprog.com/book/elixir

Programming Erlang (2nd edition)

A multi-user game, web site, cloud application, or networked database can have thousands of users all interacting at the same time. You need a powerful, industrial-strength tool to handle the really hard problems inherent in parallel, concurrent environments. You need Erlang. In this second edition of the best-selling *Programming Erlang*, you'll learn how to write parallel programs that scale effortlessly on multicore systems.

Joe Armstrong
(548 pages) ISBN: 9781937785536. $42
https://pragprog.com/book/jaerlang2

Past and Present

To see where we're going, remember how we got here, and learn how to take a healthier approach to programming.

Fire in the Valley

In the 1970s, while their contemporaries were protesting the computer as a tool of dehumanization and oppression, a motley collection of college dropouts, hippies, and electronics fanatics were engaged in something much more subversive. Obsessed with the idea of getting computer power into their own hands, they launched from their garages a hobbyist movement that grew into an industry, and ultimately a social and technological revolution. What they did was invent the personal computer: not just a new device, but a watershed in the relationship between man and machine. This is their story.

Michael Swaine and Paul Freiberger
(424 pages) ISBN: 9781937785765. $34
https://pragprog.com/book/fsfire

The Healthy Programmer

To keep doing what you love, you need to maintain your own systems, not just the ones you write code for. Regular exercise and proper nutrition help you learn, remember, concentrate, and be creative—skills critical to doing your job well. Learn how to change your work habits, master exercises that make working at a computer more comfortable, and develop a plan to keep fit, healthy, and sharp for years to come.

This book is intended only as an informative guide for those wishing to know more about health issues. In no way is this book intended to replace, countermand, or conflict with the advice given to you by your own healthcare provider including Physician, Nurse Practitioner, Physician Assistant, Registered Dietician, and other licensed professionals.

Joe Kutner
(254 pages) ISBN: 9781937785314. $36
https://pragprog.com/book/jkthp

The Pragmatic Bookshelf

The Pragmatic Bookshelf features books written by developers for developers. The titles continue the well-known Pragmatic Programmer style and continue to garner awards and rave reviews. As development gets more and more difficult, the Pragmatic Programmers will be there with more titles and products to help you stay on top of your game.

Visit Us Online

This Book's Home Page
https://pragprog.com/book/dblegacy
Source code from this book, errata, and other resources. Come give us feedback, too!

Register for Updates
https://pragprog.com/updates
Be notified when updates and new books become available.

Join the Community
https://pragprog.com/community
Read our weblogs, join our online discussions, participate in our mailing list, interact with our wiki, and benefit from the experience of other Pragmatic Programmers.

New and Noteworthy
https://pragprog.com/news
Check out the latest pragmatic developments, new titles and other offerings.

Save on the eBook

Save on the eBook versions of this title. Owning the paper version of this book entitles you to purchase the electronic versions at a terrific discount.

PDFs are great for carrying around on your laptop—they are hyperlinked, have color, and are fully searchable. Most titles are also available for the iPhone and iPod touch, Amazon Kindle, and other popular e-book readers.

Buy now at *https://pragprog.com/coupon*

Contact Us

Online Orders:	*https://pragprog.com/catalog*
Customer Service:	*support@pragprog.com*
International Rights:	*translations@pragprog.com*
Academic Use:	*academic@pragprog.com*
Write for Us:	*http://write-for-us.pragprog.com*
Or Call:	+1 800-699-7764

Milton Keynes UK
Ingram Content Group UK Ltd.
UKHW020423141024
449609UK00008B/172

9 781680 500790